The Jazz Piano Book

By Mark Levine

Copyright 1989, SHER MUSIC CO., P.O. Box 445, Petaluma, CA 94953.
All Rights Reserved. International Copyright Secured. Made in the U.S.A.
No part of this book may be reproduced in any form without written permission from the publisher.

Cover from a poster design by Sam Smidt.
Title page photo of Duke Ellington by Lee Tanner

ISBN 0-9614701-5-1

≡ ABOUT THE AUTHOR

Mark Levine has been a jazz pianist for thirty-five years, and a jazz educator for fifteen years. Born and raised in Concord, New Hampshire, he now makes his home in Berkeley, California. His education included studies with Joe Pace, Jaki Byard, Hall Overton, and Herb Pomeroy. He has worked with such jazz greats as Woody Shaw, Blue Mitchell, Harold Land, Bobby Hutcherson, Cal Tjader, Milt Jackson, Art Pepper, Charlie Rouse, Johnny Griffin, Art Farmer, Sonny Stitt, Chet Baker, Frank Morgan, Mongo Santamaria, Poncho Sanchez, and many others. He currently records for Concord Jazz Records, and has appeared on numerous albums as a sideman with Joe Henderson, Carmen McRae, Mark Murphy, Houston Person, Richie Cole, Gabor Szabo, plus five albums with Cal Tjader, one of which was a Grammy winner. His most recent album as a leader is *Smiley & Me* (Concord Jazz 352).

Mark is on the faculty of Sonoma State University in Rohnert Park, California, where he teaches jazz piano. He is active on the San Francisco jazz scene, where he leads a trio, and is much in demand by both local and touring artists.

The Jazz Piano Book by Mark Levine

©1989

≣ ACKNOWLEDGEMENTS

It has been said that writing a book is a lot like having a baby (the last chapter, like the ninth month, seems to take forever). I would like to thank several midwives who have helped bring *The Jazz Piano Book* into the world. First and foremost, I shall be forever thankful to K. Gypsy Zaboroskie for her many months of work on design, page layout, photo selection advice and preparation, patience, and general good humor.

To fellow jazz pianists Bruce Williamson and John Halle, who read through and checked the manuscript, offering much good advice along the way. Thanks, fellas—I couldn't have done it without you.

To Harry Likas, who read through the manuscript, playing the role of questioning student, thanks for your sage advice and criticism.

Muchas gracias to Rebeca Mauleón and John Santos of The Machete Ensemble, San Francisco's best salsa band, for their help in preparing the "Salsa and Latin Jazz" chapter, and the discography.

To editor-in-chief, Deborah Craig, who was just as merciless and nit-picky as I asked her to be, thanks Deb. Thanks also to Kindy Kemp, who helped with the editing, Ann Krinitsky, for her beautiful calligraphy, and artist Sam Smidt for the wonderful cover print.

Thanks to Tim Hodges and Bob Parlocha of KJAZ, America's premier jazz radio station, for letting me access the KJAZ library in preparing the discography.

Thanks to all the photographers for their sensational photos, and especially to Lee Tanner, who went above and beyond the call of duty in tracking down elusive photos of Bud Powell and Art Tatum.

Thanks also to Chuck LaPaglia, Paul Potyen, and Larry Walter, who were always available to answer computer questions. Thanks to Tom Madden of Jazz Quarter, my favorite Jazz record store in the world (it's in San Francisco), for his encyclopaedic knowledge of discography. And last—but far from least—thanks to my publisher Chuck Sher for his support and enthusiasm from start to finish.

Pianist Photographer

≡ INTRODUCTION

Welcome to *The Jazz Piano Book*. Acoustic jazz piano is a vast subject, and to cover the idiom from James P. Johnson through Cecil Taylor would take a book a thousand times the size of this one. *The Jazz Piano Book* includes beginning through advanced techniques and covers the period from Bud Powell to the present. The information offered here is based on what I learned from the pianists who have influenced and inspired me: Bud Powell, Horace Silver, Thelonious Monk, Wynton Kelly, Bill Evans, Herbie Hancock, McCoy Tyner, Chick Corea, Eddie Palmieri, Kenny Barron, and many others, including such non pianists as John Coltrane, Joe Henderson, Wayne Shorter, and Charlie Parker. I was fortunate to be able to work with, and probe the minds of, several great musicians, especially Woody Shaw and Dave Liebman. I have also had the good fortune to study with four great teachers: Joe Pace, Jaki Byard, Hall Overton, and Herb Pomeroy.

Although *The Jazz Piano Book* is meant primarily for pianists, other instrumentalists can use it as well, both as an introduction to jazz piano and as an aid to understanding harmony on their own instruments. The visual element of the keyboard makes jazz harmony more accessible than on other instruments. Many great horn players, bassists, guitarists, and drummers have been excellent pianists as well, including Charles Mingus,[1] Joe Chambers,[2] Jack DeJohnette[3] (all three of whom have recorded piano albums), and Joe Henderson.

Nobody has ever learned to play jazz from a book only. This one will help guide you while you study with a good teacher, listen to as much live and recorded jazz as you can, transcribe solos and songs from records, and, in general, immerse yourself as much as possible in the world of JAZZ.

Much of this book involves music theory. There's a good reason why music *theory* is not called music *truth*. The only truth is in the music itself. Theory is an intellectual dance we do around the music, trying to explain its dynamics. Theory varies from era to era and from musician to musician. Although there is a continuity in the evolution of jazz, the music that James P. Johnson played in the 1920s had changed radically by

---

[1] Charles Mingus, *Mingus Plays Piano*, Impulse A60.
[2] Joe Chambers, *Double Exposure*, Muse MR 5l65.
[3] Jack DeJohnette, *The Piano Album*, Landmark LLP-l504.

the time Art Tatum and Fats Waller arrived in the 1930s, Bud Powell in the 1940s, Bill Evans in the 1950s, McCoy Tyner and Herbie Hancock in the 1960s, Mulgrew Miller in the 1970s, Benny Green in the 1980s, and so on. Keep your ears, and your mind, open.

This book has an unusual format. Rather than group all voicings in one section and theory in another, the subjects alternate throughout the book, easy material progressing to more advanced techniques. Above all, I have tried as much as possible to put the musical examples within the context of tunes that are a jazz musician's daily language, from standards like "Just Friends" to Wayne Shorter's beautiful and unusual "Infant Eyes."

Art Tatum

Phil Stern Photo ©1958

▤ INTRODUCTION

Note: To use this book, you should be able to read music in both the treble and bass clef, know the major scales and key signatures, and have some basic knowledge of intervals and chords. Intervals and triads will be reviewed in Chapter One.

Tune Sources: *The New Real Book* and *The World's Greatest Fake Book*, both published by Sher Music Company, P.O. Box 445, Petaluma, CA 94953, are the two best published sources of standards and jazz originals. The very best way to learn tunes is to transcribe them off of records yourself, and as your ability to do so improves, should become your primary source.

A note on terminology and chord symbols

The unhappy fact that the chord symbols C, CΔ, Cmaj7, CM7, C6, and C69 all mean pretty much the same thing and are often used interchangeably can be discouraging to a beginner. In this book, I'll use the Δ symbol for all major chords. Many musicians use shorthand symbols, writing G7alt rather than G7b9, +9, +ll, bl3 (which would *you* rather read?), and I'll do the same. As each new chord symbol or term is introduced, I'll list alternate terms or symbols.

I'll notate raised and lowered notes within a chord as + and b (C7+ll, C7b9), instead of the equally common # or - symbols (C7#ll, C7-9).

The fourth and eleventh are, strictly speaking, the same note in a chord. I use the term "fourth" on major and sus chords (CΔ+4, Csus4), and "eleventh" on dominant and minor chords (C7+ll, C-ll).

The sixth and thirteenth are likewise the same note in a chord. I follow standard practice, using the term "sixth" on major and minor chords (C6, C-6), and "thirteenth" on dominant chords (C7bl3).

The dictionary definitions for the terms "scale" and "mode" are almost identical, and because most jazz musicians use them interchangeably, I do the same. I make a distinction when the mode is in direct reference to its parent scale, as in "the D Dorian mode of the C major scale."

Most jazz pianists use the terms "chord" and "voicing" interchangeably, and I do the same.

Intervals and Triads — Review

Intervals

A good definition of an *interval* is "the space between two notes." **Figure 1-1** shows the intervals from the half step/minor second up to the octave, all based on middle C. The most commonly used term is shown above each interval, along with any alternate terms.

Figure 1-1

The chart that follows shows all the intervals, both ascending and descending, as they occur in tunes from the standard jazz repertoire. Unless otherwise noted, the interval in question is the first two melody notes of the song. Play each example and *sing* the interval. If you can sing an interval accurately, it will be easier to play when improvising. Listen carefully to all the voicings in the examples. All of them will be covered in this book. A footnote reference after each song title lists a great recording of the tune—in many cases, the original recording.

Intervals by selected tunes

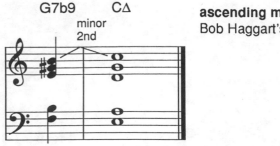

ascending minor second
Bob Haggart's "What's New?"[1]

descending minor second
Duke Ellington's "Sophisticated Lady"[2]

ascending major second
Billy Strayhorn's "Chelsea Bridge"[3]

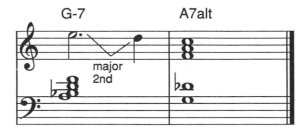

descending major second
Miles Davis' "Blue In Green"[4]

---

[1] Woody Shaw, *Setting Standards,* Muse 5318.
[2] Duke Ellington and Ray Brown, *This One's For Blanton,* Pablo 2310-721.
[3] Joe Henderson, *The Kicker,* Milestone 9008.
[4] Miles Davis, *Kind Of Blue,* Columbia 40579.

ascending minor third
Thelonious Monk's "Evidence"[5]

descending minor third
Chick Corea's "Mirror, Mirror"[6]

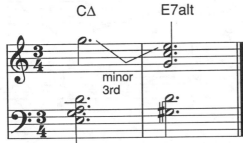

ascending major third
Chick Corea's "Windows"[7]

descending major third
John Coltrane's
"Giant Steps"[8]

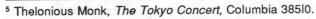

[5] Thelonious Monk, *The Tokyo Concert,* Columbia 38510.
[6] Joe Henderson, *Mirror, Mirror,* Pausa 7075.
[7] Stan Getz, *Sweet Rain,* Verve 8693.
[8] John Coltrane, *Giant Steps,* Atlantic 1311.

ascending perfect fourth
McCoy Tyner's "Search For Peace"[9]

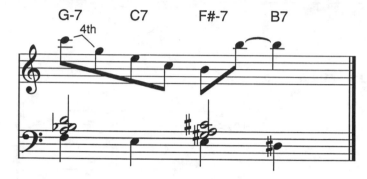

descending perfect fourth
Thelonious Monk's "Ask Me Now"[10]

ascending tritone
Joe Henderson's "Isotope"[11]

descending tritone
bars 18 and 19 of
Duke Ellington's
"Sophisticated Lady"[12]

---

[9] McCoy Tyner, *The Real McCoy,* Blue Note 4264.
[10] Thelonious Monk, *Solo Monk,* Columbia 9149.
[11] Joe Henderson, *Power To The People,* Milestone 9024.
[12] Duke Ellington and Ray Brown, *This One's For Blanton,* Pablo 2310-721.

ascending perfect fifth
Wayne Shorter's
"Angola"[13]

descending perfect fifth
intro to Wayne Shorter's "Black Nile"[14]

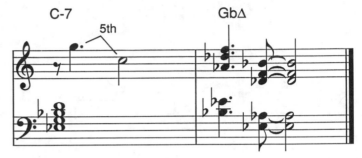

ascending minor sixth
Woody Shaw's "In A Capricornian Way"[15]

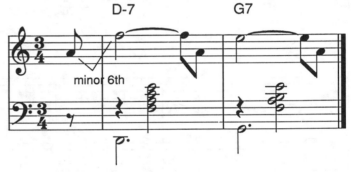

descending minor sixth
intro to Freddie Hubbard's Happy Times"[16]

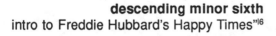

---

[13] Wayne Shorter, *The Soothsayer,* Blue Note LT-988.
[14] Wayne Shorter, *Night Dreamer,* Blue Note 4173.
[15] Woody Shaw, *Stepping Stones,* Columbia 35560.
[16] The Griffith Park Collection, *The Griffith Park Collection #2,* Elektra/Musician 60262.

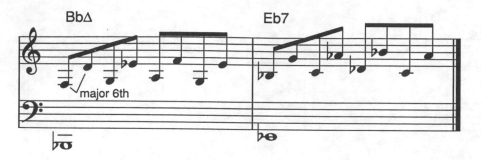

ascending major sixth
Thelonious Monk's "Misterioso"[17]

descending major sixth
Dizzy Gillespie's "Ow!"[18]

ascending minor seventh
second bar of the bridge of Duke Ellington's "Sophisticated Lady"[19]

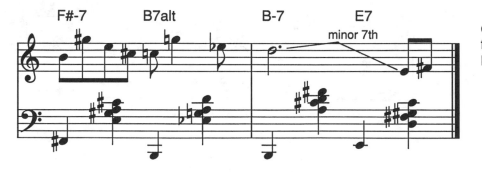

descending minor seventh
fourth bar of the bridge of Billy Strayhorn's "Chelsea Bridge"[20]

[17] Thelonious Monk, *Live At The Jazz Workshop*, Columbia 38269.
[18] *The Gifted Ones*, Pablo 2310 833.
[19] Duke Ellington And Ray Brown, *This One's For Blanton*, Pablo 2310 721.
[20] Joe Henderson, *The Kicker*, Milestone 9008.

ascending major seventh
2nd and 3rd notes of
Joe Henderson's "Serenity"[21]

descending major seventh
bar 17 of Wayne Shorter's "This Is For Albert"[22]

ascending octave
Billy Strayhorn's "Daydream"[23]

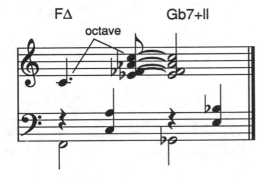

descending octave
2nd and 3rd notes of
Freddie Hubbard's "Birdlike"[24]

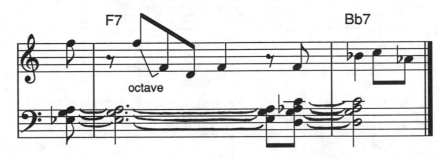

[21] Joe Henderson, *In 'n Out*, Blue Note 4166.
[22] Art Blakey, *Thermo*, Milestone 47008.
[23] Steve Lacy, *Soprano Sax*, Fantasy/OJC 130.
[24] Freddie Hubbard, *Ready For Freddie*, Blue Note 4085.

Melodic intervals greater than an octave in tunes are rare, but a few examples are shown here:

ascending minor ninth
bars 53-54 of Wayne Shorter's "Wild Flower"[25]

descending minor ninth
bar 18 of Benny Golson's "I Remember Clifford"[26]

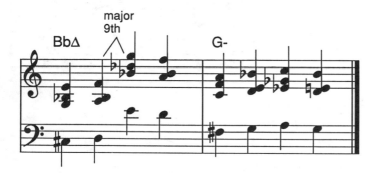

ascending major ninth
2nd and 3rd notes of Duke Ellington's "I Got It Bad And That Ain't Good"[27]

descending eleventh
15th bar of Joe Henderson's "Inner Urge"[28]

[25] Wayne Shorter, *Speak No Evil,* Blue Note 4194.
[26] The Jazztet, *Meet The Jazztet,* Argo 664.
[27] Donald Byrd, *Mustang,* Blue Note 4238.
[28] Joe Henderson, *Inner Urge,* Blue Note 4189.

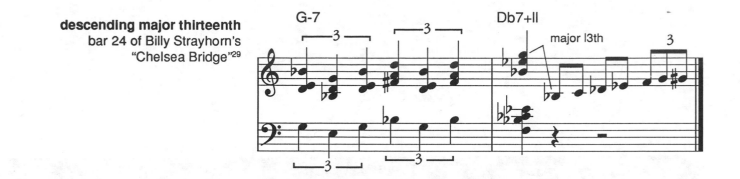

descending major thirteenth
bar 24 of Billy Strayhorn's
"Chelsea Bridge"[29]

Inverting intervals

One of the skills a pianist must have is the ability to *invert* intervals quickly. When you invert an interval, you take the bottom note and put it on top, or vice versa. A new interval results, and the rules for inverting intervals are simple.

When you invert an interval:
• major becomes minor
• minor becomes major
• perfect remains perfect
• tritone remains tritone
and the old and new intervals add up to "nine."

Look at **figure 1-2**. If you invert a major third, C with E on top, it becomes E with C on top, a minor sixth. Major becomes minor, and three plus six add up to nine. In **figure 1-3**, a minor second inverts to a major seventh. Minor becomes major, and two plus seven add up to nine. Now look at **figure 1-4**. A perfect fourth becomes a perfect fifth. Perfect remains perfect, and four plus five add up to nine. In **figure 1-5**, a tritone inverts to another tritone. Because a tritone is right in between a fourth and a fifth, you could say it is "four and a half," and four and a half plus four and a half equal nine.

Figure 1-2

major 3rd   minor 6th   **major becomes minor 3+6=9**

Figure 1-3

minor 2nd   major 7th   **minor beomes major 2+7=9**

Figure 1-4

perfect 4th   perfect 5th   **perfect remains perfect 4+5=9**

Figure 1-5

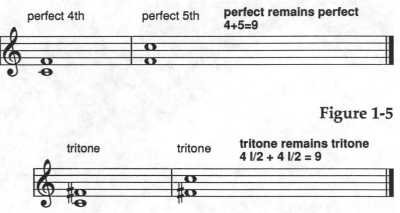

tritone   tritone   **tritone remains tritone 4 1/2 + 4 1/2 = 9**

***P**ractice tips*   Practice singing the intervals, both ascending and descending. Sing the melody, or "head," of standards, bebop, and other jazz tunes while listening to records.

[29] Joe Henderson, *The Kicker*, Milestone 9008.

Thelonious Monk

Photo © by Lee Tanner

Triads

Triads are formed by stacking one third on top of another. There are four possible combinations: major third and minor third, minor third and major third, two minor thirds, and two major thirds. A major third with a minor third on top of it forms a *major* triad. A minor third with a major third on top forms a *minor* triad. Two minor thirds make up a *diminished* triad. Two major thirds form an *augmented* triad. All four triads are shown in **figure 1-6**.

Figure 1-6

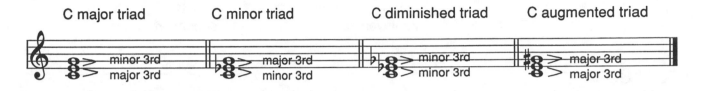

Play **figure 1-6** and listen to the effect each triad has. Be aware of your emotional response to each triad. In program music (music for TV, movies, the theatre) harmony is used to enhance whatever emotional response a scene demands. A major triad sounds happy, strong, or triumphant. A minor triad may sound sad, pensive, or tragic. A diminished triad suggests tension, agitation. An augmented triad has a floating quality, suggesting, among other things, Bambi emerging from the mist at dawn (seriously). Although these have become clichés, they still work, otherwise TV and movie composers wouldn't continue to use them. These emotional responses apply to seventh chords as well, the next chords you will learn about. It's no accident that sad tunes such as Benny Golson's "I Remember Clifford," John Lewis' "Django," and the Raye-DePaul standard "You Don't Know What Love Is" are written in minor keys, or that Bix Beiderbeck's "In A Mist"[30] uses augmented chords. As you play, you elicit an emotional response in your listener, your fellow musicians, and yourself. Be aware of it.

---

[30] Freddie Hubbard, *Sky Dive,* CTI 6018.

Triads are often inverted. An *inversion* is a chord with a note other than the root on the bottom. **Figure 1-7** shows both a C major and a C minor triad in their three possible positions: *root position,* as the term implies, with the root on the bottom; *first inversion,* with the third on the bottom; and *second inversion,* with the fifth on the bottom.

Figure 1-7

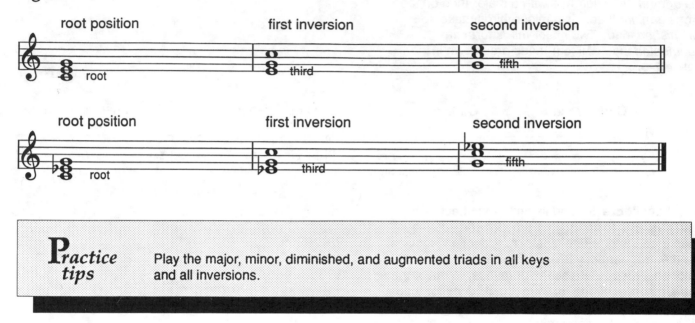

> **P**ractice **tips** Play the major, minor, diminished, and augmented triads in all keys and all inversions.

The Major Modes and II-V-I

The basic chords played in jazz harmony come from the major scale. **Figure 2-1** shows the C major scale and all of its *modes*. Each mode starts on a different note of the the major scale. The Greek names for these modes, in use for over two thousand years, are shown on the right. The Roman numerals I through VII are on the left, and correspond to the modal names on the right. In other words, Ionian is always the I mode, Dorian is always II, Phrygian is always III, and so on, the same in every major key.

Figure 2-1

The C Major Scale and Its Modes

C Ionian · D Dorian · E Phrygian · F Lydian · G Mixolydian · A Aeolian · B Locrian

From these modes come *seventh chords.* Seventh chords are constructed by playing every other note of each mode, as shown in **figure 2-2**. In the Ionian mode of the C major scale shown here, every other note has been boxed, the boxed notes forming the seventh chord shown to the right. The boxed notes are the root, third, fifth, and seventh notes of the mode, and are also the root, third, fifth, and seventh of the chord.

Figure 2-2

This particular chord is a C major seventh chord. A common symbol for this chord is the triangle, so the chord symbol used here is CΔ.[1] This chord is a major seventh chord because of the interval relationship between the root of the chord and its other notes. *A major seventh chord has a major third, a perfect fifth, and a major seventh* **(figure 2-3)**. Because this chord is built off of the first mode, it is called a I chord.

Figure 2-3

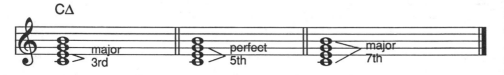

Figure 2-4

The second, or Dorian mode, of the C major scale runs from D to D **(figure 2-4)**. The boxed notes—the root, third, fifth, and seventh of this mode—again form a chord, in this case the D minor seventh chord shown on the right. The most commonly used symbol for a minor chord is the dash, so this chord is notated D-7.[2] This chord is a minor seventh chord because of the interval relationship between the root of the chord and its other notes. *A minor seventh chord has a minor third, a perfect fifth, and a minor seventh* **(figure 2-5)**. Because this chord is built off of the second mode, it is called a II chord.

Figure 2-5

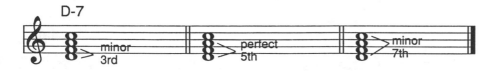

[1] Alternate chord symbols often used are: C, CΔ7, Cmaj7, Cma7, and CM7. C6 and C6/9, although slightly different chords, are often used interchangeably with CΔ.
[2] Alternate chord symbols: Dmin7, Dmi7, Dm7.

Skip now to the fifth, or Mixolydian mode, which runs from G to G. **Figure 2-6** shows this mode with the root, third, fifth, and seventh boxed to form the

Figure 2-6

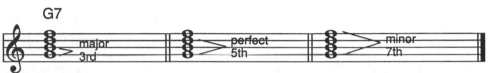

chord on the right. This is called a "G seventh" chord, or "G dominant seventh," and is notated G7. This chord is a dominant seventh chord because of the interval relationship between the root and its other notes. *A dominant seventh chord has a major third, a perfect fifth, and a minor seventh* **(figure 2-7)**. Because this chord is built off of the fifth mode, it is called a V chord.

Figure 2-7

Cecil Taylor, Randy Weston, McCoy Tyner

15

These three chords, I, II, and V—major seventh, minor seventh, and dominant seventh—are the three most commonly played chords in jazz. Since each one has a perfect fifth (there is an exception, which we'll get to soon), the third and seventh are the variables. They determine whether the chord is major, minor, or dominant, or what's called the *quality* of the chord. The following rules sum up the differences between the three chords:

- A major seventh chord has a major third and a major seventh.
- A minor seventh chord has a minor third and a minor seventh.
- A dominant seventh chord has a major third and a minor seventh.

These three chords often occur as a II-V-I chord progression.[3] II-V-I is the most common chord progression in jazz. The chords in the previous examples—D-7, G7, and CΔ—are the II-V-I progression in the key of C. Can you find II-V-I in the key of F? The second, fifth, and first notes of the F major scale are G, C, and F. The II chord is a minor seventh chord, the V chord is a dominant seventh chord, and the I chord is a major seventh chord. The II-V-I in the key of F is G-7, C7, FΔ.

The root position chords in the preceding examples use only a tiny part of the piano. To take advantage of the huge instrument at your command, you need to play chords with both hands, spreading them over a wider area of the keyboard. In the next chapter, you'll learn a simple and useful two-handed chord: the three-note voicing.

Practice **tips** — Memorize the II-V-I progression in every key. Go through all twelve keys saying the II-V-I chords aloud both sitting at, and away from, the piano. Make a mantra of it until you have the progressions memorized. *Always practice everything in every key.*

---

[3] This progression is sometimes notated ii-V7-I, the II chord in lowercase Roman numerals because it is a minor chord, the 7 after the V chord to indicate its dominant function.

Play **figure 3-1**, the first two bars of the Hill-Robinson standard "Old Folks." The chords in this example are *three-note voicings*, consisting of the root, third, and seventh of each chord. As you just learned in Chapter Two, the third and seventh of a chord determine the chord quality: major seventh, minor seventh, or dominant seventh.

Figure 3-1

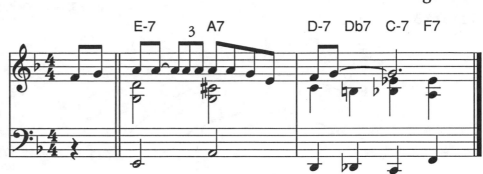

Reviewing the rules:

- A major seventh chord has a major third and a major seventh.
- A minor seventh chord has a minor third and a minor seventh.
- A dominant seventh chord has a major third and a minor seventh.

Remember, the fifth is not as important because each chord has a perfect fifth (there is an exception to this—the half-diminished chord—which we'll get to in Chapter Five). Three-note voicings reduce most chords to three essential notes: the root in the left hand, and the third and the seventh in the right hand.

Using three-note voicings enables you to play II-V-I, the basic progression in jazz harmony, with a maximum of smoothness, or good *voice leading*. Let's try playing a II-V-I in the key of C with these new voicings.

The II chord in the key of C is D-7. Play the root, D, with your left hand, and the third and seventh, F and C, with your right hand **(figure 3-2)**. While you're holding D-7, think of what the third and seventh are for the next chord, G7. The third of G7 is B, just a half step below the C you're already playing. The seventh of G7 is F, which you're already playing. Move the C down a half step while moving your left hand to the new root, G, and you're playing G7.

Now think of what the third and seventh are for the next chord, CΔ. The third of CΔ is E, a half step below the F you're already playing. The seventh is B, which you're already playing. Lower the F

Figure 3-2

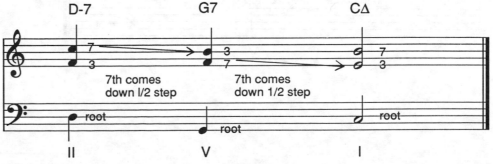

a half step while moving your left hand to the new root, C, and you've completed the II-V-I in C major.

Notice that *the seventh always comes down a half step.* Play the II-V-I progression a few more times, not looking at the music. Now try it in all twelve keys. To do this, use the *cycle of fifths*[1] **(figure 3-3).**

Figure 3-3

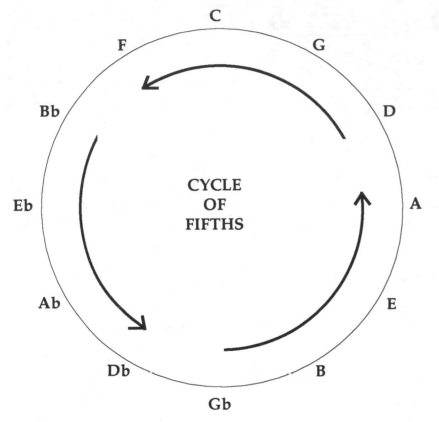

CYCLE OF FIFTHS

The cycle of fifths is an arrangement of all twelve notes of the chromatic scale, each note a fifth lower (or a fourth higher), than the preceding one. As you go around the cycle, think of each note as representing a key, the key you're going to practice in next. Start with the key of C at the top of the circle, and move counterclockwise through the keys of F, Bb, Eb, and so on. Using the cycle ensures that you practice everything in every key. More importantly, it means that your practicing approximates what happens in real life, because many chord progressions and modulations within tunes follow the cycle. For instance, the roots of a II-V-I progression follow the cycle. In the key of C, the roots of the II-V-I (D-7, G7, CΔ) are D, G, and C, which follow each other counterclockwise around the cycle. In F, the roots of the II-V-I (G-7, C7, FΔ) are G, C, and F, and they, too, follow each other around the cycle.

After you've gone through all twelve keys, reverse the notes in the right hand, starting with the third instead of the seventh on top of the II chord **(figure 3-4).** Again, as you go from II to V and V to I, the seventh comes down a half step while the third stays where it is.

Figure 3-4

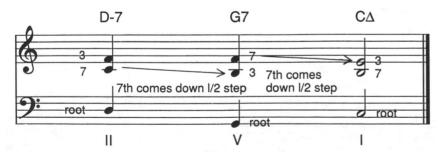

---

[1] Also known as the circle of fourths.

Practice playing the II-V-I in both positions through all twelve keys, around the cycle of fifths. When you're able to do this well, look at **figure 3-5**, a lead sheet for the Klenner-Lewis standard "Just Friends." You're going to play just the chord changes at first, so ignore the melody for now. Play the first chord, G7, with a three-note voicing. Start with the seventh on top, although the third on top would work just as well. The first two chords, G7 and CΔ, are a V-I. Remember what happens in a V-I? *The seventh always comes down a half step.* Before you go any further, look over the lead sheet of "Just Friends" and note the II-V, V-I, and II-V-I progressions (the designation for each chord is shown below the staff). The chords in a II-V-I all have to be from the same key. The C-7, F7, GΔ chords in bars 3-5 are not a II-V-I. C-7 and F7 are the II-V in the key of Bb, but GΔ is the I chord in the key of G. The B-7, E-7 chords in the second and third bars of the first ending are not a II-V. They are both II chords.

Play the first two chords in "Just Friends" again. Now go on to the next chord, C-7. The third and seventh of C-7 are Eb and Bb, just a half step below the E and B you're already playing on CΔ. Continue through the tune, always moving your right hand to the closest third and seventh of the next

Figure 3-5

Just Friends   Klenner & Lewis

Figure 3-6

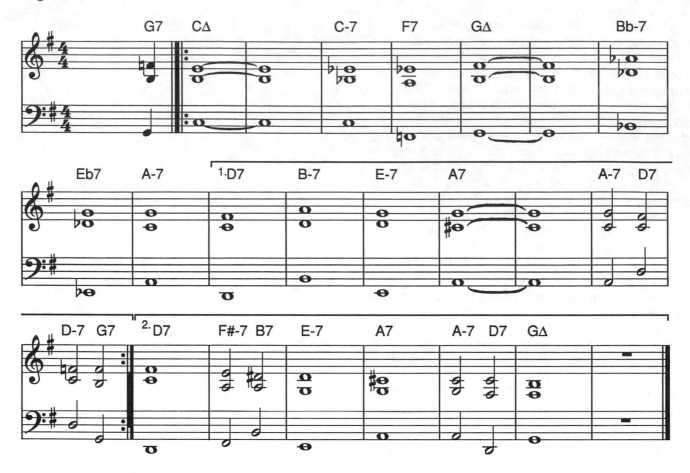

chord. **Figure 3-6** shows the complete tune with three-note voicings.

You're now ready to add the melody to "Just Friends." This doesn't necessarily mean adding a fourth note. If the melody note *is* the third or seventh, don't add an extra note, just make sure that the melody note is on top, where the melody belongs. The melody note in the pickup bar of "Just Friends," B, is the third of the G7 chord. Don't add a note, just voice that note on top. B, the melody note in bar I, is the seventh of the C△ chord. Again, don't add a fourth note, just voice the chord with B on top. You won't need to play a fourth note until bar 5, where the melody note A is the ninth of the G△ chord. **Figure 3-7** shows the complete "Just Friends" with the melody added to the three-note voicings.

So far, we've only talked about roots, thirds, fifths, and sevenths. If you continue to build a chord by adding more thirds, you get ninths, elevenths, and thirteenths **(figure 3-8)**. The ninth corresponds to the second note of the mode of each chord, the eleventh to the fourth, and the thirteenth to the sixth. Although the second and the ninth are the same

Figure 3-7

Just Friends

Klenner & Lewis

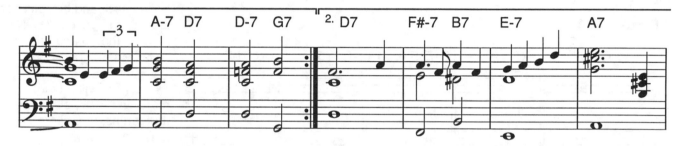

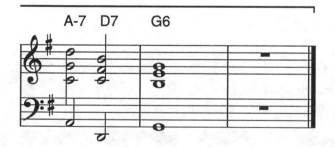

Figure 3-8

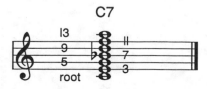

21

Figure 3-9

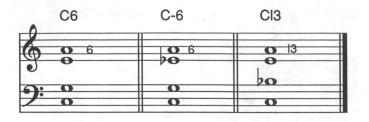

Figure 3-10

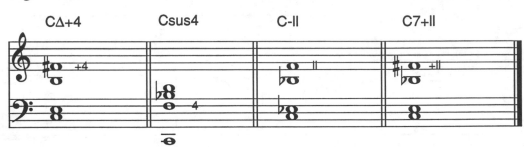

Figure 3-11

note, the term "ninth" is used for all chords, and "9" in chord symbols. Although the sixth and the thirteenth are the same note, most musicians use the term "sixth" when notating major and minor chords, and "thirteenth" when notating dominant seventh chords **(figure 3-9)**. Although the fourth and the eleventh are the same note, many musicians use the term "fourth" on major and sus chords, and "eleventh" for minor and dominant chords **(figure 3-10)**. Note that the fourth in the CΔ+4 chord has been raised, as has the eleventh in the C7+11 chord. Natural fourths or elevenths are seldom played when voicing major and dominant chords. When a note has been raised or lowered in a chord, the note is said to be *altered*. Other altered notes are the b9, +9, b5, +5, and b13, all shown in **figure 3-11.** Note that the +5 and b13 are the same note.

There will be much more on ninths, elevenths, thirteenths, and altered notes in Chapter Five.

Practice **tips**   Play the II-V-I progression in both positions through all twelve keys, around the cycle of fifths. Analyze tunes by chord type—is each chord a II, V, or I chord?

Suggested tunes to work on

Tune-Up	All The Things You Are
Ask Me Now	Satin Doll
Come Sunday	Countdown
Four	Darn That Dream
Here's That Rainy Day	Cherokee
Lazybird	Moment's Notice
Little B's Poem	Giant Steps

Sus And Phrygian Chords

Although Duke Ellington was playing them in the 1930s, *sus* chords have been an everyday sound in jazz only since the 1960s. The simplest voicing—whether you're playing a standard or Herbie Hancock's "Maiden Voyage"—is to play the root with your left hand while playing a major triad a whole step below the root with your right hand, as in **figure 4-1**.

Figure 4-1

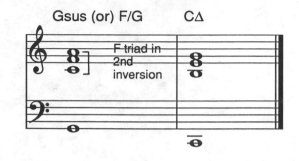

Because G is the root of this sus chord, the triad in your right hand would be F major, a whole step below G. Note that the triad is in second inversion, meaning that the fifth of the triad (C), is on the bottom, instead of the root (F). Triads often sound stronger inverted than in root position, especially so when in second inversion. The Gsus chord resolves smoothly to a CΔ chord.

Figure 4-2

The "sus" here refers to the *suspended fourth* of the chord, in this case the note C. In traditional harmony, this note usually resolves down a half step, the sus chord becoming a dominant seventh chord **(figure 4-2)**. In modern music, the fourth often doesn't resolve, which gives sus chords a floating quality.

Figure 4-3

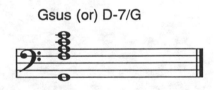

You might see this same Gsus chord notated as G7sus4, Gsus4, F/G, or D-7/G. The last two variations are *slash chords*, the upper-left part of the symbol indicating what chord is to be played over the bass note in the lower-right part of the symbol. F/G describes exactly what's happening in **figure 4-1**: an F triad in the right hand over the note G in the left hand. D-7/G describes the *function* of the sus chord, because a sus chord is like a II-V progression contained in one chord. The II-V progression in the key of C is D-7, G7. In **figure 4-3**, your right hand plays a common D-7 left-hand voicing (which will be covered in Chapter Seven) over a G root, combining D-7 and G7 into a single chord, D-7/G, or Gsus.

Figure 4-4

Two songs recorded in the 1960s did a lot to popularize sus chords among jazz musicians: John Coltrane's "Naima,"[1] and Herbie Hancock's "Maiden Voyage."[2] "Maiden Voyage" was a revolutionary tune for its time, because it consists entirely of sus chords. Herbie's vamp on the first two bars is shown in **figure 4-4**. The Dsus chord is voiced with a C major triad in the right hand a whole step down from

---

[1] John Coltrane, *Giant Steps*, Atlantic SD-1311.

[2] Herbie Hancock, *Maiden Voyage*, Blue Note BST-84195.

Herbie Hancock   Photo ©1986 Brian McMillen

Figure 4-5

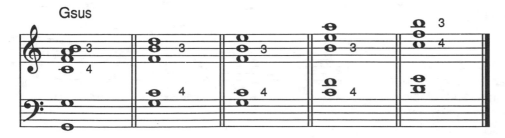

the root, D. One note in the triad has been doubled, and the fifth has been added in the left hand to strengthen the chord.

A persistent myth about sus chords is that "the fourth takes the place of the third." Jazz pianists, however, often voice the third with a sus chord, as you can see in the examples in **figure 4-5**. Note that in each example the third is voiced above the fourth. You could play the fourth above the third, as in **figure 4-6**, but the result would be a much more dissonant chord. In a tune like "Maiden Voyage," however, where each sus chord lasts for four bars, you have more freedom to use dissonance, so the voicing in **figure 4-6** might not sound quite so harsh by the fifth or sixth chorus. Let your taste be your guide.

Phrygian chords

Figure 4-6

Gsus

A *Phrygian* chord is a dominant seventh chord with the thirteenth instead of the root in the bass. **Figure 4-7** shows first a new G7 voicing with the root in the bass; then the same G7 voicing, but with the thirteenth, E, in the bass; and then the same chord, now analyzed as an E Phrygian chord. You might see this Phrygian chord notated with any of the three symbols shown—Esusb9, E Phryg, or G7/E—since there is no single commonly accepted chord symbol for a Phrygian chord.

Figure 4-7

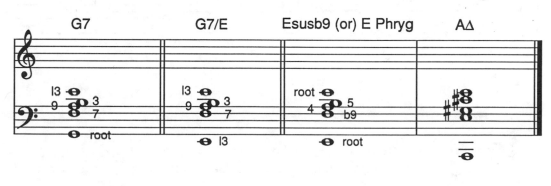

As you learned in Chapter Two, Phrygian is the third mode of the major scale, so E Phrygian is derived from the third note of the C major scale. The alternate chord symbol G7/E gives a clue to what's happening here. Instead of playing G in the bass, you substitute E, the Phrygian note in the key of C. Notice how smoothly the E Phrygian chord resolves to the AΔ chord. Even though G7 is a V chord in the key of C, the V-I relationship here is between E and A.

A beautiful example of Phrygian harmony is the Eb Phrygian chord that McCoy Tyner plays on the intro to John Coltrane's "After The Rain."[3] Another example is the Eb Phrygian chord in bars four, twelve, and twenty-eight in Wayne Shorter's haunting slow waltz "Penelope."[4] And yet another example is the A Phrygian chord in the fourth bar of Duke Ellington's "Melancholia."[5]

---

[3] John Coltrane, *Impressions*, MCA/Impulse MCA-5887.
[4] Wayne Shorter, *Etcetera*, Blue Note LT-l056, Herbie Hancock on piano.
[5] Duke Ellington, *Piano Reflections*, Capitol ll058.

You can use sus and Phrygian chords to reharmonize II-V progressions as a single chord, as shown in **figure 4-8**, the first few bars of Victor Young's "Stella By Starlight." The original chords in the first two bars—E-7 and A7, a II-V in the key of D—have been combined into an A Phrygian chord, while C-7, F7—the II-V in the third and fourth bars—are now a single Fsus chord.

Figure 4-8

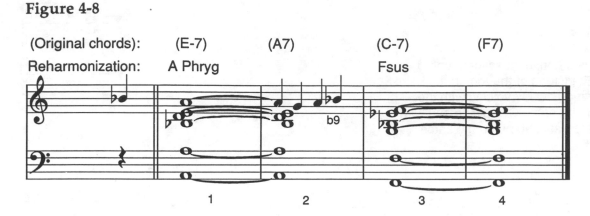

(Original chords): (E-7)   (A7)   (C-7)   (F7)
Reharmonization: A Phryg   Fsus

Practice **tips**

Go through tunes in *The New Real Book* and *The World's Greatest Fake Book*, reharmonizing II-V progressions using sus and Phrygian chords.

Suggested tunes to work on

Stella By Starlight	I Didn't Know What Time It Was
Star Eyes	Yesterdays
April In Paris	Out Of This World
Think On Me	What Is This Thing Called Love?
Ebony Moonbeams	Festival
Fly With The Wind	Highway One
Eighty One	

Adding Notes to Three-Note Voicings

Play **Figure 5-1**, the first four bars of John Coltrane's "Moment's Notice."[1] **Figure 5-2** shows the same four bars with several notes added, and in some cases altered, to the basic three-note voicings.

The easiest way to start adding notes to three-note voicings is shown in **figure 5-3**. When you have *unaltered* II-V-I chords (chords that have no b9, +9, +4, +II, b5, +5, bI3, ø, or "alt" in the chord symbol), add the following notes:

- To the II chord add the fifth.
- To the V chord add the ninth (or the b9).
- To the I chord add the fifth and the ninth.

The fifth of the II chord and the ninth of the V chord are the same note, which makes going from II to V very easy.

In the second line of **figure 5-3**, the V chords all have a b9. Practice **figure 5-3** through all the keys until it becomes second nature for you to add fifths and ninths to three-note voicings.

[1] John Coltrane, *Blue Trane*, Blue Note BST-8l577.

Figure 5-1

Figure 5-2

Figure 5-3

Look at **figure 5-4**, Wayne Shorter's beautiful ballad "Infant Eyes."[2] Notice all the new chords not found in "Just Friends," including sus, b9, alt, Phrygian, and +4 chords. You're going to play just the chord changes for now, so omit the melody. Voice the first chord, G-7, with a three-note voicing, putting the seventh on top, although the third on top would work just as well. Continue through the tune, always going to the voicing for the next chord that's closest for your right hand. Ignore for now the altered notes b9 in bar 4, +4 in bar 12, and b9 in bar 18. For the Fsus chord in bar 6, play the basic sus voicing you learned in Chapter Four.

Figure 5-4

Infant Eyes — Wayne Shorter

[2] Wayne Shorter, *Speak No Evil*, Blue Note BST-84194 (Herbie Hancock is the pianist on this great album).

Bar II contains an Eb Phrygian chord. Phrygian is the third mode of the major scale and Eb is the third note of the Cb major scale, which means that Eb Phrygian is in the key of Cb. The V chord in the key of Cb is Gb7, which explains the alternate chord symbol Gb7/Eb. Voice the Phrygian chord as you learned in Chapter Four, playing the root with your left hand and playing the b9, fourth, fifth, and root with your right hand **(figure 5-5)**.

Continue through the tune, always going to the closest notes in the right hand for the next chord. **Figure 5-6** shows the complete "Infant Eyes" arranged with three-note voicings.

Figure 5-5

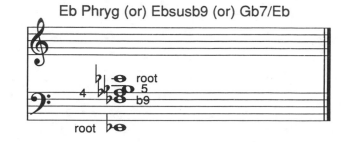

Eb Phryg (or) Ebsusb9 (or) Gb7/Eb

Figure 5-6

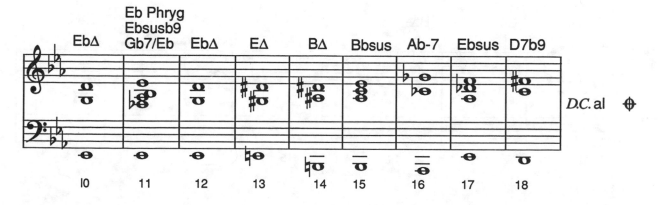

You're now ready to add the melody to "Infant Eyes." Remember, you don't have to add a fourth note if the melody already is the third or seventh of the chord. Because you'll be be playing four, five, six, or more notes from now on, it's OK to start playing two notes in the left hand instead of just the root. **Figure 5-7** shows "Infant Eyes" with the melody added.

Figure 5-7

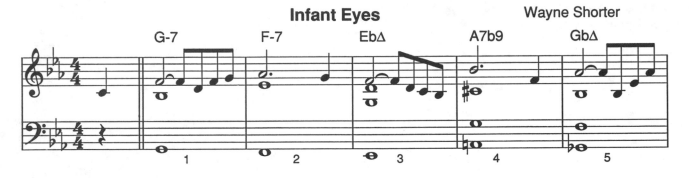

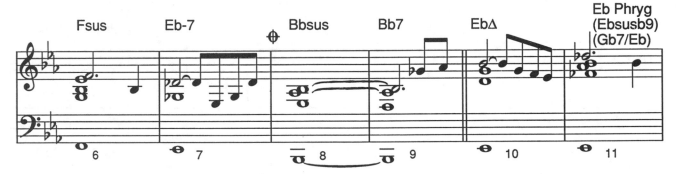

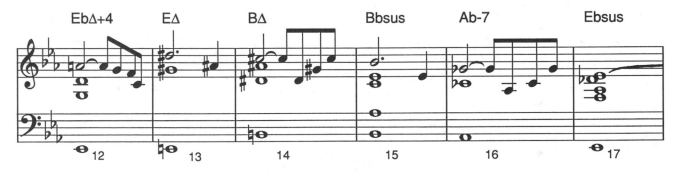

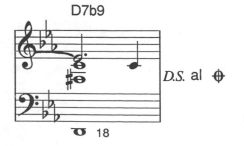

Notice that the melody note is often the altered note in the chord symbol, as in bars 4 (b9), 12 (+4), and 18 (b9). In the Bbsus chord in bar 8 there appears to be a note missing. In the basic sus voicing you learned in Chapter Four, your right hand plays a major triad a whole step below the root of the chord. A whole step below Bb is Ab, but the voicing in bar 8 has only Ab and Eb of the Ab triad, with the C missing. Try playing the C and you'll hear why it is omitted—it's too low and sounds muddy.

Cecil Taylor

Photo © by Jerry Stoll

Figure 5-8

Infant Eyes

Wayne Shorter

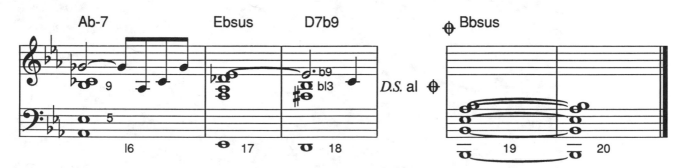

You can enhance "Infant Eyes" by adding just a few notes here and there to the three-note voicings. Play through **figure 5-8** and notice how much richer the tune now sounds.

The II chords in bars 1 and 2 have both the fifth and ninth added, the same combination you played in **figure 5-3**. In bar 3, the sixth and ninth have *replaced* the major seventh on the EbΔ chord. Even though the chord symbol specifically calls for the major seventh, you can usually substitute the sixth and ninth for the major seventh. The GbΔ chord in bar 5 includes the sixth, ninth, *and* the major seventh. Notice how well the thirteenth in bar 4 goes with the b9. These two notes often are played together in dominant seventh b9 chords. The seventh is omitted on the D7b9 voicing in bar 18 because it appears as the melody note on the fourth beat.

Note the doubled notes in bars 2, 6, 8-11, 13, 15, 17, and 19-20. They strengthen and enhance the voicings. If your left hand can't reach the tenths in bars 10 and 12, try "rolling" the tenths, as in **figure 5-9**.

There are no hard-and-fast rules for when to add what notes to a given chord. There are too many variables—what note is in the melody; whether you want a dense chord with lots of notes or a spacy, skeletal, or spread-out chord; how "dark" or "light" you want the chord to be; whether you're high or low on the keyboard; and so on. What follows is a chart of the *possible* notes that you can add to three-note minor seventh, dominant seventh, and major seventh voicings:

minor seventh	dominant seventh	major seventh
5	5	+4
b5 (on ø chord)	9	5
9	b9	+5
11	+9	6
6	+11	9
b6 (rare)	13	
+7 (on minor major chord)	b13 (or +5)	

As you can see, you have lots of choices. Some of the notes not listed deserve an explanation. On a I chord, for example, the minor third, fourth, minor seventh, or b9, all tend to destroy the tonal feeling of "major," so they are not commonly played. Anything is possible in music, however, depending on the context. Cecil Taylor might not hesitate to

Figure 5-9

EbΔ

Ped...............

play a major seventh on a dominant seventh chord, for example, and even such chord-based improvisers as Joe Henderson and Wayne Shorter can do it and make it sound good. If you played a major seventh on a dominant seventh chord while accompanying Ella Fitzgerald, however, you would probably be out of a job very fast. The context determines what is acceptable to your audience, your fellow musicians, and, most important, yourself.

Figures 5-10a through **5-10g** show a D-7 chord with many of the added or altered notes listed above. Adding the b5 **(figure 5-10b)**, gives you a *half-diminished chord*, a minor seventh chord with a b5, which is often notated with the symbol ø.

The sixth is sometimes played in place of the seventh **(figure 5-10e)**, but both the sixth and the seventh can also be played together **(figure 5-10f)**. A minor sixth chord doesn't really function as a II chord, but rather as a minor I, or *tonic minor*, chord. You could play a minor sixth chord as the first chord on George Gershwin's "Summertime," Bronislau Kaper's "Invitation," or Kenny Dorham's "Blue Bossa."

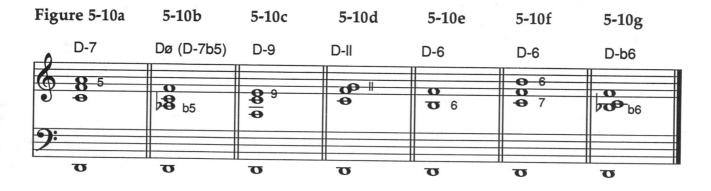

Figure 5-10a	5-10b	5-10c	5-10d	5-10e	5-10f	5-10g
D-7	Dø (D-7b5)	D-9	D-ll	D-6	D-6	D-b6

Figures 5-11a through **5-11h** show a G7 chord with many of the added or altered notes listed above. The b13 and the +5 are the same note, and can be notated either way **(figure 5-11g)**. The +9 and b13 often go together **(figure 5-11h)**, and are usually notated as "alt," which is shorthand for "altered." Altered means much more than just the +9 and the b13: it implies a scale that has four alterations (more on alt chords in Chapter Nine).

Figures 5-12a through **5-12f** show a CΔ chord with many of the added or altered notes listed above. Note that the raised fifth, G#, in **figure 5-12c**, together with the third and seventh, E and B, form an E major triad. This chord is often notated E/C.

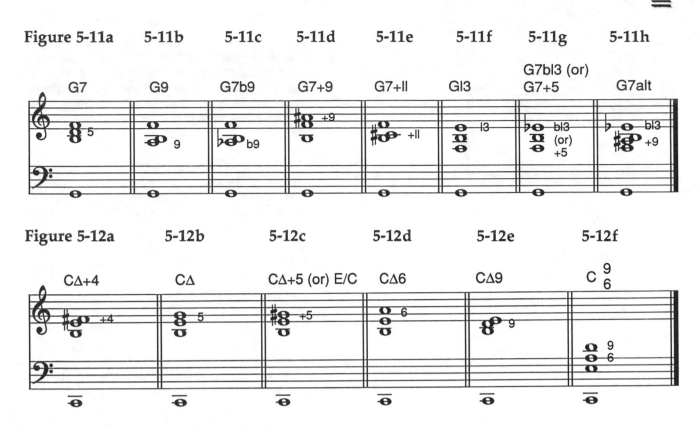

Figure 5-11a   5-11b   5-11c   5-11d   5-11e   5-11f   5-11g   5-11h

Figure 5-12a   5-12b   5-12c   5-12d   5-12e   5-12f

Play through lots of tunes, adding and altering notes to three-note voicings. You'll soon start to get a feel for what works.

There are a few chords not found in either "Just Friends" or "Infant Eyes," some playable as a three-note voicing, others needing a fourth note. The *minor-major* chord **(figure 5-13)** is shown both in close position and as a three-note voicing with an added fifth and ninth. Notice the two different ways to notate the chord. The first chord in Horace Silver's "Nica's Dream"[3] is a minor-major chord. *A minor-major chord always has a minor third, a perfect fifth, and a major seventh.* Although it's a minor chord, it's not a II chord—it functions as a minor I, or tonic minor, chord. There will be more on minor-major chords in Chapter Nine.

Another chord, especially common in old standards, is the *diminished seventh* chord **(figure 5-14)**, shown both in close position and as a two-handed voicing. In traditional theory, this chord is made up of a root, minor third, diminished fifth, and doubly diminished seventh. However, it's much easier to think of the diminished seventh chord as a *series of minor thirds stacked on top of each other.* The diminished seventh chord is usually notated either with a small circle, as in Co, or as Co7.

Figure 5-13

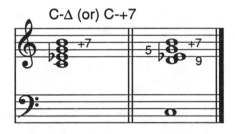

Figure 5-14

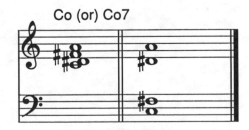

---

[3] Horace Silver, *Horace-Scope*, Blue Note 4042.

Figure 5-15

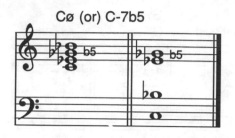

Cø (or) C-7b5

Figure 5-16

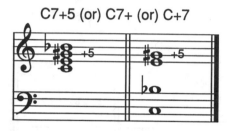

C7+5 (or) C7+ (or) C+7

Diminished chords occur in the third bar of the bridge of Duke Ellington's "Sophisticated Lady," the second bar of Antonio Carlos Jobim's "Wave," and in bar 28 of Chick Corea's "Mirror, Mirror." Diminished chords usually function as a kind of disguised dominant seventh b9 chord. There will be more on diminished seventh chords in Chapter Nine.

The *half-diminished chord*, mentioned briefly before, is shown in **figure 5-15**, both in close position and as a two-handed voicing. Half-diminished is a shorthand term for a minor seventh b5 chord. In older music, you're likely to see this chord written as C-7b5. In newer music, you'll probably see the same chord notated as Cø. The first chord in McCoy Tyner's "Search For Peace,"[4] Horace Silver's "Peace,"[5] and Dave Brubeck's "In Your Own Sweet Way"[6] are all half-diminished chords. *A half-diminished chord always has a minor third, a flatted fifth, and a minor seventh.* Half-diminished chords function as II chords, and are often played when the I chord in a II-V-I progression is a tonic minor chord, as in Dø, G7alt, C-∆.

The *whole-tone chord*, shown in **figure 5-16** both in close position and as a two-handed voicing, is usually notated C7+5, and sometimes as C7b13 (+5 and b13 are the same note). The chord symbol C7+5 is often shortened to C7+ and sometimes to C+7. This can be confusing, since the + has nothing to do with the 7. G7+5 occurs in bar 17 of "Stella By Starlight," although G7alt is sometimes played there instead. There will be more on both alt and whole-tone chords in Chapter Nine. *A whole-tone chord always has a major third, an augmented fifth, and a minor seventh.* Whole-tone chords function as V chords.

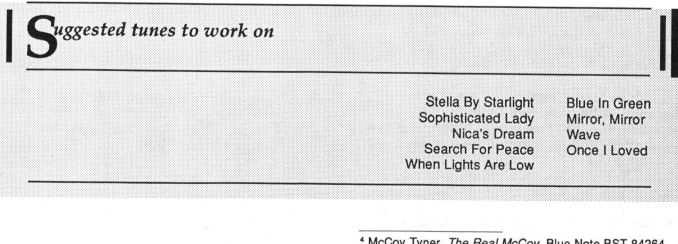

*S*uggested tunes to work on

Stella By Starlight	Blue In Green
Sophisticated Lady	Mirror, Mirror
Nica's Dream	Wave
Search For Peace	Once I Loved
When Lights Are Low	

---

[4] McCoy Tyner, *The Real McCoy*, Blue Note BST 84264.

[5] Horace Silver, *Blowin' The Blues Away*, Blue Note 84017.

[6] Miles Davis, *Workin' and Steamin'*, Prestige 24034 (Red Garland on piano).

CHAPTER SIX
Tritone Substitution

Play **figure 6-1**, the first four bars of Jerome Kern's "All The Things You Are." Now play **figure 6-2**. What's your reaction to the reharmonization in the third bar? Does it sound more "modern"? Does the progression sound smoother? Do you like it? What you're hearing is *tritone substitution*.

Jazz musicians like to use substitute chords. A substitute chord is just what it sounds like: a chord that substitutes for another chord. The most common type of substitute chord is tritone substitution. **Figure 6-3** shows a II-V-I progression in the key of C, immediately followed by the same progression, with a Db7 chord substituting for G7, a tritone substitution. Play both progressions and listen to the difference. Substituting Db7 for G7 makes the bass line chromatic. Bass players love tritone substitution for this reason.

This is how tritone substitution works: Remember from Chapter Two that the two most important notes in seventh chords are the third and the seventh. The interval between the third and seventh of a dominant chord is a tritone **(figure 6-4)**. Since this interval doesn't occur in major seventh or minor seventh chords, its presence *defines* the dominant chord. If you play just the two notes of the tritone, they strongly suggest a V chord, incomplete though it may be. What's so unusual about the tritone is that it's the third and seventh of *two* different dominant seventh chords **(figure 6-5)**. B and F, the third and seventh of G7, are the same notes as Cb and F, the seventh and third of Db7. Because of this, G7 and Db7 can substitute for each other. Incidentally, notes such as B and Cb, which are the same but are spelled differently, are called *enharmonic*.

Figure 6-1

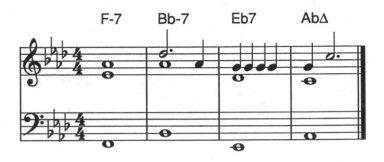

Figure 6-2

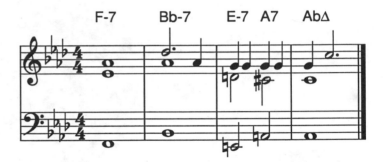

Figure 6-3 .

Figure 6-4   **Figure 6-5**

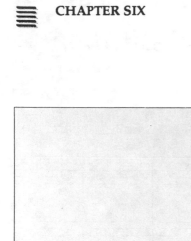

Bud Powell

Photo © by Chuck Stewart

The tritone, and the V chord that it is part of, are very unstable and want very much to resolve, as in **figure 6-6**. If you play a tritone ten times in a row before you go to bed tonight **(figure 6-7)**, you probably won't be able to fall asleep—you'll have to get up, run to the piano, and resolve it to a I chord **(figure 6-8)**. Because the tritone belongs to two dominant seventh chords, you could also resolve it to its *other* I chord **(figure 6-9)**.

B and F, the third and seventh of G7, are also Cb and F, the seventh and third of a Db7 chord. The third and seventh of a V chord always form the interval of a tritone, no matter which note is on top. Remember, this is because the tritone is exactly half an octave, and inverts to another tritone (recall from Chapter One that a tritone inverts to a tritone, 4 and 1/2 plus 4 and l/2 equal nine). The roots of the G7 and Db7 chords are also a tritone apart.

Other than smooth bass motion, another reason to use tritone substitution is that it often makes the melody more interesting. Bars 3l-33 of "All The Things You Are" are shown in **figure 6-10**. The melody note on the F7 chord, G, is the ninth of the chord. In **figure 6-11,** B7 substitutes for the original F7 chord, not only making for chromatic bass motion, but also changing the melody note from a ninth to a +5. Reharmonization such as this transforms old standards into tunes that sound fresher and more modern.

Figure 6-6

Figure 6-7

etc.

Figure 6-8

Figure 6-9

Figure 6-10

Figure 6-11

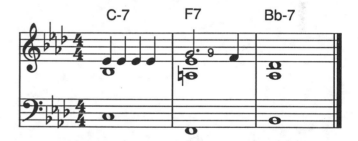

Figure 6-12

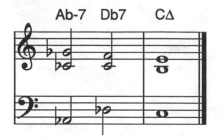

Figure 6-13

The early bebop musicians extended tritone substitution, often preceding the substitute V chord with its II chord. Not only can you substitute Db7 for G7, you can also precede Db7 with Ab-7 to make a II-V progression **(figure 6-12)**. Look back at **figures 6-1** and **6-2** to see this idea in action. A7 substitutes for Eb7, and is preceded by E-7 to make a II-V progression—E-7, A7—in **figure 6-2**. Charlie Parker, Bud Powell, Thelonious Monk, and others used this idea in their original compositions as well as when reharmonizing standards, as shown in **figure 6-13**, bars 9-10 of Bud's "Dance Of The Infidels."[1] The G-7 bar is followed not by the expected C7, which would create a II-V progression, but by Gb7, the tritone substitution of C7. Gb7 is preceded by Db-7, making a II-V, Db-7, Gb7—the II-V tritone substitution of C7.

A cautionary note is necessary here. You can overdo tritone substitution, which can sound terrible if it results in an awkward bass line or clashes with the melody. Don't forget to use your taste as you learn new techniques.

Suggested tunes to work on

Just Friends	All The Things You Are
Tune Up	I Should Care
A Foggy Day	Tea For Two
Yesterdays	Sweet And Lovely

---

[1] Bud Powell, *The Amazing Bud Powell, Vol. I*, Blue Note 1503.

Left-Hand Voicings

Voicing chords with your left hand gives your right hand the freedom to play the melody or improvise. Play **figure 7-1** and experience this new freedom. Your left hand provides a harmonic cushion for your right hand to play a line over, despite the lack of a root in the chord. Art Tatum, Errol Garner, and Ahmad Jamal occasionally played these non-root position chords, and by the mid-1950s, Red Garland was playing them often. Bill Evans and Wynton Kelly then developed them further, and by the late-1950s were playing them much more consistently. Before that, most bebop pianists followed Bud Powell's lead, playing two- or three-note root position voicings (see Chapter Seventeen).

   None of the chords in **figure 7-1**—D-7, G7alt or CΔ—has a root in its voicing. The C "major seventh" chord doesn't even have a major seventh! Left-hand voicings give you a lot more flexibility. You're not tied to playing the root, and your left hand is higher up on the keyboard, playing chords that include ninths and thirteenths. Don't worry about the lack of a root in the chord. When playing in a rhythm section, the bass player will often play the root on the first beat of a given chord, and jazz pianists even use these voicings when playing solo piano.

Figure 7-1

Figure 7-2

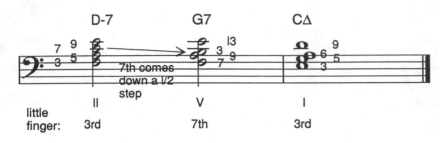

little
finger: 3rd   7th   3rd

Figure 7-3

There are many left-hand voicings, but I'll begin with the basic ones. Look at **figure 7-2**, a II-V-I progression in the key of C. Play the D-7 chord. Your left hand is playing F-A-C-E, the third, fifth, seventh, and ninth of D-7. Remember, although this chord looks like a root position FΔ chord, these are rootless voicings—it's really D-7. If you're not used to playing chords without the root, reach over with your right hand and play a low D to reassure yourself that, indeed, this is truly a D-7 chord. Now play it again, this time without the root. You should quickly get used to hearing the voicing without the root underneath.

Remember what happens in a II-V when you play three-note voicings? *The seventh comes down a half step.* The same thing happens with left-hand voicings. Three notes of the D-7 voicing stay the same when you resolve to the G7 chord. Only the seventh, C, resolves down a half step to B, the third of the G7 chord. You now have the seventh, ninth, third, and thirteenth of G7. Again, reach over with your right hand and play the root, G, to hear how the chord sounds with a root on the bottom.

Go on to the CΔ chord—playing the third, fifth, sixth, and ninth with your left hand—and you have the complete II-V-I. There's no B, or major seventh, in this C "major seventh" chord, but you can freely substitute the sixth and ninth for the major seventh. Sometimes an arranger specifically wants this effect and writes the chord symbol C69.

Some pianists, McCoy Tyner for example, play the third, fifth, seventh, and ninth on a I chord **(figure 7-3)**. For now, choose which voicing you like best for the I chord and stick to it, returning later to learn the other one.

Some pianists call these the "A" position left-hand voicings. Practice them through all twelve keys around the cycle of fifths. Keep your little finger between middle C and the C an octave below. Remember, the II chord looks like a root position major seventh chord and you only have to move the seventh down a half step to get to the V chord. Go slowly, be accurate, and *remember what key you're in*. As an example, if you find yourself playing E natural on a Db7 chord you'll know that something is wrong because there's no E natural in the key of Gb. When in doubt, reach over and play the root with your right hand.

Notice what note of the chord your little finger is playing on each of these II-V-I voicings. The sequence is third-seventh-third **(figure 7-2)**. The "B" position voicings are just the opposite, the little finger playing the seventh-third-seventh. For D-7 in the "B" position, take the same four notes you played in the "A" position and rearrange them so that the seventh is on the bottom, as in **figure 7-4**. The example is written in the treble clef for ease of reading, but play the chords with your left hand. In the "B" position, the bottom two notes of D-7 in the "A" position have been transposed to the top of the voicing. Reading from the bottom up, you now have the seventh, ninth, third, and fifth of D-7. Again, the seventh comes down a half step, and you have G7, the V chord. The G7 chord has exactly the same notes it had in the "A" position, but now, arranged from the bottom up, you have the third, thirteenth, seventh, and ninth.

For the I chord, play the seventh, root, third, and fifth, and you'll have the entire II-V-I in "B" position. Think of the I chord here as a major triad with the major seventh tacked on to the bottom. This I chord *has* the major seventh, B, unlike the I chord in the "A" position. Also, the root, C, is in the voicing, but not on the bottom where you'd normally expect a root to be. Some pianists play seventh, ninth, third, and fifth for the I chord **(figure 7-5)**. This option is OK, but use it with care. By itself it sounds more like a G6 chord than a C△ chord. If you precede it with a G7 chord, it will sound like a C△ chord. If you precede it with some other chord, however, it could sound too much like G6. If you or your bass player play C, the root, underneath, the chord will sound like C△. You may be playing solo piano, however, with no bass player. Even if you do have a bass player, *bass players don't always play the root*.

Play the II-V-I in "B" position again **(figure 7-4)**, and practice it through all twelve keys, going around the cycle of fifths. Note the symmetry of the II chord. The bottom interval is a major third, as is the top interval, and they are separated by a half step **(figure 7-6)**. "Seeing" the chord in this way helps you get past the arithmetic stage of theory. Try to be aware of what the chord *looks* and *feels* like (its hand position), as you play it. When McCoy Tyner is playing a million notes a minute, he's not thinking "left-hand voicing, 3-5-7-9, seventh down a half step." He's done that already, many years ago. He knows what the chord looks and feels like when he plays it. Aim for that state of grace, when you no longer have to think about theory. In order to reach that point of mastery, however, you'll have to think about theory a great deal.

Figure 7-4

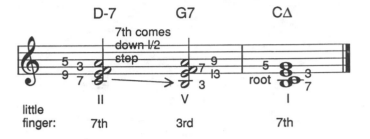

Figure 7-5

Figure 7-6

Figure 7-7

Tune-Up

Miles Davis

Figure 7-8

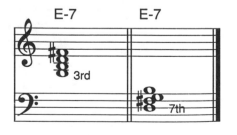

After you've gone through the cycle a few times in both positions, look at the lead sheet of Miles Davis' composition "Tune-Up"[1] **(figure 7-7)**.

"Tune-Up," first recorded in the 1950s, is a popular jam session tune. Ignore the melody for now. You're going to play E-7, the first chord, with a left-hand voicing, but should you start with your little finger on the third or on the seventh? Try both **(figure 7-8)**. The voicing with the seventh on the bottom is a bit muddy, probably too low to start with, so go with the one that has the third on the bottom. The first three chords in the tune are a II-V-I, so play the third-seventh-third sequence you just learned. You should end up with your little finger on the F# of the DΔ chord. The chord after DΔ is D-7. What's the closest D-7, little finger on the third or on the seventh? Since your little finger is on F#, and the third of D-7 is F natural, the choice is easy. Again, you have a II-V-I. The chord following CΔ is C-7,

[1] Miles Davis, *Relaxin'*, Fantasy/OJC I90 (with Red Garland on piano).

and again, go to the closest C-7 and complete another II-V-I. Stop at this point, go back to the top and play through the first eleven bars again, comparing what you've played with the first eleven bars in **figure 7-9**.

The next chord, in bar l2, is Eb△. What's the closest Eb△? Little finger on third or seventh? The closest voicing is the one with the seventh on the bottom. Try it and you'll find that you're in "muddy waters." If you're playing a nine-foot Steinway, this voicing might sound OK. On most pianos, however, it's a bit too low. If you shift up to the other voicing, with the third on the bottom, you'll be in a better range of the piano. **Figure 7-9** shows the complete "Tune-Up" with left-hand voicings.

Now add the melody to "Tune-Up." If you play the melody exactly where it's written in the lead sheet **(figure 7-7)**, your hands will bump into each other almost immediately. The solution is to play the melody an octave up. The melody on a lead sheet is usually written in the middle register of the treble clef *for ease of reading only*. You can play the melody anywhere you want on the piano. Most pianists switch octaves often, playing the melody where it's written for eight bars and then taking it up an octave for the next eight bars, as an example. This provides contrast and enables you to play different voicings during similar sections of the tune.

Figure 7-10 shows the complete "Tune-Up" with the melody added.

Figure 7-9

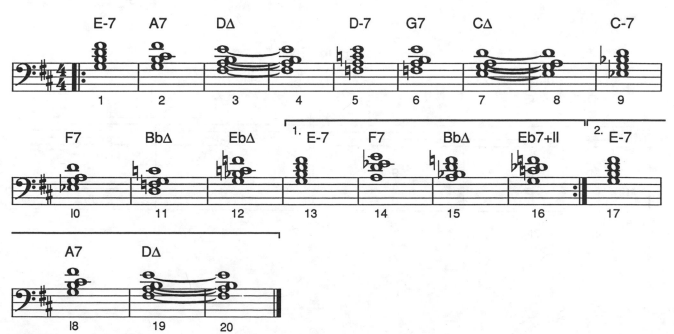

Figure 7-10

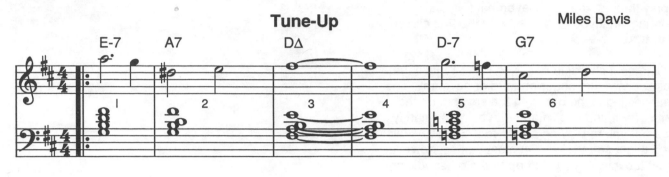

Tune-Up

Miles Davis

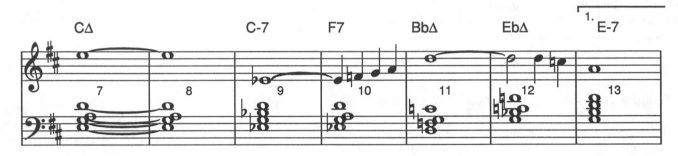

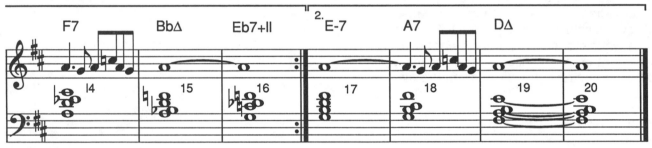

Figure 7-11

Left-hand voicings for II-V-I

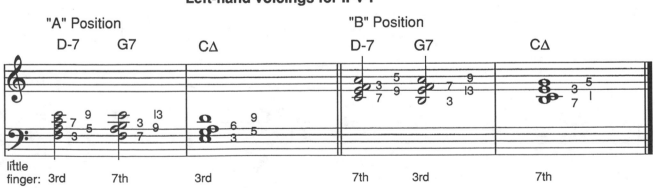

Practice tips

As you voice the chords in a tune, ask yourself two questions:

1) Is this a II-V? If so, all you have to do is lower the seventh a half step.
2) If it's not a II-V, what's the closest position for the next chord, little finger on the third or seventh?

Until you have all the numbers memorized, use the complete left-hand voicing chart (**figure 7-11**).

You might find that a V chord not preceded by its II chord is a little hard to find. If so, practice the V chords separately, as follows:

1) Play the V chords, third in the little finger, through the cycle.
2) Play the V chords, seventh in the little finger, through the cycle.
3) Alternate the V chords, first with the seventh in the little finger, then with the third in the little finger (**figure 7-12**).
4) Alternate the V chords, first with the third in the little finger, then with the seventh in the little finger (**figure 7-13**).

A final note: You can also play left-hand voicings with the right hand, the left hand playing the root in the bass (**figure 7-14**). This would be most appropriate when accompanying a singer or a horn player in a duo situation, with no bass player.

Figure 7-12

Figure 7-13

Figure 7-14

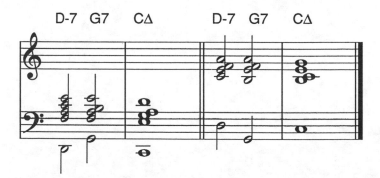

Bill Evans and Tony Bennett

Photo © by Phil Bray

Suggested tunes to work on

Just Friends	Autumn Leaves
Autumn In New York	Beatrice
Invitation	Tune-Up
Satin Doll	Take The "A" Train
Giant Steps	

Altering Notes in Left-Hand Voicings

Play **figure 8-1**. The left-hand voicings you learned in Chapter Seven have been altered in this example. Listen to these new sounds.

Figure 8-2 shows five new voicings for the *half-diminished* chord. Half-diminished means a minor seventh chord with a b5. The first two shown are left-hand voicings that you have already learned for a D-7 chord: third in the little finger and seventh in the little finger, but with the fifth flatted. The third voicing shown has the root in the little finger. The fourth voicing has the b5 in the little finger. The last voicing has the fourth (or eleventh, they are the same note) on the bottom. Which of these new voicings you choose when playing Dø depends on what chord you're coming from, what chord you're going to, where you are on the keyboard, what the melody note is, and more.

Some of these new half-diminished voicings may look familiar. The first one is the same as a root position F-Δ chord. The third one is the same as one of the voicings you learned for a Bb7 chord, with the third in the little finger. The fourth one is the same as a minor-major voicing for F-Δ with the third in the little finger. *You can play the same left-hand voicing for several different chords.*

Figure 8-3 shows two left-hand voicings for a G7b9 chord, with the seventh and third in the little finger, respectively.

Figure 8-4 shows two left-hand voicings for a G7+5 chord, with the seventh or the third in the little finger. In Chapter Seven, all of the left-hand voicings that you learned for dominant seventh chords had a thirteenth but no fifth. When there is a +5 in the chord symbol, you have to flat the thirteenth because +5 and b13 are the same note. The +5 and b13 of a G7 chord—D# and Eb—are the same note. Remember, that means they are *enharmonic.* The G7+5 symbol is often shortened to G7+, and sometimes is notated G+7, which can be confusing because the + refers to the fifth, rather than the seventh.

Figure 8-1

Figure 8-2

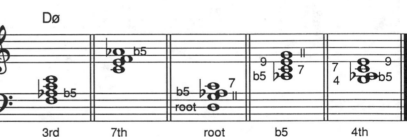

Figure 8-3

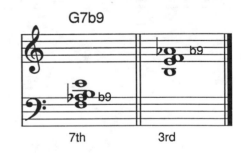

Figure 8-4

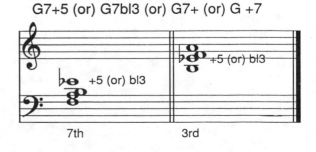

Figure 8-5

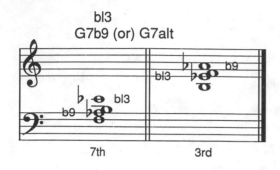

bl3
G7b9 (or) G7alt

7th   3rd

Figure 8-5 shows two voicings for a G7b9, bl3 chord, seventh or third in the little finger. This chord might be also notated as G7alt, but the next example illustrates two more commonly used voicings for an alt chord.

Figure 8-6

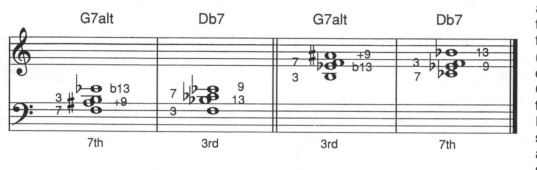

G7alt   Db7   G7alt   Db7

7th   3rd   3rd   7th

Figure 8-6 shows two G7alt chords, both with a +9 and a bl3. "Alt" is short for "altered," and means much more than just +9 and bl3. It implies a scale with *four* alterations, the b9, +9, +ll, and bl3 of a dominant chord (scales will be covered in the next chapter). For now, when you see a dominant seventh chord with "alt" as part of the chord symbol, raise the ninth and flat the thirteenth in the left-hand voicing. Both of these G7alt voicings are enharmonically the same as the Db7 chords shown to their right. Although they're spelled differently (the A# and B in the G7alt chords are spelled Bb and Cb in the Db7 chords), the two voicings—G7alt and Db7—have exactly the same notes. This is also an example of tritone substitution: G7 and Db7 share the same third and seventh, or tritone, and G and Db are a tritone apart.

Figure 8-7

G7   G7alt   Db7   Db7alt   G7

As shown in figure 8-7, it may be easier for you to find a G7alt voicing by thinking that the "tritone substitution for G7alt is Db7," rather than by thinking "G7: sharp the ninth, flat the thirteenth." In the figure, the left-hand voicing for G7 has it's ninth sharped and thirteenth flatted, turning it into a G7alt chord, which is enharmonically the same as a left-hand voicing for Db7. Then the Db7 has it's ninth sharped and its thirteenth flatted, turning it into a Db7alt chord, awkwardly spelled F-A-Cb-E, which is enharmonically the same as F-A-B-E, and you're back to G7 again!

Suppose that the chord symbol were G7+ll. None of the dominant seventh voicings you learned in Chapter Seven had an eleventh. The eleventh of G7 is C (don't forget, the eleventh and fourth are the same note), so the +ll would be C#. You don't have to change anything because +ll is always an *optional* alteration in a dominant seventh voicing. If you do want the +ll, however, there are two commonly used left-hand voicings. In the first version, move the closest note in the voicing to the +11. The closest note to C# in a G7 voicing is B, the third, so move B to C# and you'll have G7+11 (**figure 8-8**), shown here with both the little finger on the seventh, and the little finger on the +11. If you're not used to the sound of this chord, reach over and play the root, G, a couple of octaves below. Now play the chord without the root.

The second way to play G7+11 is, reading up from the bottom, the seventh, third, +4, and thirteenth (**figure 8-9**). You can also invert this chord, playing the third in the little finger, but this voicing sounds cramped.

The G7+11 voicings in **Figure 8-8** have no third. An often-repeated myth is that "you have to have both the third and seventh in a dominant seventh chord." That's true of *unaltered* dominant chords, but once you start altering notes on dominant chords, the boundaries of what defines a dominant seventh chord become more flexible, and strange (and beautiful) sounds will happen.

Figure 8-10 shows two voicings for a C7+9 chord, third or seventh in the little finger. Dominant seventh +9 chords usually have a fifth but no thirteenth in the voicing, as in both of these examples. The second voicing, with the seventh in the little finger, is seldom played because the voicing with the third in the little finger sounds so much stronger.

The *minor-major* chord, discussed briefly in Chapter Five, is a minor chord with a major seventh. Unlike minor seventh chords, minor-major chords don't usually function as II chords, but as minor I chords, also called *tonic minor* chords. A common chord symbol for minor-major chords is a dash with a triangle, as in D-Δ. An alternate chord symbol is a dash with a +7 above or after the dash, as in D- +7. You can usually substitute D-Δ when the chord symbol says D- or D-6, unless the melody note is the sixth or the seventh. In **figure 8-11**, D minor-major is shown in two positions, third or seventh in the little finger. Note that these two voicings are exactly the same as the two voicings for G7+11 in **figure 8-8**. The G7alt and Db7 voicings in **figure 8-5** also shared the same voicing, but they were both dominant chords, and dominant chords a tritone apart can substitute for each other. How can a minor chord and a dominant chord have the same voicing? Once the harmony starts to become complex, the usual distinctions between major, minor, and dominant begin to blur, making possible many things that don't occur in traditional harmony.

Figure 8-8

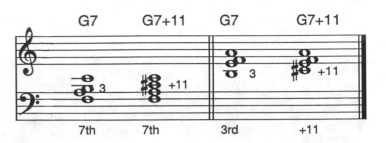

Figure 8-9

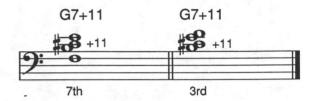

Figure 8-10

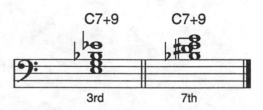

Figure 8-11

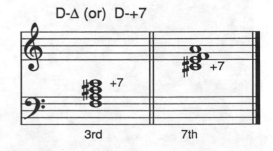

Wynton Kelly, Paul Chambers, Jimmy Cobb

Photo © by Lee Tanner

For the *diminished seventh chord*, also mentioned briefly in Chapter Five, first play the chord in root position, a series of minor thirds stacked on top of each other (**figure 8-12**). This sounds a bit tame, so raise the top note a whole step for a much hipper left-hand voicing. This gives you exactly the same voicing as G7b9.

Figure 8-13 shows three handy left-hand voicings for a Gsus chord. The first voicing has only three notes and is often played because of the extra "space" that a sus chord evokes. The second and third voicings shown are identical to the D-7 left-hand voicings that you learned in the previous chapter. Since a sus chord acts like a II-V contained in a single chord, a Gsus chord is like D-7 and G7 combined into D-7/G, which is how it's often notated.

Figure 8-14 shows a left-hand voicing for a Phrygian chord. Reading up from the bottom, it consists of the root, b9, fourth, and fifth.

It's time to put into practice some of these new voicings. Look at **Figure 8-15**, an arrangement of the Jimmy Van Heusen-Johnny Mercer standard, "I Thought About You."[1] This version has been reharmonized somewhat, in part to create opportunities for you to play the new voicings. Glance through the chord symbols—you'll see half-diminished, alt, +ll, b9, and minor-major chords.

Figure 8-12

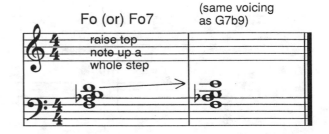

Figure 8-13

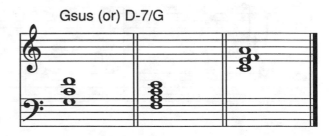

Figure 8-14

E Phrygian
(or) Esusb9
(or) G7/E

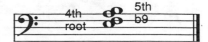

---

[1] Miles Davis, *Someday My Prince Will Come*, Columbia PC 8456. The piano solo on the title track is one of Wynton Kelly's best.

Figure 8-15

I Thought About You

Jimmy Van Heusen &
Johnny Mercer

Figure 8-15 (Continued)

The first chord in "I Thought About You" is Bø. You went through five choices for a half-diminished chord in **figure 8-2**. You could start with your little finger on the third, D, but that would be pretty low on the piano. You could start with your little finger on the seventh, A, but since the top note of the voicing would be the same as the melody note, your hands would bump into each other. You could start with your little finger on the root, B, but that would put you even higher on the piano, forcing you to play the melody an octave higher. That's a viable option, but for now play the melody exactly where it's written. Putting your little finger on F, the b5, places you right in the middle of the range for left-hand voicings (roughly from middle C to the C below), allows room for your right hand to play the melody, and, most important, *sounds good*.

Play through "I Thought About You." Except for the last two bars, all of the chords are left-hand voicings. The basic criteria used here for deciding which voicings to play as you move from chord to chord are:

- Smoothness of motion.
- Keeping your hands from bumping into each other.
- Keeping your left hand in the best range for left-hand voicings, with your little finger, for the most part, between middle C and the C an octave below.

Play through the arrangement a few times, getting used to what may be some very new sounds for you. Then read through the following notes:

bar 2:   The optional +II of the Eb7+II chord is in the melody, so you can omit it from your left-hand voicing.

bar 4:   The optional +II of the Ab7+II chord is played here, while the right hand improvises a line on the chord (the same thing happens in bar 20).

bar 5:   The left hand plays only three notes on the G-7 voicing to keep your hands from bumping into each other (the same thing happens in bar 21).

bar 10:   Coming from the previous
              chord, the closest Bb-7
              would be with your little
              finger on a low Db. That's
              too low and sounds muddy,
              so play Bb-7 with your little
              finger on the seventh.

bar 11:   After the FΔ, the closest
              G-7 would be with the third
              in the little finger. The
              voicing with the seventh
              in the little finger is played
              here because it moves
              more smoothly into the next
              two chords.

bar 14:   Because there was another
              Bø chord in the previous
              bar, the voicing with the
              seventh in the little finger is
              played here for variety.

bars 17-18:   The Bb7+ll, A7alt, and Ab7
              voicings played here are
              enharmonically the same
              as the E7alt, Eb7+ll, and
              D7alt chords in bars 1-2.
              What's the difference
              between them? None,
              unless you have a bass
              player, and the *bass
              player plays the root on
              all three chords.* Bass
              players love to play tritone
              substitution on dominant
              chords however, so don't
              count on it.

bar 22:   There is a shift upward,
              going from E-7 to A7alt,
              to avoid going too low
              on the A7alt.

bar 23:   This is a reharmonization,
              using D-Δ in place of D-7,
              the original chord.

bar 25:   This is a new voicing for a
              major seventh chord, with
              the little finger on the fifth.

Don't be overwhelmed by the sudden abundance of new voicings. As you go through a tune, many voicings will eliminate themselves as choices by being either too high or too low, not smooth-flowing going from chord to chord, or because your hands would bump into each other. After a few practice sessions, you'll have many of these voicings memorized. In addition, you'll gravitate toward a few of your favorites, a process that marks the beginning of a personal "style" in your playing.

There are more left-hand voicings, which will be covered in Chapter Sixteen.

Suggested tunes to work on

Blue In Green	Stella By Starlight
Search For Peace	Inner Urge
Old Folks	Woody'n You
What Is This Thing Called Love?	Quiet Now
Peace	

Introduction: why scales?

Take yourself back to the year 1940 B.C.P. (Before Charlie Parker). You're a young jazz musician struggling to learn how to improvise. You've been hanging around older, more experienced musicians with the hope that they will show you some of their secrets. Your first theory lesson consists of the following: "On a D-7 chord you can play D-F-A-C, the root, third, fifth, and seventh of the chord." A few days later, a more educated musician tells you that you can also play E-G-B, the ninth, eleventh, and thirteenth. Play **figure 9-1**, the root, third, fifth, and seventh with your left hand, the ninth, eleventh, and thirteenth with your right hand.

Jazz education has come a long way since 1940, but most musicians still play the same notes on a D-7 chord. What has changed is the way we think about the notes. Because we learned the alphabet as A-B-C-D, and so on, it's not easy to think of every *other* letter of the alphabet, as in D-F-A-C-E-G-B. And because we learned numbers as I-2-3-4, and so forth, it's not easy to think of every *other* number, as in I-3-5-7-9-II-I3. D-7 isn't too difficult to visualize on the piano, because it's all white notes. Ab-7 is a little tougher, because it's a mix of black and white notes. If the chord were C#7alt, with a b9, a +9 that looks like a minor third, a +II, bI3, and no fifth, it would be even more difficult. At this point, many students exclaim "This is too hard," and give up. Fortunately, there's an easier way.

Take another look at **figure 9-1**. This time drop your right hand an octave, superimposing it over your left hand **(figure 9-2)**. Play all seven notes at the same time. You now see the seven notes of a scale, or mode, the D Dorian mode, shown to the right. A scale is much easier to remember than a grouping of thirds, as in **figure 9-1**. *That's the reason jazz musicians think of scales, or modes, when they improvise, because it's easier than thinking chords.*

Scales have a negative connotation for many people, because they conjure up the image of a classical pianist banging away in a rote fashion for eight hours a day. You'll certainly have to practice scales in order to use them when you improvise, but the best jazz musicians think of them more as an

Figure 9-1

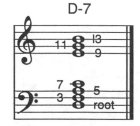

Figure 9-2

D Dorian mode

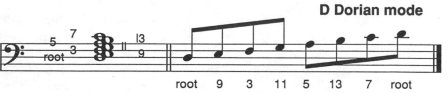

root   9   3   11   5   13   7   root

"available pool of notes" to play on a given chord, rather than as "do-re-me-fa-sol," and so on. Try this out yourself. Play a left-hand voicing for C∆ and improvise with your right hand, playing all the notes in C major, but trying *not* to play them as a scale. Granted, C major is the easiest key to do this in, but after you've practiced this technique for a while, you'll find that it's just as easy in any key.

As you can see in **figure 9-2**, the notes in an extended D-7 chord are exactly the same as the notes in the D Dorian mode. Remember this, because everybody uses the expression "play this scale on that chord" as if the scale and the chord were two different things. *The scale and the chord are, for the most part, two forms of the same thing.* Since we're going to be thinking of scales and chords as being the same thing, let's review the rules for the three basic chords: major seventh, minor seventh, and dominant seventh. The same rules will apply for most scales.

- A major seventh chord has a major third and a major seventh.
- A minor seventh chord has a minor third and a minor seventh.
- A dominant seventh chord has a major third and a minor seventh.

Major scale harmony

Because you can play more than one scale on a given chord, the scales presented here are in the category of "basic first choices." Different musicians play different scales on the same chords. Bud Powell and Herbie Hancock, two giants of jazz piano, played different scales on half-diminished chords, for instance. Keep an open mind—and open ears.

Look at the Major Scale Harmony chart **(figure 9-3)**.[1] The C major scale is shown here in all its modes, Ionian, Dorian, Phrygian, Lydian, and so on. The first, or Ionian, mode goes with some kind of C chord. What kind of a third and seventh does it have? Because it has a major third and a major seventh, it's the mode for a C∆ chord. Now look at the second, or Dorian, mode, which runs from D to D. It goes with some kind of D chord. Because it

---

[1] Reprinted in appendix as "Appendix A."

Figure 9-3

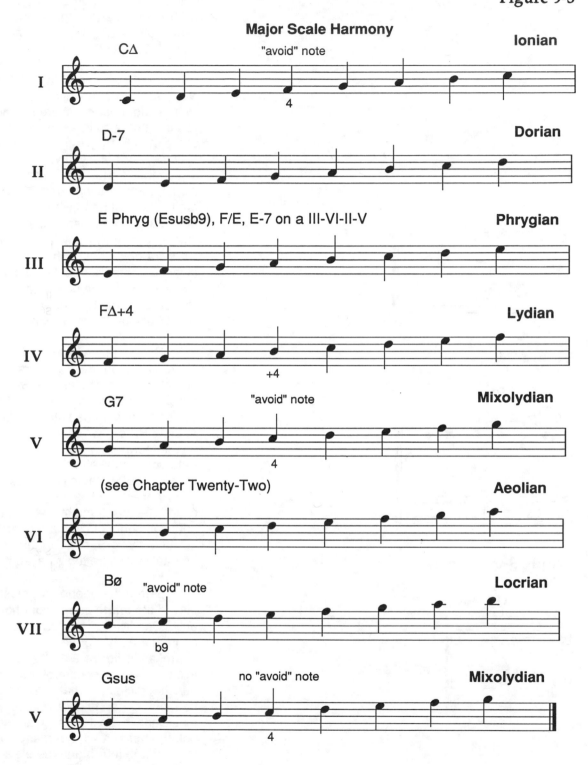

has a minor third and a minor seventh, it's the mode for a D-7 chord. Now skip to the fifth, or Mixolydian, mode, which runs from G to G. Because it has a major third and a minor seventh, it's the mode for a G7 chord. These are the scales, or modes, to play over D-7, G7, C△, the II-V-I in the key of C.

Figure 9-4

CΔ

Figure 9-5

BbΔ

Figure 9-6

CΔ+4

At this point, a logical question is: "Why bother with scales and modes? The D Dorian, G Mixolydian, and C Ionian modes all have the same notes. Why not just think 'play in C major,' on D-7, G7, CΔ?"

Good question. Play a left-hand voicing for CΔ with your left hand while playing the C Ionian mode with the right hand. There is a note in the mode that you can't play quite as freely as the other six notes of the mode. Play the left-hand voicing while you play the fourth, F, with your right hand. Hear the dissonance? This is a so-called "avoid" note. Play the left-hand voicing again, this time playing a short run in the right hand with F in the middle of it, as in **figure 9-4**. The dissonance is hardly noticeable this time, because F is now a *passing note*, and is not struck or held against the chord. "Avoid" note is not a very good term, because it implies that you shouldn't play it. A better name would be "handle with care" note. Unfortunately, that's not as catchy, so I'll (reluctantly) stick with "avoid" note.

The context will determine how much dissonance you play. The first note in the ninth bar of Victor Young's "Stella By Starlight" is a fourth on a major seventh chord **(figure 9-5)**, the "avoid" note, but it resolves immediately to the major third. Andrew Hill or Don Pullen might not hesitate to stay on the fourth on a major seventh chord, but Oscar Peterson is unlikely to play it except as a passing note. If you're playing an "outside," or free piece, or one where there is a long section of just a single chord, the fourth might just be the most interesting note you could play on a Δ chord. If you're accompanying Sarah Vaughn, however, she probably won't be too pleased if you play the fourth.

Before the bebop era, most jazz musicians played the fourth of a major chord as a passing note only. Charlie Parker, Bud Powell, Thelonious Monk, and other early pioneers of bebop often *raised* the fourth, as in **figure 9-6**. It's hard to believe now, but this note was very controversial at one time, and purists proclaimed that "jazz is dead" as modern harmony began to be widely played by jazz musicians in the 1940s. The raised fourth is notated here as +4, but many musicians call it +11 instead (the fourth and the eleventh are the same note). Back in the 1940s, it was called a b5, but as more and more jazz musicians started thinking of scales while improvising, the term b5 has slowly given way to +4 or +11. As you can see in **figure 9-7**, the fourth of the C major scale has been raised, rather than the fifth lowered.

The new scale, or mode, in **figure 9-7** is the same as the G major scale, except that it starts on C, the fourth note of the scale. The fourth mode of the major scale is Lydian, which makes this the C Lydian mode. Even though the chord symbol reads CΔ+4, you're actually in the key of G. Learn to *think key, not chord*, as much as possible. You don't have to wait to see +4 in a chord symbol to play a raised fourth on a major seventh chord, however. You can play it on most major seventh chords. Well, almost. A Δ+4 chord would probably sound out of character on a Willie Nelson tune. I almost said "on a Beatles tune," but Oliver Nelson used Δ+4 chords in his arrangement of Lennon & McCartney's "Yesterday" on Lee Morgan's album *Delightfulee*.[2]

Figure 9-7

C Lydian Mode

CΔ+4

+4

We usually think of Lydian chords as being very "modern," but George Gershwin used a Lydian chord as the first chord in the bridge of "Someone To Watch Over Me." And the chord in the sixth bar of "Happy Birthday" is a Lydian chord!

Look back at the fourth, or Lydian mode, in the major scale harmony chart **(figure 9-3)**. What kind of third and seventh does it have? Because it has a major third and a major seventh, it must go with an FΔ chord. If you saw the chord symbol FΔ, however, the first scale you would think of would be the F major scale. How does the F Lydian mode differ from F major? Instead of a Bb, it has a B natural, or a raised fourth, so +4 has been added to the chord symbol.

Look now at the fifth, or Mixolydian mode, in **figure 9-3**. The Mixolydian mode is also known as the *dominant scale*. Play a left-hand voicing for G7 while playing the G Mixolydian mode in your right hand. There is another "avoid" note here, C, the fourth note of the mode. Play C with your right hand while playing the left-hand voicing; you'll hear the dissonance. Again, if you play C as a passing note, you'll hardly notice any dissonance. You will hear it only if you strike C as your left hand plays G7, or hold C against the chord. And again, the context will decide whether or not you play C on a G7 chord. You might specifically *want* to play something dissonant, or you might want to play the fourth and then resolve it down a half step to the third, as in the

[2] Lee Morgan, *Delightfulee*, Blue Note BST 84243. McCoy Tyner is the pianist on this, one of Lee's best albums.

Figure 9-8

Figure 9-9

Figure 9-10

Figure 9-11

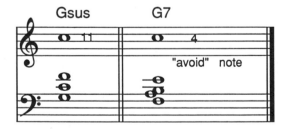

Figure 9-12

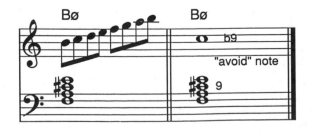

example from "Stella By Starlight." Whatever you do, don't think of dissonance as being "bad." Dissonance is not a pejorative term. Dissonance is often what makes music interesting, providing tension, resolution, and energy.

As with the "avoid" note on the I chord, most jazz musicians in the pre-bebop era played the fourth on a V chord strictly as a passing note. Bird, Bud, Monk, and other innovators of the bebop era often *raised* the fourth on a V chord, as in **figure 9-8**. The chord is notated here as G7+11. Some musicians, instead, write this chord as G7+4 (the fourth and the eleventh are the same note). In the 1940s it was called a b5. However, that term has slowly given way to +11 or +4. As you can see in **figure 9-9**, the fourth note of the G Mixolydian mode has been raised, rather than the fifth lowered.

This new scale does not have the same notes as any another major scale. It has one accidental, C#, but there is no major scale with a key signature of C# only. At this point, you've left major scale harmony and moved on to another type of harmony based on an entirely different scale, the melodic minor scale. Melodic minor harmony will be covered in the second part of this chapter.

Look at the last line of **figure 9-3**. The fifth, or Mixolydian, mode appears here again, but this time with a new chord symbol, Gsus. This is the scale, or mode, that is usually played over a Gsus chord. This is the difference between G7 and Gsus, the two chords that share the same G Mixolydian mode: Sus chords are voiced such that the fourth doesn't sound like an "avoid" note. Play the G Mixolydian mode first over a Gsus voicing and then over a G7 voicing **(figure 9-10)**, and you'll hear the difference. Play the C by itself over each voicing **(figure 9-11)**, and the difference is more pronounced.

Look at the seventh, or Locrian, mode in **figure 9-3**. The chord symbol above this mode is Bø, or B half-diminished, which is shorthand for B-7b5. Play **figure 9-12**. Notice that the second note in this mode, C, sounds very dissonant over a Bø left-hand voicing. C is the b9 of the chord. There is a natural ninth, C#, in the left-hand voicing, but C will sound dissonant even if the left-hand voicing has no C# **(figure 9-13)**. C is another "avoid" note. Until the mid-1950s, most jazz musicians thought vertically instead of

Figure 9-13

horizontally—chords instead of scales. When they did think of a scale for a half-diminished chord, Locrian was their choice, although Bud Powell often used the harmonic minor scale on half-diminished chords. There is another mode, found in melodic minor harmony (covered in the second part of this chapter), that works on half-diminished chords and has no "avoid" note. On half-diminished chords some musicians play the Locrian mode, others the mode from melodic minor harmony. Many musicians play both, so you have a choice. For now, suspend judgement until we get to that other half-diminished mode.

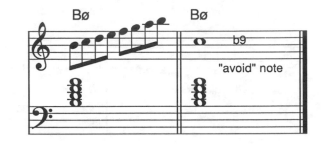

Bobby Hutcherson and Andrew Hill   Photo © by Lee Tanner

Figure 9-14

Figure 9-15

Look at the third, or Phrygian, mode in **figure 9-3**. This mode is played on Phrygian chords (see Chapter Four). However, it's also often played on a III chord, as in the progression E-7, A7, D-7, G7. Jazz musicians call this progression a "III-VI-II-V"[3] in the key of C. **Figure 9-14** shows an improvised line over a III-VI-II-V in the key of C, the notes on the E-7 chord running up the Phrygian mode. Now play **figure 9-15** and listen to the same four bars but with the E Dorian mode played on the E-7 chord instead. Which do you like better? Both examples have Bud Powell-style voicings in the left hand, root position voicings that will be covered in Chapter Seventeen. The left-hand voicing for an E-7 chord that you learned in Chapter Seven won't work too well when you're playing an E Phrygian line. This is because E Phrygian has two notes—F and C—that sound very dissonant against the left-hand voicing for E-7 **(figure 9-16)**. In fact, they sound like "avoid" notes.

Figure 9-16

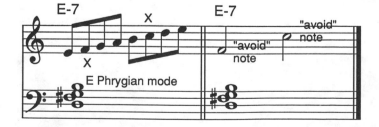

---

[3] In classical theory, it would be called III-V/II-II-V, because A7 is the V of D-7.

The Phrygian mode is very characteristic of Spanish music. In **figure 9-17**, an F/E chord—an F triad over an E pedal—resolves to an E major triad, a typical cadence in Spanish music. The E Phrygian mode is the best scale to play over the F/E chord. Now play the F/E chord by itself without resolving it (**figure 9-18**). Does it sound like a I chord? A V chord? It doesn't fit neatly into our preconceived notions of what I or V chords sound like. Gil Evans and Miles Davis used this chord extensively in Miles' album *Sketches Of Spain*,[4] especially on Gil's "Solea."

All of the major scale modes have been covered except Aeolian, the sixth mode. Aeolian chords are rare, and I'll save Aeolian theory for Chapter Twenty-Two. For now, it's time to move on to a type of harmony more exotic than anything the major scale has to offer, one that typifies the sound of modern jazz; the melodic minor scale.

Figure 9-17

Figure 9-18

P*ractice tips*

Play each of the new modes over the appropriate left-hand voicings around the cycle of fifths. As you learn each new mode, explore its melodic possibilities. Check out the color and relative dissonance of each note by playing it over a left-hand voicing. Create short phrases and melodies and try to get away from always playing "do-re-mi" phrases.

S*uggested tunes to work on*

Just Friends	Tune-Up
All The Things You Are	Satin Doll
I Got Rhythm	Stompin' At The Savoy

---

[4] Columbia 40578.

Melodic minor scale harmony

Play **figure 9-19**, the same example that opened Chapter Eight, and listen to the sound of melodic minor harmony. Half-diminished, altered, and minor-major chords are all derived from the melodic minor scale. Look at **figure 9-20**, the chart called Melodic Minor Scale Harmony.[5] The melodic minor scale is almost identical to the major scale, except that it has a minor third.[6] Like the major scale, it has seven modes.

Figure 9-19

---

[5] Reprinted in appendix as "Appendix B."

[6] In classical theory, there are two melodic minor scales, one to be played ascending, and another to be played descending. Because the descending melodic minor scale is identical to the Aeolian mode of the major scale, jazz musicians think of the *ascending* scale as "the melodic minor scale."

Figure 9-20

Melodic Minor Scale Harmony

Look at the first, or minor-major mode. This mode goes with some kind of C chord. It has a minor third and a major seventh, making it a *minor-major* chord, or C-Δ (often notated as C-+7). Play the left-hand voicing you learned for this chord in Chapter Eight **(figure 9-21)**, while playing the scale with your right hand. Notice how much more exotic sounding melodic minor harmony is than major scale harmony. The first chord in Horace Silver's "Nica's Dream"[7] and Billy Strayhorn's "Chelsea Bridge"[8] are minor-major chords. *The minor-major mode, the first mode of the melodic minor scale, is played when improvising on minor-major chords.*

Figure 9-21

Skip ahead to the fourth mode in **figure 9-20**, which runs from F to F. This mode goes with some kind of F chord. Because it has a major third and a minor seventh, it appears to be a dominant seventh chord, suggesting a chord symbol of F7. If you saw an F7 chord symbol, you would normally think of F Mixolydian, the fifth mode of the Bb major scale. How does this mode differ from F Mixolydian? It has a B natural, a raised eleventh (or raised fourth—remember, fourth and eleventh are the same notes), therefore +11 has been added to the chord symbol. This mode is called the *Lydian dominant* mode, Lydian because of its raised fourth, and dominant because it goes with a dominant chord, unlike the Lydian chord from major scale harmony, which goes with a major seventh chord. *The Lydian dominant mode, the fourth mode of the melodic minor scale, is played when improvising on dominant seventh +11 chords.*

Now look at the sixth mode in **figure 9-20**; it runs from A to A. This mode goes with some kind of A chord. Since it has a minor third and a minor seventh, it appears to be a minor seventh chord, suggesting a chord symbol of A-7. If you saw an A-7 chord symbol, you would normally think of A Dorian, the second mode of the G major scale. The mode shown here is obviously not from G major, since it has an E flat and no F sharp. How does it differ from A Dorian? It has a b5 (Eb), and a b6 (F). This

---

[7] Art Blakey, *The Original Jazz Messengers*, Columbia Odyssey 32l60246.

[8] Many musicians play Eb7+11 instead as the first chord on "Chelsea Bridge." Strayhorn himself often played Bb-Δ at first, then Eb7+11 later in the same performance.

suggests a chord symbol of A-7b5, b6. Most musicians, when confronted with chords that have two alterations or more, prefer to simplify the chord symbol. The traditional symbol, omitting the b6, is A-7b5. Many musicians go even further, using the shorthand symbol Aø, or A half-diminished. The symbol A-7b5, b6 has seven "bits" of information for your brain to process. A-7b5 has five "bits." Aø has only two "bits." When you're playing a fast tune with lots of changes, short and simple chord symbols make life much easier.

Figure 9-22

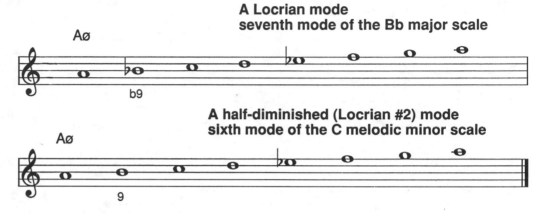

**A Locrian mode
seventh mode of the Bb major scale**

**A half-diminished (Locrian #2) mode
sixth mode of the C melodic minor scale**

The half-diminished mode is often called the *Locrian #2* mode, because it has the same interval steps as the major scale's Locrian mode, except that the second note of the mode is a major second above the root, unlike the Locrian mode's minor second. Most of the early bebop musicians played the Locrian mode on half-diminished chords, and it is still the first choice of many musicians for ø chords. **Figure 9-22** shows both the A Locrian mode and the A half-diminished mode. As you can see, the only difference between the two is a single note, Bb in the Locrian mode, B natural in the half-diminished mode. **Figure 9-23** shows first Bb, then B natural, played over a root position Aø chord. Hear the difference? The Bb sounds fine when played as a passing note, but is very dissonant when struck or held on the ø chord. It sounds like an "avoid" note. The B natural, on the other hand, is arguably the prettiest note you can play on an Aø chord. *The half-diminished mode, the sixth mode of the melodic minor scale, is played when improvising on half-diminished chords.*

Figure 9-23

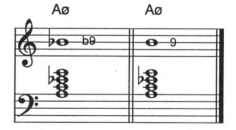

Look at the seventh, or *altered* mode, which runs from B to B. This mode goes with some kind of "B" chord. It appears to have a minor third, D, but notice that the note after D in the scale, Eb, is a *major* third above B, the root. A major third above B is D#, and Eb is just an enharmonic spelling for D#. Chords usually don't have both a minor and a major third. The true third here is Eb, a major third above B. Along with a major third, the mode has a minor seventh, so it must go with some kind of B7 chord. If you saw the chord symbol B7, you would normally think of the B Mixolydian mode, the fifth mode of the E major scale. Since the key signature for E major is four sharps, this mode obviously doesn't come from E major.

Now look at **figure 9-24**, which compares the B Mixolydian mode of E major with the seventh mode of C melodic minor. Underneath each note is the note's position in a B7 chord. Where the B Mixolydian mode has a ninth, the B altered mode has both a b9 and a +9 (the note that looks like a minor third). Where the B Mixolydian mode has an eleventh, the B altered mode has a +ll. The B Mixolydian mode has a thirteenth, the altered mode a bl3. B mixolydian has a fifth, B altered has no fifth. The complete chord symbol, reflecting all of these changes, would be B7b9, +9, +ll, bl3. Can you imagine playing a fast tune and having to read that chord symbol? Again, shorthand is called for, and the preferred chord symbol is B7alt. "Alt" stands for "altered," and is also the name of the mode.

Figure 9-24

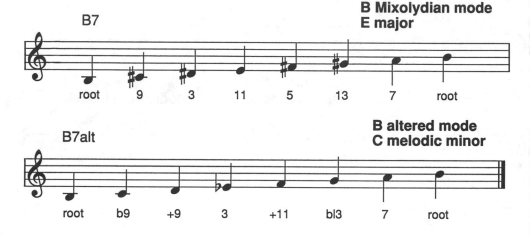

This chord is called "altered" because, as a B7 chord, it has been altered in every possible way. The ninth has been both lowered and raised, the eleventh has been raised (the eleventh can't be lowered, it would then become the major third), and the thirteenth has been lowered (the thirteenth can't be raised, it would then become the minor seventh). If you change B, the root, or Eb, the third, or A, the seventh, you won't have a B7 chord any more. Within the confines of B7, you've made the maximum number of alterations.

Some musicians use the symbols b5 and +5 in place of +ll and bl3. And some musicians call this the *diminished whole-tone* scale, because it starts out like a diminished scale and ends up like a whole-tone scale (these scales will be covered later in this chapter). *The altered mode, the seventh mode of the melodic minor scale, is played when improvising on altered dominant seventh chords.*

Some jazz theory books list two other possible names for the altered scale: the *super-locrian* mode (because, like the Locrian mode, it is the seventh mode, although of the melodic minor scale); and the *Pomeroy* scale, named after Berklee School of Music's guru Herb Pomeroy. I've never heard a real live working jazz musician use either of these terms, however, so I'd stick with either "altered," or "diminished whole-tone." Two terms are enough for the same scale.

Look now at the third mode in **figure 9-20**, which runs from Eb to Eb. This mode goes with some kind of Eb chord. Because it has a major third and a major seventh, it suggests an EbΔ chord. Normally, if you saw an EbΔ chord symbol, you'd think of the Eb Ionian, or major, scale. How does this mode differ from Eb major? It has both a raised fourth, A natural, and a raised fifth, B natural. The complete chord symbol would be EbΔ+4, +5. The common shorthand symbol for this chord is EbΔ+5. This chord, and its mode, are called *Lydian augmented*, Lydian because of its raised fourth, augmented because of its raised fifth, as in an augmented triad. Bud Powell played Lydian augmented chords in his great composition "Glass Enclosure."[9] Another beautiful example of a Lydian augmented chord is the AbΔ+5 chord in the fourth bar of the bridge of Duke Pearson's "You Know I Care."[10] *The Lydian augmented mode, the third mode of the melodic minor scale, is played when improvising on major seventh +5 chords.*

The second mode in **figure 9-20** is the mode you play over an altered sus chord. There is no standard symbol for this chord, although susb9 is the one most commonly used. This chord and its mode only began to be played in the 1960s, by such musicians as John Coltrane, McCoy Tyner, and Wayne Shorter.[11] The symbol susb9 is also used for Phrygian chords, so it can be confusing. A comparison of the three sus chords—sus, Phrygian, and second mode melodic minor—appears in Chapter Twenty-Two.

As you can see, these six chords played in modern jazz—minor-major, susb9, Lydian augmented, Lydian dominant, half-diminished, and altered—all share the same melodic minor scale. This is similar to major scale harmony, where the major seventh, minor seventh, Phrygian, Lydian, dominant seventh, and sus chords all share the same scale. There is a very big difference between the two types of harmony, however. For the most part, there are no "avoid" notes in melodic minor harmony. The lack of "avoid" notes means that almost everything in any melodic minor key is interchangeable with everything else in that key.

---

[9] *The Amazing Bud Powell, Vol. II,* Blue Note 81504. A transcription of "Glass Enclosure" by Bill Dobbins appears in the October-November 1989 issue of *The Piano Stylist.*

[10] Joe Henderson, *Inner Urge,* Blue Note 4189, McCoy Tyner on piano, and one of the best records of the 1960s.

[11] Bar 7 of Wayne Shorter's tune "Dance Cadaverous," *Speak No Evil,* Blue Note 4194.

As an example, look at **figure 9-25**. The left-hand voicing that was played in **figure 9-21** for C-Δ is repeated here. Play it with your left hand while reaching over with your right hand to play a C in the root for a C-Δ chord. Play D in the root and you'll have a Dsusb9 chord. Change the root to Eb and you'll hear an EbΔ+5 chord. Play F in the root and you'll have F7+ll. Change the root to A and you'll hear an Aø chord. Play B in the root and you'll have B7alt. The same voicing works for all six chords. Because there are no "avoid" notes in melodic minor harmony, almost all voicings are interchangeable. The only difference in these chords is the root, *and if you're not playing the root, there is no difference.*

Figure 9-25

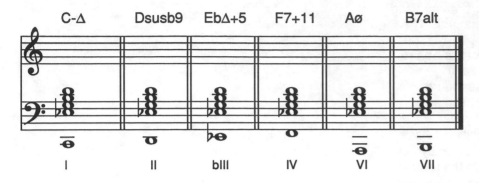

You don't have this interchangeability with chords from the major scale. As an example, although both D-7 and CΔ are from the key of C, you can't play a D-7 voicing for a CΔ chord because the D-7 voicing has an F, the "avoid" note of a CΔ chord.

This interchangeability is the reason that so many of the chords you learned in Chapter Eight shared the same voicings. If you have a background in traditional theory, this requires some rethinking about harmony. As an example, in traditional harmony, the third and seventh are of paramount importance, especially on dominant seventh chords. The voicing in **figure 9-25** lacks a third when you play it on an F7+ll or Aø chord, and lacks the seventh on a B7alt chord. If you play it for Dsusb9, it has neither the third nor the seventh. When you play chords from melodic minor harmony, unless you specifically play the root underneath the chord, you're really playing the entire *key*, not just the chord.

Figure 9-26

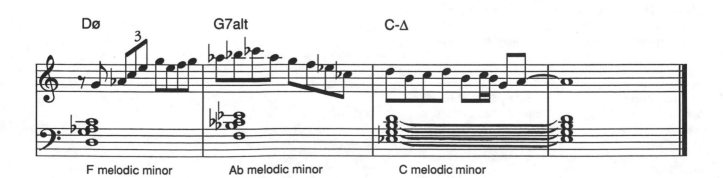

Look at **figure 9-26**. The chords in this example—Dø, G7alt, C-Δ—are known as a *minor II-V-I*. All three chords are derived from melodic minor harmony, and the notes from the line played over the left-hand voicings are derived from the melodic minor scale of each chord. The notes played over the Dø chord are from F melodic minor, the notes over the G7alt chord are from Ab melodic minor, and the notes over the C-Δ chord are from C melodic minor. Note that the left-hand voicing for Dø moves up a minor third to become the G7alt chord. This will always work, no matter what voicing you are playing for the Dø chord, because Ab melodic minor—the key the G7alt chord is derived from—is a minor third above F melodic minor—the key the Dø chord is derived from. Again, think key, not chord. *In a IIø/Valt progression, the voicing for the ø chord can be moved up a minor third and played for the alt chord.*

As was the case with the Aeolian mode of major scale harmony, one mode—the fifth—has been omitted from this survey of melodic minor harmony. The fifth mode is played very rarely, but I'll return to it in Chapter Twenty-Two.

Practice **tips**

Play all of the new modes over the appropriate left-hand voicings around the cycle of fifths, as in C7alt, F7alt, Bb7alt, Eb7alt, and so forth. Explore the color of individual notes that may be new to you, such as the natural ninth and b6 on a ø chord. Create phrases and melodies, and as you get better at using each new mode, try to get away from playing "do-re-mi" phrases. Use each mode as a pool of available notes for your ear and taste to select.

Suggested tunes to work on

Stella By Starlight	Blue In Green
I Thought About You	Search For Peace
Peace	Woody'n You
Nica's Dream	Invitation

Diminished scale harmony

Play **figure 9-27**. This is the sound of *diminished scale harmony*. **Figure 9-28**[12] shows two diminished scales, the first one alternating half steps and whole steps, the second one alternating whole steps and half steps. Although one starts on G and the other starts on F, they both have exactly the same notes. Unlike the seven-note major and melodic minor scales, diminished scales have eight notes. The diminished scale has another unique characteristic that makes it easier to use by far than either the major or melodic minor scales: it is *symmetrical*.

The diminished scale shown in the first bar of **figure 9-28** alternates half steps and whole steps in a symmetrical pattern, unlike the asymmetrical major and melodic minor scales. For example, the major scale steps are whole, whole, half, whole, whole, whole, half. There are always twelve different asymmetrical scales, like the twelve major and twelve melodic minor scales. There are always *less* than twelve of a symmetrical scale. For example, the chromatic scale is a symmetrical scale, constructed entirely of half steps. How many different chromatic scales are there? Only one. A chromatic scale starting on any note has exactly the

Figure 9-27

Figure 9-28

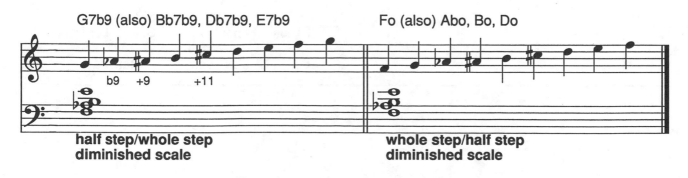

half step/whole step diminished scale   whole step/half step diminished scale

---

[12] Reprinted in appendix as "Appendix C."

same notes as a chromatic scale starting on any other note. Because diminished scales are symmetrical, there are less than twelve of them.

Play the diminished scale again, this time without looking at the music. Start on G and alternate half steps and whole steps. Go up one octave and then come down. Play the scale a few times until you've memorized it. Now start on Bb and again alternate half steps and whole steps. This scale has the same notes as the G diminished scale. Try it now starting on Db. Again, same notes. Start on E. Again, same notes. The G, Bb, Db, and E half step/whole step diminished scales all have the same notes. These four starting notes are a minor third apart. That's the key element of diminished scale harmony. *In diminished scale harmony, everything repeats at the interval of a minor third.*

Because the G, Bb, Db, and E diminished scales are the same, the Ab, B, D, and F diminished scales will also be the same, since they, too, are a minor third apart. Ditto for the A, C, Eb, and F# diminished scales. In other words, there are only three different diminished scales.

Look at the first bar of **figure 9-28** again. This scale, running from G to G, goes with some kind of G chord. What kind of third and seventh

Horace Silver

Photo © by Lee Tanner

Figure 9-29

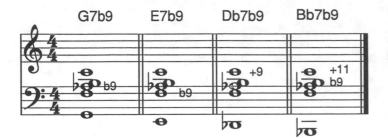

Figure 9-30

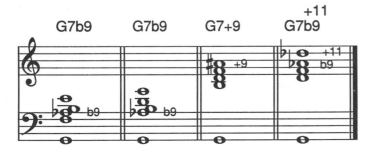

does it have? Although A# is a minor third above G, there is a B, or major third, right after it. As you learned from the altered mode, when a scale looks as though it has both a minor and a major third, the "minor third" is really a +9. Since the true third is B, and F is the minor seventh, this scale goes with some kind of G7 chord. What are the alterations? Ab is the b9, A# the +9, C# the +11. The complete chord symbol would be G7b9, +9, +11. Again, shorthand is desirable, and the usual symbol is G7b9, although G7+9 is used also. Play the left-hand voicing for G7b9 shown in **figure 9-28** while playing the scale with your right hand.

As in melodic minor harmony, diminished scale harmony has no "avoid" notes. As a result, everything harmonically contained within this scale is interchangeable: chords, voicings, "licks," patterns, and so on. Since the G, Bb, Db, and E diminished scales are identical, G7b9, Bb7b9, Db7b9, and E7b9 chords are largely interchangeable. The only difference between them is the root, and if you're not playing the root, they are fully interchangeable. You can test this out in two ways. First, play the left-hand voicing again, as shown in **figure 9-29**, and reach over with your right hand to play the four different roots shown below it. Putting G in the bass gives you a G7b9 chord. Playing E in the bass gives you E7b9.

Playing Db in the bass gives you a Db7b9 chord, with a +9, but no b9. How can this be a Db7b9 chord when there's no b9 in the voicing? Remember, many chord symbols are shorthand symbols. Db7b9 is shorthand for Db7b9, +9, +11. Any combination of those three alterations may be present in the voicing. If you specifically want the +9 in the voicing, use +9 in the chord symbol—otherwise, b9 is the generally acceptable shorthand symbol for the chord. Playing Bb in the bass makes the chord Bb7b9, with a +11 present in the voicing along with the b9. One voicing works for four different dominant seventh b9 chords, all sharing the same scale.

For students trained in classical theory, the absence of the seventh in the E7b9 voicing and the third in the Bb7b9 voicing may be troubling. Designating a note as the third or seventh is somewhat arbitrary on diminished scale chords, however. Playing chords in diminished scale harmony means playing in a "key" much more than playing a chord—the key being a diminished scale that encompasses four different chords.

Figure 9-30 shows the same G7b9 left-hand voicing transposed up in minor thirds, giving four different voicings for the same dominant seventh b9 chord. Play each one with the same root, G, underneath. Now play them without the root. A good place to use this idea is when a V chord lasts for a couple of bars. This gives you enough space to move through different voicings of the same chord, increasing or decreasing the tension, as in **figure 9-31**. As the left-hand voicing for F7b9 moves up in minor thirds, the right hand plays a four-note motif that moves downwards in minor thirds **(figure 9-32)**. When your hands move in opposite directions, it's called contrary motion. *Remember, in diminished scale harmony, everything repeats at the interval of a minor third.*

Figure 9-31

Figure 9-32

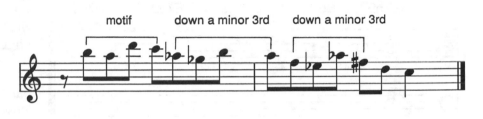

There are endless diminished scale "licks." Three more are shown in **figure 9-33**. Because their symmetry makes diminished patterns so "perfect," sometimes it's difficult not to sound mechanical when playing them. Music, like life, needs a few

Figure 9-33

Figure 9-34

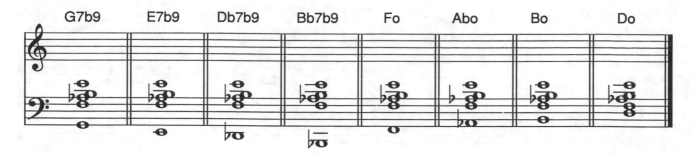

Figure 9-35

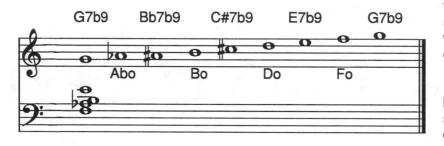

Figure 9-36

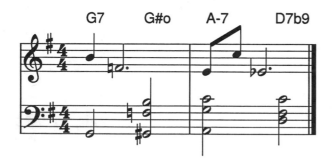

Figure 9-37

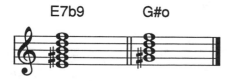

Figure 9-38

jagged edges to be interesting. Listen to Herbie Hancock solo over diminished scale chords on "Empyrean Isles,"[13] and what John Coltrane plays over them on "Blue Train."[14]

Go back now and look at the second bar of **figure 9-28**. This is the whole step/half step diminished scale, just the opposite of the half step/whole step pattern in the first bar. This scale goes with *diminished seventh* chords. Note that this scale, running from F to F, has exactly the same notes as the G to G half step/whole step scale, and can use the same left-hand voicing as the G7b9 chord. Again, everything repeats at the interval of a minor third, so Fo is interchangeable with Abo, Bo, and Do. The same left-hand voicing goes with *eight* chords, four of them dominant seventh b9 chords, four of them diminished seventh chords **(figure 9-34)**. **Figure 9-35** shows the same thing from a different angle, a diminished scale with the symbol of the chord built off of each note.

Diminished chords are often played in place of dominant seventh b9 chords to get chromatic bass motion. Look at **figure 9-36**, bars 3-4 of the bridge of Duke Ellington's "Sophisticated Lady." The G#o chord precedes an A-7 chord. The dominant seventh chord normally preceding any A chord would be E7. Compare the E7b9 and G#o chords in **figure 9-37**. As you can see, G#o is E7b9 without the E. The same thing happens in the 28th bar of Chick Corea's "Mirror, Mirror" **(figure 9-38)**. In both examples, playing a diminished chord in place of a dominant seventh b9 chord produces chromatic bass motion. When you come across a diminished chord in a tune, check to see if it is equivalent to the dominant seventh b9 chord of whatever chord

[13] Herbie Hancock, *Empyrean Isles*, Blue Note 84175.
[14] John Coltrane, *Blue Train*, Blue Note 81577.

comes next. Although this is the most common use of diminished chords, there are some exceptions. The second bar of Antonio Carlos Jobim's "Wave" contains a diminished chord that is not a substitute for the dominant seventh b9 chord of the following chord **(figure 9-39).** In classical terminology this is called an "irregular diminished seventh." There will be more on this chord in Chapter Nineteen.

Figure 9-39

Every time you play something from diminished scale hamony, you're playing in several tonalities at the same time. You can't always assume that the bass player will play the root, so what note the bassist plays underneath can effect the tonality. Because bass players play tritone substitution often, and play passing notes as well as roots, the G7b9 chord you think you're playing may end up sounding like Bb7b9, Db7b9, E7b9, Fo, Abo, Bo, or Do, depending on what note the bassist plays underneath. Bass players have lots of power, so be nice to them.

Practice
tips

Play the left-hand voicing for each dominant seventh b9 chord around the cycle while playing the half step/whole step scale in the right hand. Do the same with the whole step/half step scale. As you play each chord and scale, name all the other chords that share that same scale. Make up some diminished scale melodies, using the "everything repeats at a minor third" method, and then make up some more melodies trying *not* to repeat phrases a minor third away. Also, try repeating phrases at the interval of a tritone, which is two minor thirds.

Figure 9-40

G7+5

Figure 9-41

G7+5 (or) G7b̶3

+11 +5

Whole-tone scale harmony

Play **figure 9-40** and listen to the sound of *whole-tone harmony*. **Figure 9-41** shows the whole-tone scale.[15] Because the whole-tone scale is a symmetrical scale, consisting entirely of whole steps, you know that there are fewer than twelve of them. In fact, there are only two different whole-tone scales. The G whole-tone scale shown has the same notes as the A, B, C#, D#, and F whole-tone scales. The Ab whole-tone scale has the same notes as the Bb, C, D, E, and F# whole-tone scales.

There are no "avoid" notes in whole-tone harmony, so everything is interchangeable within the harmony of a given scale. Anything you play on G7+5 will work on A7+5, B7+5, C#7+5, D#7+5, and F7+5. Whole-tone harmony lacks half of the intervals that occur in major, melodic minor, and diminished scale harmony. No matter how you rearrange the notes, there can be no minor seconds, minor thirds, perfect fourths, perfect fifths, major sixths, or major sevenths in whole-tone harmony. This can make whole-tone harmony pretty boring, so it's best played in short doses. You could look through 100 tunes and find only a few with whole-tone chords. Two good examples are Wayne Shorter's "JuJu,"[16] a waltz with ten bars of whole-tone chords at the beginning, and the whole-tone chords on the bridge of McCoy Tyner's "Search For Peace."[17]

Occasionally, someone will write a tune with mostly whole-tone harmony, such as Bix Beiderbeck's "In A Mist,"[18] Lee Morgan's "Our Man Higgins,"[19] and John Coltrane's "One Up, One Down,"[20] but that's rare. A whole-tone chord is often played on bar 17 of "Stella By Starlight," and bar 24 of "All The Things You Are," but many musicians prefer alt chords there instead.

---

[15] Reprinted in appendix as "Appendix D."

[16] Wayne Shorter, *JuJu*, Blue Note BST 84182.

[17] McCoy Tyner, *The Real McCoy*, Blue Note 4264.

[18] Freddie Hubbard, *Sky Dive*, CTI/CBS Associated ZK-44171.

[19] Lee Morgan, *Cornbread*, Blue Note BIIE-84222. Alto saxophonist Jackie McLean's first couple of choruses on "Our Man Higgins" is one of the best examples of whole-tone soloing ever recorded. *Cornbread* also has one of Herbie Hancock's most beautiful solos, on Lee's bossa nova "Ceora."

[20] John Coltrane, *New Thing At Newport*, Impulse 94.

Figure 9-42

Look at the third and seventh of the whole-tone scale. Because this scale, running from G to G, has a major third and a minor seventh, it goes with a G7 chord. C# is the +II, D# the +5. The complete chord symbol is G7+II, +5. The traditional shorthand for this chord is G7+5, often further shortened to G7+, and occasionally written G +7. The notation G +7 is confusing, because the + refers to the fifth, not shown in the chord symbol, and has nothing to do with the seventh. Because +5 and b13 are enharmonic, the same chord is often notated G7b13.

The key element of whole-tone harmony is the fact that everything repeats at the interval of a whole step. **Figure 9-42** shows three "licks" on a G7+5 chord. The symmetry and lack of intervalic variety can make it difficult to be original when playing on whole-tone chords. The most inventive improviser on whole-tone chords was probably Thelonious Monk. He could play patterns that would sound like clichés coming from anyone else. His quirky and angular sense of time gave what can be a very boring type of harmony a tremendous feeling of energy. His solo on "Evidence"[21] is one of the best examples of soloing over whole-tone chords.

[21] Thelonious Monk, *The Complete Blue Note Recordings Of Thelonious Monk*, Mosaic 101.

Keep in mind that scales are the ABCs, not the poetry, of jazz. Mindlessly running up and down scales is the trademark of the boring player. Scales should be just another tool at your disposal. Always think of singing through your instrument. Play with passion, fire, and tenderness—and practice your scales!

Practice tips   Practice whole-tone scales over left-hand voicings around the cycle of fifths. Invent new whole-tone licks. Try improvising on whole-tone chords and *not* playing symmetrical licks.

Putting Scales To Work

So you've practiced your scales—but can you use them on that Dø, G7alt, C-Δ progression coming up? You need an exercise that will transform scales into music. Play **figure 10-1**. This is, in classical terminology, a *sequence*. A sequence is a melodic phrase repeated at a different pitch. The four-note motif spirals upward from one chord to the next, creating unexpected tension and resolution. Practicing sequences is a great way to learn how to improvise using scales. To be able to do this fluently, let's start with an easier example.

Figure 10-1

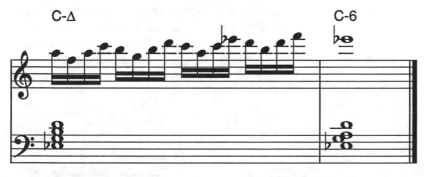

Figure 10-2

Figure 10-2 shows the changes for the first four bars of "Stella By Starlight." In the bass clef are left-hand voicings for the chords. The chord in bar I, Eø, is from the G melodic minor scale. Arbitrarily starting on the note A from that scale, your right hand walks up the scale step-wise in quarter notes for the remainder of bar I, the last note in the bar being D.

The chord in bar 2, A7b9, is from the A half step/whole step diminished scale. What would be the the next note after D—the last note in bar I—that belongs to the A7b9 scale? It's D#, the +II of the A7b9 chord. That becomes the first note in bar 2. Notice that the line in bar 2 alternates half steps and whole steps, because this is a diminished scale.

Had your first note in bar 2 been E, you would have alternated whole steps and half steps instead. The line continues up, the last note in bar 2 being G.

The chord in bar 3, C-7, is from the C Dorian mode of Bb major. What would be the next note after G—the last note in bar 2—that belongs to the C Dorian mode? It's A, and so on. If there are two chords per bar, play just two notes per chord. When you get to the C an octave below the top of the keyboard, turn around and come back down. Continue down and don't reverse directions again until your hands are about to bump into each other.

This exercise allows you to practice several different things at the same time: left-hand voicings, the scale for each chord, and most important, *linking the scales together*. It also makes you enter each new scale on the note right after the last note of the previous chord, rather than the root. This takes you away from thinking of each scale as always starting on the root, and helps to equalize in your mind the importance of each note in every scale.

Before you do this exercise, however, it would be a good idea to go through all of the changes to "Stella," playing the scale for each chord. **Figure 10-3** shows all four scales, ascending and descending, for the chords in bars I-4 . The complete set of changes for "Stella" is shown in **figure 10-4**.[I]

Figure 10-3

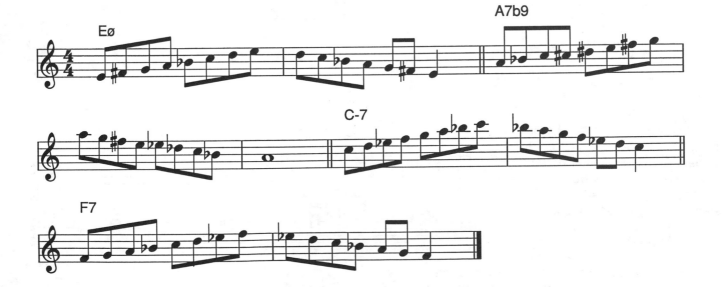

[I] This set of changes for "Stella" has been altered somewhat to provide opportunites to use as many scales as possible. The original chord change in bar II, D-7, has been changed to D-Δ. The original chord change in bars 23 and 24, BbΔ, has been changed to BbΔ+5.

Figure 10-4

As you play through "Stella," ask yourself what type of harmony each chord is derived from. Major? Melodic minor? Diminished? Whole-tone? If a chord is from major scale harmony, is it a I chord? A II chord? A V chord? If it's from melodic minor harmony, is it minor-major? Altered? Half-diminished? Memorize the melodic minor modal numbers: minor-major is I, susb9 is II, Lydian augmented is III, Lydian dominant is IV, half-diminished is VI, alt is VII.

Identifying the right scale tells you what notes will sound good with each chord. Actually, in real life you have a good deal more freedom to interpret chord symbols. You might opt to reharmonize on the spot and change a G-7, C7, FΔ progression to Gø, C7b9, FΔ+4, for instance. While you're first learning how to use scales, however, it's a good idea to think of chord symbols as *scale-specific*. That is, interpret each symbol literally, and think of each chord as implying only a single scale.

When you get to an "avoid" note, raise it **(figure 10-5)**. This means raising the fourth on all major chords and the eleventh on all unaltered V chords. In real life, you won't always want to do this because "avoid" notes are not necessarily "bad" notes. Practicing this technique now trains you to watch for opportunities to do so in real life.

Figure 10-5

Pick some more tunes from *The New Real Book* or *The World's Greatest Fake Book* and go through them as you did on "Stella," playing the appropriate scale over a left-hand voicing for each chord. Look for tunes with +ll, b9, +9, alt, ø, +4 and +5 chords. Practice, and you'll soon get much better at linking the appropriate scale to each chord. Notice how your reaction time improves. It might take you ten seconds at first to think "Bø is from D melodic minor." Get your reaction time down to three seconds, one second, a half-second, a tenth of a second, until it's instantaneous. Some musicians use flash cards when learning to associate chords with the right scales. You don't even need to sit at the piano to practice this. As an example, go through all the alt chords around the cycle of fifths, linking each one to its appropriate melodic minor scale—"C7alt is from Db melodic minor; F7 alt is from F# melodic minor"; and so on. You can even do this when you're driving on the freeway (but don't miss your exit).

Vary the exercise in **figure 10-2** by playing eighth notes **(figure 10-6)**. Then play eighth notes broken into thirds **(figure 10-7)**, then play thirds reversing direction **(figure 10-8)**, then triplets **(figure 10-9)**, then triplets made up of a step and a skip **(figure 10-10)**. Be inventive and make up some of your own patterns.

Figure 10-6

Figure 10-7

Figure 10-8

Figure 10-9

Figure 10-10

Some of these patterns are very musical, and you might want to play them when you're soloing. If you did this all of the time, your playing would sound pretty mechanical. As part of an otherwise more lyrical and free-flowing solo, however, patterns and sequences can add a lot of structure and organization to your playing. For a great example of Herbie Hancock sequencing patterns, listen to his solo on Cole Porter's "All Of You," from Miles Davis' album *My Funny Valentine*.[2] About halfway through his solo, he starts to spin pattern after pattern through the changes to the tune, creating long, flowing lines of increasing and decreasing tension. Tenor saxophonist Joe Henderson, using just a three-note motíf, plays a brilliant solo using the same approach on Lee Morgan's "Ca-lee-so," from Lee's album *Delightfulee Morgan*.[3]

What left-hand voicing did you play on the Eø chord in bar 25 of "Stella"? Whatever it was, if you transpose it up exactly a minor third, it will go with the A7alt chord in the next bar. This will work no matter what voicing you played for Eø. **Figure 10-11** shows three examples of this idea. Why does this work? Remember, there are no "avoid" notes in melodic minor harmony. Everything from a particular melodic minor scale, including chords and voicings, is interchangeable. You're really playing the *key* more than the *chord*. Eø is from G melodic minor, A7alt is from Bb melodic minor. Bb is a minor third above G. *Whenever you have a II-V in which the II is half-diminished and the V is alt, any ø voicing moved up a minor third will fit the alt chord.*

Figure 10-11

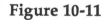

[2] Columbia PC-9l06.
[3] Blue Note BST 84243.

Practice tips

Practice all of the preceding patterns through various chords and progressions. Aebersold records are especially handy for this, particularly *II-V-I* (Vol. 3), and *Gettin' It Together* (Vol. 21).

Suggested tunes to work on

Up Jumped Spring	Blue In Green
I Thought About You	The Shadow Of Your Smile
Social Call	Witchcraft
Nardis	Woody'n You
Little B's Poem	Invitation
Airegin	Rapture
Yesterdays	

The traditional method of practicing scales—two hands moving up and down four octaves—is great for technique but doesn't do much to improve your skills as an improviser. Because you're always starting on the root, reversing directions on the root, and ending on the root, you're using only one seventh of the possibilities inherent in each scale. Beginning jazz musicians often sound like **figure 11-1** on their first attempt at playing a II-V-I. This root-bias will never do. You need a better method of practicing scales, and a good way to start is with the exercise shown in **figure 11-2**. By going up the Ionian mode, down the Dorian, up the Phyrgian, down the Lydian, and so on, you're starting on each note, reversing directions on each note, and ending on each note of the C major scale.

Figure 11-1

Figure 11-2

You've only covered half the possibilities, however. Reverse everything, as in **figure 11-3**, going down the Ionian, up the Dorian, down the Phrygian, up the Lydian, and so on. Use the same pattern to practice melodic minor scales.

Figure 11-3

If you practiced this exercise every day, you'd still be starting the C major scale on C every day. I think it helps to take this idea even further, starting the C major scale on C one day, D the next, E the next, and so on. If this seems like taking things to extremes, remember, the goal is to de-program yourself from years of root-bias conditioning.

The eight-note diminished scale **(figures 11-4, 11-5)** and six-note whole-tone scale **(figures 11-6, 11-7)** use slightly different patterns when practiced in this way.

Figure 11-4

Figure 11-5

Figure 11-6

Figure 11-7

Figure 11-8

Right-Hand Scale Fingerings for Major Keys

Major Key	Fingering	Fourth finger on
C, D, E, G, A, B	12312345	7th
	(1-	
F	12341234	Bb
	(1-	
Bb	21231234	Bb
Eb	21234123	Bb
Ab	23123123(4)	Bb
Db	23123412	Bb
Gb	23412312	Bb

Right-Hand Fingerings for Melodic Minor Keys

Melodic Minor Key	Fingering	Fourth finger on
All keys except F#	(same as major scales)	
F#	23123412	D#

Left-Hand Scale Fingerings for Major Keys

Major Key	Fingering	Fourth finger on
C, F, E, A, D, G	54321321	2nd
Bb, Eb, Ab, Db	32143213	4th
Gb	43213212	root
	(4-	
B	43214321	5th

Left-Hand Fingerings for Melodic Minor Keys

Melodic Minor Key	Fingering	Fourth finger on
All keys except Bb, Eb, F#	(same as major scales)	
Bb, Eb	21432132	3rd
F#	43213214	root

Correct scale fingering is important, although some great jazz pianists, like Thelonious Monk, had their own unique scale fingerings. If you're playing a convoluted line through several chord changes, playing the correct Hanon fingerings may not be very practical. For the most part, however, it's wise to stick with the traditional fingerings that have worked well for the last several hundred years. **Figure 11-8** is a fingering chart for major and melodic minor scales.

The number in the half parentheses at the end of some of the scale fingerings means to use that finger on the root if you're going beyond one octave. The (4) at the end of the Ab major scale, right hand, means use the fourth finger on the second note of the scale (Bb), if going beyond one octave.

The majority of fingering mistakes are made with the fourth finger. Fourth finger notes are shown on the right. The note indicated isn't the *only* note you'll use your fourth finger on, but your fourth finger should be used on that note most of the time.

Common sense will tell you when to break fingering rules. The first four notes of the C major scale are usually fingered I-2-3-I for the right hand. If you're not going beyond F, however, it doesn't make much sense to go thumb under for just one note. I-2-3-4 is much more efficient **(figure 11-9)**.

Figure 11-9

There are no Hanon fingerings for diminished and whole-tone scales. Not many pianists in Hanon's day were familiar with these scales. The whole-tone scale didn't come along until Debussy used it in his compositions in the late 19th century, and the diminished scale has always been an oddity in classical music. The fingerings in the following chart **(figure 11-10)** are my own, and please feel free to change them if they're not right for you. Some pianists have big hands, some pianists have small hands, and no one fingering is right for everybody. The diminished scale fingerings are shown in groups of four, as in C, Eb, F#, and A, since they all have the same notes. The same is true for the whole-tone fingerings. Since there are only two different whole-tone scales, they are shown in groups of six each.

Figure 11-10

Right-Hand Fingerings for Diminished Scales

half step/whole step

Diminished scale	Fingering	Notes
C	l23l2l234	3rd finger on Bb & Eb
	(l-	
Eb	3l2l23l23	(same)
F#	2l23l23l2	(same)
A	23l23l2l2	(same)
C#	2l2l234l2	3rd & 4th fingers on Bb & Ab
E	2l234l2l2	(same)
G	234l2l2l2	(same)
Bb	2l2l2l234	(same)
D	23l23l2l2	3rd finger on Eb & Ab
F	l23l2l234	(same)
	(l-	
Ab	2l2l23l23	(same)
B	2l23l23l2	(same)

Right-Hand Fingerings For Whole-Tone Scales

Whole-Tone Scale	Fingering	Notes
C	l2l2345	2nd, 3rd, & 4th finger on Gb, Ab, & Bb
	(l-	
D	2l234l2	(same)
E	l234l23	(same)
	(l-	
F#	234l2l2	(same)
Ab	34l2l23	(same)
Bb	2l2l234	(same)
Db	23l23l2	2nd & 3rd finger on Db & Eb
Eb	3l23l23	(same)
F	l23l234	(same)
	(l-	
G	23l23l2	(same)
A	2l23l23	(same)
B	l23l234	(same)
	(l-	

 Practice tips — Practice all scales *in all keys* using the correct fingerings. Use the "up one mode, down the next" idea when practicing scales.

Figure 12-1

Play **figure 12-1**, and listen to the sound of "So What" chords as played by McCoy Tyner in the first few bars of his "Peresina."[1] "So What," a Miles Davis tune from the 1950s, helped introduce modal jazz to the world.[2] **Figure 12-2** shows the two "So What" chords that Bill Evans played on Miles' recording. The D-7 "So What" chord is analyzed in **figure 12-3**. Reading up from the bottom, it consists of the root, eleventh, seventh, third, and fifth of a minor seventh chord. It's much easier to play if you see it intervalically **(figure 12-4)**, as a series of three perfect fourths with a major third on top. Notice that the top note of the voicing is the fifth of the chord. *When voicing melodies with So What chords, look for minor seventh chords with the fifth in the melody.*

The So What chord works just as well as a non-root position major seventh chord **(figure 12-5)**. Reading from the bottom up, this chord consists of the third, sixth, ninth, fifth, and major seventh. Play it while holding down the sustain pedal, and reach down and play a low Bb to hear what the chord sounds like with the root. Notice that the top note of the voicing is the major seventh of the chord. *When voicing melodies with So What chords, look for ∆ chords with the major seventh in the melody.*

The So What chord also works very well as a non-root position Lydian chord **(figure 12-6)**. Reading from the bottom up, it consists of the major seventh, third, sixth, ninth, and +4. Again, play it while holding the sustain pedal down. Then reach down and play a low Eb to hear what the chord sounds like with the root. Notice that the top note of the voicing is the +4 of the chord. The first chord in Miles Davis' "Blue In Green" can be voiced (although in a different key), with this chord. *When voicing melodies with So What chords, look for Lydian chords with the +4 in the melody.*

Figure 12-2

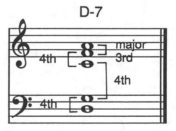

Figure 12-3

D-7

Figure 12-4

D-7

Figure 12-5

Bb∆

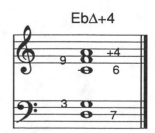

Figure 12-6

Eb∆+4

---

[1] McCoy Tyner, *Expansions*, Blue Note BST 84338.
[2] Miles Davis, *Kind Of Blue*, Columbia CJ-40579.

Figure 12-7

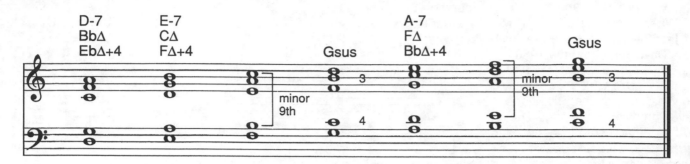

Figure 12-7 shows the So What chord extended diatonically up the C major scale. Play through these chords and listen to how each one sounds. Some of them have a tritone instead of a perfect fourth, and a minor third on top instead of a major third. A couple of them are fairly dissonant. When playing a modal tune with long stretches of a single minor seventh chord, you might want to play some or all of these for variety, even though they're not traditionally thought of as minor seventh voicings. This could keep you from being bored on a modal tune that stays forever on just one or two chords. "So What," Freddie Hubbard's "Little Sunflower,"[3] and John Coltrane's "Impressions"[4] are typical modal tunes, all with long sections of D-7. Each one is a great tune, but they've all been played several million times, and it's easy to run out of ideas after nineteen choruses of D-7.

Playing some of these more dissonant So What voicings helps to create needed tension and interest. Practicing **figure 12-7** in all major keys will also help you to see each key in a new way. In particular, it will make you more aware of the position of the tritone—the fourth and seventh—in each key.

Note the presence of the two new sus chord voicings. Both sus chord voicings include the major third of the chord, which in both cases is voiced above the fourth.

Play the third voicing, the one with F on the bottom, and the next-to-last one, the one with B on the bottom. These two voicings are much more dissonant than the others because they each have an interval of a minor ninth. The minor ninth is "the last dissonant interval." The evolution of Western music (I don't mean Country & Western Music) has

---

[3] Freddie Hubbard, *Backlash*, Atlantic 90466l.
[4] John Coltrane, *Impressions*, MCA/Impulse MCA-5887 (McCoy Tyner on piano).

seen a gradual relaxation of what is considered
dissonant. During the Inquisition, for example,
using a tritone could get you excommunicated, or
worse. Minor seconds and major sevenths were
relatively rare in classical music until the late
nineteenth century. In Jazz, the same two intervals
were rarely played until the 1930s, and if you listen
to records from that decade you'll hear many more
major sixth than major seventh chords. The natural
ninth on a half-diminished chord was considered a
no-no until fairly recently.

Play the two voicings again, the one with F on
the bottom and the one with B on the bottom. Would
you play either of these on a sixteen-bar D-7 section
of a modal tune? It might make for some interesting
sounds. Would you play either of them behind
Carmen McRae on the D-7 chord in the first bar of
the Arthur Schwatrz standard "Alone Together"?
Probably not. Minor ninths sound consonant in
some situations, highly dissonant in others.

Figure 12-8 shows the first five bars of Freddie
Hubbard's "Little Sunflower." The next few examples
show "Little Sunflower" voiced with So What chords
or variations of them. **Figure 12-9** uses diatonic So
What chords, everything staying within the key of C.
Some of the chords have tritones and minor thirds,
others perfect fourths and major thirds.

Figure 12-8

Figure 12-9

Figure 12-10

Figure 12-11

Starting with **figure 12-10**, the examples that follow show chords moving in *parallel motion*. As you play through these examples, don't try to read every note. Instead, try to see the chords intervalically, each note moving in parallel motion. Notice your hand position and what each chord looks like. Notice especially the interval between your thumbs, whether it's a fourth, a minor third, a whole step, or a half step.

In **figure 12-10**, each melody note is voiced with the same basic "fourth-fourth-fourth major third" So What voicing moving parallel with the melody, and going in and out of several keys. In **figure 12-11**, the bottom two notes of the basic So What chord are raised a whole step. This gives the chord a very dark "bite" because of the minor ninth between the bottom note in the left hand and the middle note in the right hand. In **figure 12-12**, the bottom two notes are raised another half step. This voicing brings left hand and right hand within a whole step of each other and sounds like space music. In **figure 12-13**, the bottom two notes are raised another half step. The left and right hands are now only a half step apart, and the voicing sounds extremely dissonant. The concept of a So What chord is stretched, with interesting results. Play all five of these versions, and see what your reactions are to dissonance, parallelism, and odd voicings. The key element here is parallelism. Parallel voicings are very effective in modal tunes.

Figure 12-12

Figure 12-13

People respond favorably to music that is highly structured, and the use of parallelism heightens the effect of structure. As an example, often before a gig I'll sit down and noodle around at the piano just to see if it's in tune, playing exactly the same voicing, but moving it around the keyboard. Whether I'm playing a consonant voicing, as in **figure 12-14**, or a dissonant one, as in **figure 12-15**, someone will frequently come up and say: "Gee, that's nice. Did you write that?" McCoy Tyner used parallelism beautifully in the two bars of "Peresina" which you played at the beginning of this Chapter in **figure 12-1**.

Figure 12-14

Figure 12-15

McCoy Tyner

Photo © by Jerry Stoll

Figure 12-16

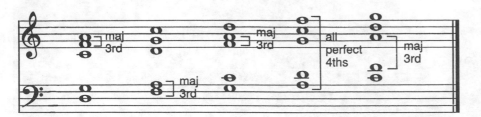

Figure 12-17

As with any other chord, So What chords can be inverted. Since the So What chord has five notes, it has five possible inversions **(figure 12-16)**. When you're 'comping on a D-7, FΔ, or BbΔ chord that lasts a few bars or more, you may want to play the So What chord through some of its inversions to provide a little variety, as in **figure 12-17**. Note the changing position of the major third in each inversion in **figure 12-16**. In the next-to-last voicing, the third has disappeared. All of the intervals are now perfect fourths. We've moved into the area of a new voicing—fourth chords, the subject of the next chapter.

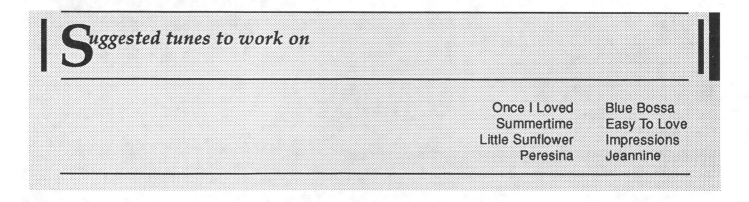

Practice tips

Read through tunes in *The New Real Book* and *The World's Greatest Fake Book*, looking for opportunities to play So What voicings on minor seventh chords with the fifth in the melody, major seventh chords with the major seventh in the melody, and Lydian chords with the +4 in the melody. Practice the So What chords diatonically up and down each major scale, as in **figure 12-7**.

Suggested tunes to work on

Once I Loved	Blue Bossa
Summertime	Easy To Love
Little Sunflower	Impressions
Peresina	Jeannine

CHAPTER THIRTEEN
Fourth Chords

Play **figure 13-1** and listen to the sound of *fourth chords*. McCoy Tyner in the early 1960s was the first jazz pianist to play fourth chords extensively, although the Powell brothers, Bud and Ritchie, were playing them over a decade earlier. On Bud's "So Sorry Please,"[1] he can be heard not only playing fourth chords, but also voicing parts of the melody in parallel fourths **(figure 13-2)**. "So Sorry Please" is also an early example of the use of pentatonic scales by a jazz musician (pentatonic scales will be covered in Chapter Fifteen). Bill Evans also played parallel fourths, as in the example shown from his version of Cy Coleman's "See Saw" **(figure 13-3)**.[2] Kenny Barron plays a similar figure near the end of his version of Vernon Duke's "Autumn In New York."[3] Bud Powell's brother Ritchie can be heard playing fourth chords as he 'comps behind Clifford Brown and Harold Land on Bud's "Parisian Thoroughfare."[4]

Figure 13-1

Figure 13-2

Figure 13-3

[1] Bud Powell, *The Genius Of Bud Powell*, Verve 82l690.
[2] Bill Evans, *Since We Met*, Fantasy 950l.
[3] Kenny Barron, *Autumn In New York*, Uptown UP27.26.
[4] Clifford Brown & Max Roach, *Jordu*, Trip TLP-5540.
  Richie Powell, an outstanding bebop pianist, was killed in the same auto accident that took Clifford Brown's life.

Figure 13-4

Figure 13-5

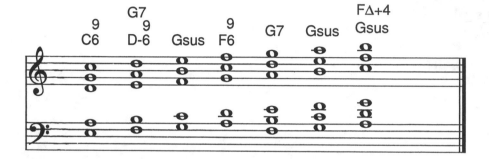

Play the chord shown in **figure 13-4**, a voicing for a C 6/9 chord. From the bottom up, it consists of the third, sixth, ninth, fifth, and root. It's much easier to "see," however, as a series of perfect fourths with the third of the chord on the bottom and the root on the top. Learn this major 6/9 voicing by practicing it around the cycle of fifths. **Figure 13-5** shows fourth voicings extended diatonically all the way up the C major scale. Most of the voicings include a tritone, rather than just perfect fourths. If you're playing a modal tune like "So What," "Little Sunflower," or "Impressions," you might want to play some or all of these voicings while you're 'comping or soloing, to create some tension in what is otherwise very unchanging harmony.

The second chord in **figure 13-5**, with F on the bottom, works very well as a D-6/9 chord. Reading from the bottom up, the voicing consists of the third, sixth, ninth, fifth, and root. D-6/9 is a *tonic minor* chord—that's a minor chord that acts more like a minor I than a II chord, and usually doesn't have a seventh. The first chord in George Gershwin's "Summertime," Kenny Dorham's "Blue Bossa," Bronislau Kaper's "Invitation," and Dietz-Schwartz's "Alone Together" could all be voiced with a tonic minor chord. Play this chord again, hold the sustain pedal down, and reach down and play a low D to hear what the chord sounds like with the root on the bottom. Practice this voicing around the cycle of fifths.

The D-6/9 voicing also works well as a G7 chord. Play it with the sustain pedal down, and reach down and play a low G underneath to hear the chord with the root. As a G7 chord, from the bottom up it reads seventh, third, thirteenth, ninth, and fifth. Now look at the third chord from the right in **figure 13-5**. It's the same chord, but with one more fourth added on top. This is a classic six-note dominant seventh chord that just about everybody plays. It's a fat sounding chord, with, from the bottom up, the seventh, third, thirteenth, ninth, fifth, and root. It sounds great as the first chord in a blues. Practice this voicing around the cycle of fifths.

Figure 13-5 also shows three new sus chord voicings. They all include a major third.

You don't have to play all of the notes in these five- and six-note chords for them to sound good. **Figure 13-6** shows the chords from **figure 13-5**, but with the top note omitted from each voicing. This gives you more choices when voicing melodies. If you have a CΔ chord with the root in the melody, you can voice it with the first chord shown in **figure 13-5**. If you have a CΔ chord with the fifth in the melody, you can play the first chord shown in **figure 13-6**. The different G7 voicings in **figure 13-5** and **figure 13-6** give you the choice of the fifth, root, or ninth in the melody.

Figure 13-6

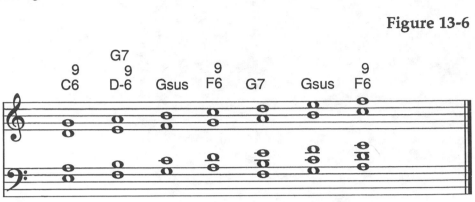

Fourth voicings work well together, as in **figures 13-7** and **13-8.** These voicings suggest the styles of McCoy Tyner and Chick Corea. If you try to read these voicings note for note, you'll tie yourself up in knots (unless you're The World's Greatest Sight Reader). Instead, try to see the chords intervalically. The example in **figure 13-8** consists of four different voicings, which are analyzed in **figure 13-9**. The first one has a tritone on the top; the second has a tritone on the bottom; the third and fourth ones consist of perfect fourths only. Try to "see" and "feel" them this way with your eyes and hands as you play them.

Figure 13-7

So far, we've only talked about two-handed fourth chords. McCoy Tyner uses three-note fourth voicings in his left hand, often after striking the octave or octave and fifth on the first beat of the bar, as shown in **figure 13-10**. There will be more on left-handed fourth chords in Chapter Sixteen.

Figure 13-8

Figure 13-9

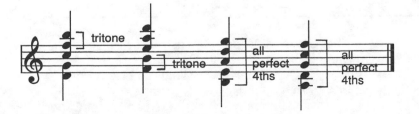

Figure 13-10

Kenny Barron   Photo © by Tom Copi All Rights Reserved

Practice tips   Practice the fourth voicings up and down the major scales in all keys, as in **figure 13-5**. In each key, note where the tritone is. Look for opportunities to voice melodies playing fourth chords.

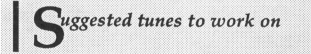

Suggested tunes to work on

That Old Devil Moon	Triste
On Green Dolphin Street	Mr. Day
Solar	What Am I Here For?
Softly, as In A Morning Sunrise	Caravan
Footprints	The Green Street Caper

CHAPTER FOURTEEN ≣
Upper Structures

Upper structures basic

Play **figure 14-1**, an arrangement of the first few bars of "Stella By Starlight," and listen to the sound of *upper structure* chords. All of the chords except the C-7 chord on the first beat of the third bar are voiced with upper structures. There are nine different upper structure chords. The first section of this chapter will concentrate on the four shown in **figure 14-2**.

A good definition of an upper structure is "a triad over a tritone." Look at the first upper structure in **figure 14-2**, a D triad over E and Bb, the third and seventh, or tritone, of a C7 chord. The three notes of the D triad (D, F#, A) are the ninth, +ll, and thirteenth of the C7+ll chord. Try finding this same voicing on F7+ll. Did you play a G major triad over A and Eb? Did you know to play a G triad because on the C7+ll chord the D triad is a major second above C? That's why this chord is called *upper structure II*, because the root of the triad is a major second above the root of the V chord. The upper structure number refers to the interval between the root of the triad and the root of the dominant chord. Each upper structure number is shown below the chord in Roman numerals. *Upper structure II is played on V7+ll chords.*

Figure 14-1

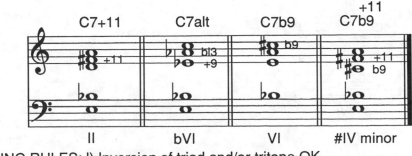

Figure 14-2

VOICING RULES: I) Inversion of triad and/or tritone OK.
2) Doubled notes OK at or near top of voicing only.

Figure 14-3

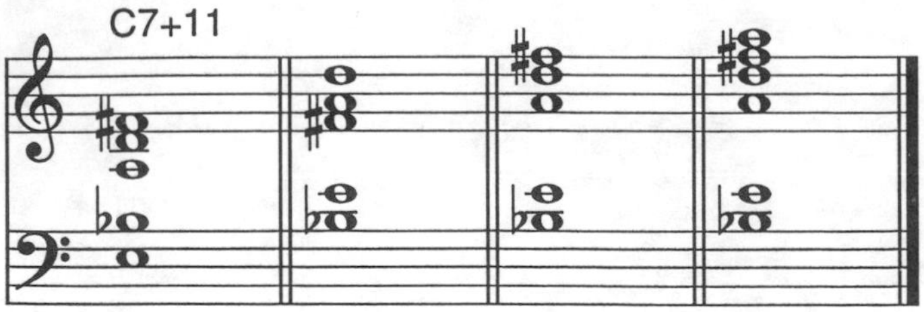

C7+11

You can invert either or both the triad and the tritone. **Figure 14-3** shows several inversions of upper structure II on C7+II, with the triad and/or the tritone inverted. Remember this, because in several of the upper structures shown here, the triads will be in first or second inversion. They can also be played in root position, as is the C7+II upper structure II in **figure 14-2**.

Look at the second chord in **figure 14-2**, upper structure bVI. This chord is an Ab triad in second inversion over the tritone of a C7 chord. The notes Eb and Ab in the triad are the +9 and b13 of a C7 chord, and instead of notating the chord C7+9, b13, we'll use the shorthand symbol C7alt. Ab, the root of the triad, is a minor sixth above C, so this chord is called *upper structure bVI*. Try finding the same chord for an F7alt chord. Did you play a Db major triad over A and Eb in the left hand? *Upper structure bVI is played on alt chords.*

The third chord in **figure 14-2**, upper structure VI, is an A triad in second inversion over the tritone of a C7 chord. The C# in the triad is the b9 of a C7 chord, so this chord is notated C7b9. A, the root of the triad, is a major sixth above C, so this chord is called *upper structure VI. Upper structure VI is played on V7b9 chords.*

Figure 14-4

C7b9

VI

Figure 14-5

C7b9

VI

Upper structure VI, as shown in **figure 14-2**, has only four notes. Both the A triad and the tritone of C7 have the note E, which raises the possibility of a doubled note in the chord. Play C7b9 as it appears in **figure 14-4.** Notice that this voicing doesn't sound quite as good as the C7b9 in **figure 14-2**. This is because in **figure 14-4** the doubled note, E, is at the bottom and in the middle of the chord. A doubled note in an upper structure usually sounds good only if one of them is at or near the top of the chord. Play **figure 14-5**. The E is doubled again, but one E is on the top of the chord, which sounds much better. The reasons why this is so can be found in the study of acoustics and the overtone series, which are beyond the scope of this book. For now, remember a simple rule: *Use doubled notes on upper structures with caution, except on or near the top of the chord, where they will always sound good.*

These first three—II, bVI, and VI—are by far the most frequently played upper structures. You can see why just by looking at their chord symbols: C7+II, C7alt, and C7b9. The three most common alterations played on V chords are +II, alt, and b9.

Look at the last upper structure in **figure 14-2**: an F# minor triad in second inversion over the tritone, a C7b9, +ll chord. The notes C# and F# in the triad are the b9 and +ll of a C7 chord. F#, the root of the triad, is a raised fourth above C, so this chord is called *upper structure #IV minor*. This voicing sounds great when used to harmonize melodies in parallel motion, as in the two examples shown in **figure 14-6**. The first example shown is bars 25-28 of Herbie Hancock's "Dolphin Dance."[1] In the second example, the upper structure #IV minor chords are on the third and fourth beats of the sixth bar of Thelonious Monk's "Ask Me Now"[2] (these are both just examples of how to use upper structure #IV minor chords—they are not what Herbie and Monk played on their records).

Don't try to "read" all of the notes as you play these examples. The upper structure voicings are all identical, moving in parallel motion. Be aware of your hand positions, what they feel and look like. Your right hand is playing a minor triad in second inversion. Your left hand is playing a tritone. The interval between your thumbs is a minor third. "See" the chord this way and just read the top line. *Upper structure #IV minor is played on V7b9, +ll chords.*

Figure 14-6

"Dolphin Dance"

"Ask Me Now"

---

[1] Herbie Hancock, *Maiden Voyage*, Blue Note BST-84195.
[2] Thelonious Monk, *Solo Monk*, Columbia 9149.

Figure 14-7

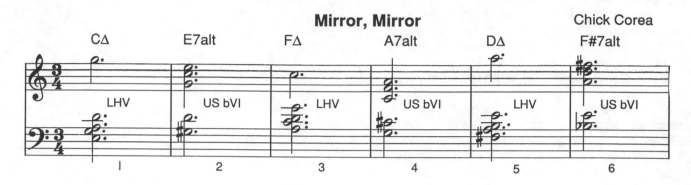

Mirror, Mirror

Chick Corea

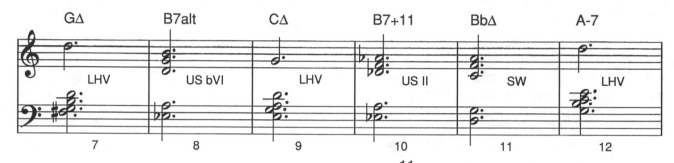

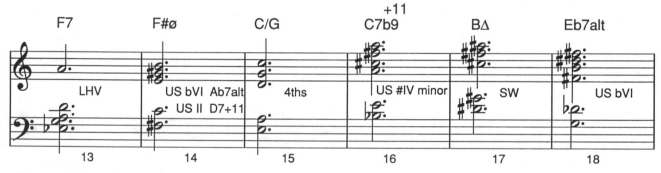

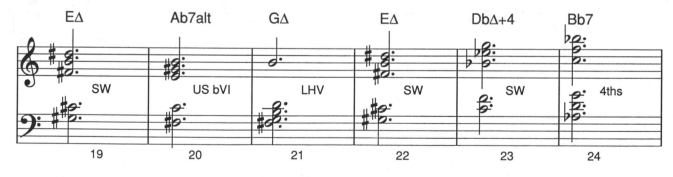

Figure 14-7 (Continued)

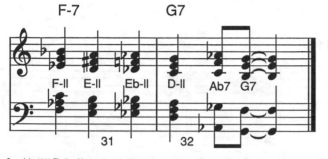

Play through **figure 14-7**, an arrangement of Chick Corea's pretty waltz "Mirror, Mirror."[3] This tune is voiced using the four upper structures just covered—II, bVI, VI, and #IV minor—along with So What chords, fourth chords, and left-hand voicings.

Chord type	Voicing
• Dominant chord with altered notes	Upper structure
• Minor seventh chord with fifth in the melody	So What
• Major seventh chord with seventh in the melody	So What
• Lydian chord with +4 in the melody	So What
• Major chord with root in the melody	Fourths
• Dominant chord with root in the melody	Fourths
• Half-diminished chord	(See Notes below)
• Diminished chord	(See Notes below)
• Almost everything else	Left-hand voicing

---
[3] Joe Henderson, *Mirror, Mirror*, Pausa 7075.

Notes on "Mirror, Mirror"

An upper structure is played on the F#ø chord in bar 14. How is this possible? All of the upper structures shown in **figure 14-2** are based on V chords. As you learned in Chapter Nine, however, a chord derived from a melodic minor scale is interchangeable with almost any other chord from the same scale because of the absence of "avoid" notes in melodic minor harmony. F#ø is from A melodic minor, as are Ab7alt and D7+11, so an upper structure for Ab7alt or D7+11 will work for an F#ø chord.

Figure 14-8

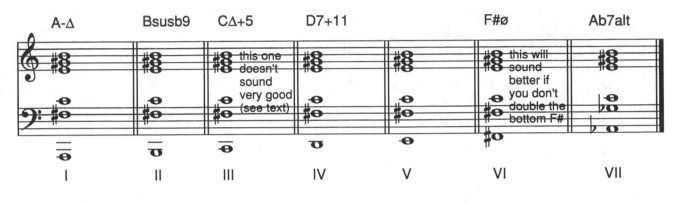

Figure 14-9

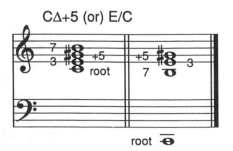

C△+5 (or) E/C

Let's expand on this idea of interchangeable voicings again. Look at **figure 14-8**. Play the F#ø voicing again, hold the sustain pedal down, and reach down and play a low A to make it an A-△ chord. Play the voicing again, this time reaching down and playing a low B, then C, D, and so on, up the A melodic minor scale. This one voicing works for all of the chords of A melodic minor. Well, almost. The "classic" voicing for a Lydian augmented chord, the third mode of melodic minor, has just four notes. These are the root, third, +5, and major seventh, as in the two voicings shown in **figure 14-9**. Notice the alternate chord symbol, E/C, which describes exactly what's played: an E triad over a C root. For many musicians, adding a fifth note tends to take away from the purity of the Lydian augmented chord. For this reason, playing a five-note upper structure for C△+5 may or may not work for now. I say "for now" because harmony is constantly evolving. Jazz musicians didn't even begin to play Lydian augmented chords with any frequency until the mid-1960s. In five years, the "classic" Lydian augmented chord in **figure 14-9** may be considered hopelessly tame, and relegated to pop music. Stay tuned.

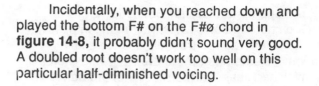

Incidentally, when you reached down and played the bottom F# on the F#ø chord in **figure 14-8,** it probably didn't sound very good. A doubled root doesn't work too well on this particular half-diminished voicing.

Notice the two new chords in **figure 14-8**, the ones with B and E in the bass. The chord with E in the bass is rarely used, but I'll come back to it in Chapter Twenty-Two. The chord with B in the bass was rarely played until just a few years ago. There's no standard symbol for this chord, but you'll probably see it notated as Bsusb9. This symbol suggests its function, because it acts like an altered sus chord. Unfortunately, Bsusb9 is also a common way to notate a B Phrygian chord, so "susb9" can be confusing. Eventually, we'll all agree on a chord symbol. For now, just note how smoothly this chord resolves down a fifth to EΔ **(figure 14-10)**. We'll come back to this chord in Chapter Twenty-Two.

The chord change in bar l5 of "Mirror, Mirror" is C/G. Following the F7 and F#ø chords in the previous two bars, this makes a chromatic bass line (F, F#, G) in bars l3-l5. In this arrangement, however, you're playing non-root position chords, so the "G" part of the C/G chord symbol is mainly to tell the bass player what to do. If you were playing a solo gig, with no bass player, you might want to voice the three chords in root position to bring out what Chick Corea intended.

In the original version of "Mirror, Mirror," there is no melody in bar 25, just three beats rest and an A7alt chord. For this reason, the chord is voiced fairly low so that the top note won't sound like a melody note.

Figure 14-10

An upper structure for Bb7b9 is played on the G#o chord in bar 28. As their name implies, diminished chords are from diminished scale harmony. Remember, there are no "avoid" notes in diminished scale harmony. Any chord derived from a diminished scale is interchangeable with any other chord from the same scale. The scale for the G#o chord, the G# whole step/half step diminished scale, is the same as the scale for Bb7b9, the Bb half step/whole step diminished scale. Any voicing for Bb7b9—in this case upper structure VI—will also work for G#o. You may wonder "how can I remember all that?" and "can anybody really think that fast?" The answer is yes. The trick is to learn all the chords from a particular diminished scale as a group, so that you can relate them to each other rapidly. G7b9, Bb7b9, Db7b9, E7b9—minor thirds apart—and G#o, Bo, Do, and Eo—also minor thirds apart—are derived from the same diminished scale. Take a look at **figure 14-11**, which shows this particular diminished scale as a continuum of chords, all related and all with interchangeable voicings

Figure 14-11

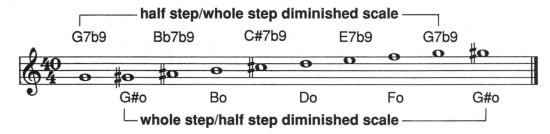

The D7+11 chord in bar 30 of "Mirror, Mirror" suggests an upper structure II. However, the melody note, C, is not a note in the E triad. Instead, it sits on top of the E triad. If this voicing is too dissonant for your taste, play a left-hand voicing instead.

The voicings in bar 31 and on the first beat of bar 32 consist of thirds stacked on top of each other: the root, third, fifth, seventh, ninth, and eleventh of a minor seventh chord (more on this voicing in Chapter Sixteen).

Notice the contrary motion between the top and bottom notes in the chords from bars 9 through 11.

This is just one way to play "Mirror, Mirror." It shows how smoothly left-hand voicings, So What chords, fourth chords, and upper structures all flow together.

Upper structures completed

There are five additional upper structures, shown in **figure 14-12**. Note that, unlike the four you learned previously, three of the five shown here have the root, C, on the bottom. The first, an Eb major triad over the C7 tritone, is the upper structure for a C7+9 chord. Because Eb, the root of the triad, is a minor third above C, this chord is called *upper structure bIII. Upper structure bIII is played on V7+9 chords.*

Figure 14-12

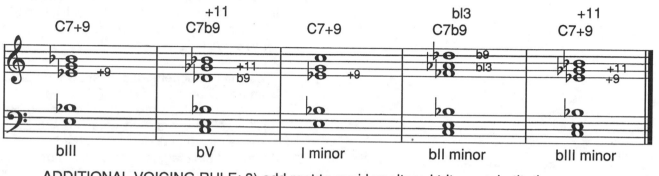

ADDITIONAL VOICING RULE: 3) add root to avoid unaltered tritone substitution

The second upper structure shown, a Gb major triad in second inversion over the C7 tritone, has the root, C, added in the bass. If you play this voicing without the root, as in **figure 14-13**, you'll hear why the root was added. This very "hip" C7b9, +11 voicing is exactly the same as a very tame F#7 chord. In fact, *all* C7 upper structures are also F#7 chords, because C7 and F#7 share the same tritone (review Chapter Six, "Tritone Substitution," if you've forgotten). However, the Gb major triad upper structure bV sounds like an *unaltered* tritone substitution in **figure 14-13**, a plain F#7 chord. When this happens, you must add the the root in the bass for the chord to sound like the C7b9, +11 chord that was intended. The Db and Gb in the triad are the b9 and +11 of a C7 chord. Because Gb, the root of the triad, is a flatted fifth above C, this chord is called *upper structure bV. Upper structure bV is played on V7b9, +11 chords.*

The last three examples in **figure 14-12** are all minor triad upper structures. Upper structure I minor, a C minor triad in first inversion over the C7 tritone, is the upper structure for a C7+9 chord. The note Eb in the triad is the +9 on a C7+9 chord. Compare its sound to upper structure bIII, which can also be played for a C7+9 chord. They're both good voicings. Which one do you like best? Because the C minor triad has the same root as the C7 chord, this upper structure is called *upper structure I minor. Upper structure I minor is played on V7+9 chords.*

Figure 14-13

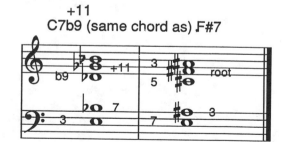

The fourth upper structure shown in **figure 14-12** is bII minor, a Db minor triad in first inversion over the tritone of C7. It needs the root on the bottom, otherwise it will sound like a plain F#7 chord, an unaltered tritone substitution. Because Db, the root of the triad, is a minor second above C, this chord is called *upper structure bII minor*. The notes Db and Ab in the triad are the b9 and b13 of a C7 chord. You could use C7alt as shorthand, although alt voicings usually have a +9 rather than a b9. Without the +9, this chord sounds a little tame for an alt chord, but it's still a pretty chord (change the Fb in the right hand to Eb and listen to the difference). *Upper structure bII minor is played on V7b9, b13 chords.*

The last upper structure shown in **figure 14-12** is an Eb minor triad over the C7 tritone, and requires the root on the bottom so it doesn't sound like an unaltered F#7 chord. The notes Eb and Gb in the triad are the +9 and +11 of a C7 chord. Because Eb, the root of the triad, is a minor third above C, this chord is called *upper structure bIII minor. Upper structure bIII minor is played on V7+9, +11 chords.*

Figure 14-14 shows the complete upper structure chart,[4] with all nine voicings shown. Look at the boxed areas in **figure 14-14**, where you'll see F#7 chord symbols. Almost all of these C7 upper structure voicings can also be played as F#7 chords, because C7 and F#7, a tritone away from each other, also share the same third and seventh, or tritone. Look at the first chord in **figure 14-14**, upper structure II, a C7+11 chord. Analyzing this as an F#7 chord shows it to be F#7alt. As F#7alt, this chord's upper structure number is bVI, because D, the root of the triad, is a minor sixth above F#. Since upper structure II is also upper structure bVI of the chord a tritone away, the opposite will be true: Look at upper structure bVI, C7alt. Analyzing this as an F#7 chord shows it to be F#7+11, upper structure II, because Ab is a major second above F# (don't let the enharmonic spelling throw you off).

The same interchangeability happens with upper structures bIII and VI. C7+9, upper structure bIII, is also F#7b9, upper structure VI. C7b9, upper structure VI, is also F#7+9, upper structure bIII.

Minor triad upper structures I minor and #IV minor are also interchangeable. C7+9, upper structure I minor, is also F#7b9, +11, upper structure #IV minor. C7b9, +11, upper structure #IV minor, is also F#7+9, upper structure I minor.

---

[4] Reprinted in appendix as "Appendix E."

Figure 14-14

Upper Structures

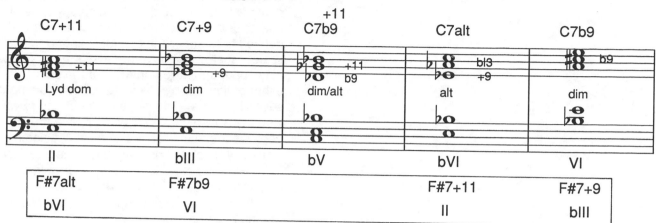

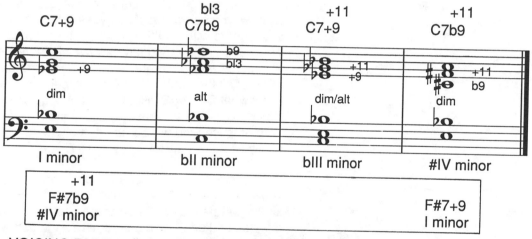

VOICING RULES: 1) Inversions of triad and tritone OK
2) Doubled notes OK at or near top of voicing only
3) Add root to avoid unaltered tritone substitution

Since the root, C, was added to upper structures bV, bII minor, and bIII minor, they will sound like C7 chords only, and can't be played as F#7 chords.

In other words, most of the upper structures function as two different dominant seventh chords, a tritone apart.

Remember how an upper structure was played on the F#ø chord in bar 14 of "Mirror, Mirror?" And an upper structure was played on the G#o chord in bar 28? Upper structures first evolved as dominant chords, so their terminology is tied to their use as dominant chords. Because they are all derived from either the melodic minor or diminished scales, scales that have no "avoid" note, you can play upper structures on most of the chords found in either of those two scales, not just on dominant seventh chords. The same upper structure will work for A-Δ, Bsusb9, D7+11, F#ø, and Ab7alt, because these chords are all from A melodic minor. Don't say "I can't think that fast." The trick is to learn all of the chords from a melodic minor or a diminished scale together. That way, you think of the chords as a group and know that their voicings are interchangeable.

The "numbers" part of all this is just temporary. By now, you can probably play a left-hand voicing for a D-7 chord without thinking about it very much. When you first learned left-hand voicings, however, you had to analyze that D-7 chord very carefully to pick out all the notes. At this point, because you know what D-7 *looks* like, you can just go ahead and play it. Upper structures are just another voicing. With practice, you will be able to play them just as easily as a left-hand voicing for D-7.

Try this: Play upper structure II on C7+11, as shown in **figure 14-14**. Play it a few times without looking at the music. Then come back to it in a few minutes and see if you can remember it *just by the way it looks*. Because this upper structure is from G melodic minor, it will also work for other chords in G melodic minor, such as G-Δ, Eø, and F#alt. Learn to think of these chords as a family, and soon the math part of music theory will be behind you.

Upper structures and scales

All nine upper structures are derived from just three scales: the Lydian dominant and altered modes of melodic minor harmony, and the half step/whole step diminished scale. Neither melodic minor nor diminished scale harmony have "avoid" notes, so upper structures from the same scale can be substituted for each other. As an example, upper structures bIII, VI, I minor, and #IV minor are interchangeable because all are derived from diminished scale harmony. For variety's sake, you might want to 'comp on a different one each chorus of a tune that has a V7b9 chord.

To be able to tell which of the three scales an upper structure is derived from, first look at **figure 14-15**, a comparison of the three scales in question: the Lydian dominant, altered, and half step/whole step diminished scales. All three scales shown here are based on C, and go with some type of C7 chord. The differences between them are in their fifths, ninths, and thirteenths. The Lydian dominant scale has a natural ninth, a natural fifth, and a natural thirteenth. The altered scale has both a b9 and a +9, no fifth, and a bl3. The half step/whole step diminished scale has both a b9 and a +9, a natural fifth, and a natural thirteenth. Note that all three scales have a +ll.

The complete upper structure chart **(figure 14-14)**, shows the scale (in abbreviation) for each upper structure between the staffs. Note that upper structure bV and blll minor are derived from *both* the diminished and altered scales. That's a clue to how they are often used. In the lead sheet for an old standard, a chord symbol might just say "C7." Most jazz musicians will interpret that very freely, and alter the chord in some way. b9 and alt are two common ways of altering a V chord, and if you are in doubt as to which one the soloist is going to play, 'comping on an upper structure bV will solve the problem, because its notes are derived from both scales.

As you get used to 'comping behind a soloist, you can begin to predict the alterations they will make to the chords with a fair degree of accuracy. Even though Wynton Kelly for the most part 'comped the same chords that Coltrane soloed on, there were times when Wynton played C7b9 and 'Trane played C7alt. And even though it's a good idea for everyone to more or less play the same chords, making things *too* specific takes away from the spontaneity of the music. How come Coltrane and Wynton still sounded so good when one was playing C7b9 and the other was playing C7alt? Both players were rhythmically very strong, and harmonically very clear. When they diverged briefly from playing exactly the same changes, what you hear is bitonality, or two types of harmony at the same time. The best players keep a balance of "playing the right changes," and not being imprisoned by them. That's a desirable goal. To get to that point, however, you must spend a lot of time "playing the right changes."

Figure 14-15

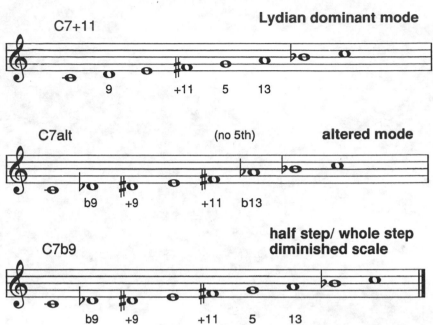

Chick Corea

Photo © by Lee Tanner

Four upper structures—bIII, VI, I minor, and #IV minor—are derived solely from diminished scale harmony. Two of them—VI and #IV minor—function as you would normally expect a V chord to, that is, they resolve smoothly to a chord a fifth lower (**figure 14-16**). bIII and I minor, however, function very differently. Although they are, strictly speaking, V chords, they both have the same tonic, rather than dominant, feeling as the first chord in a blues. **Figures 14-17** and **14-18** show rhythmic patterns on a C7+9 chord. The first one is voiced as an upper structure bIII, the second as an upper structure I minor. Notice the bluesy feeling of both voicings. Neither C7+9 has any inclination to resolve downward a fifth to an F chord.

The ability to move around by minor thirds on diminished scale chords is especially useful when playing upper structures. As long as you move in minor thirds, you won't leave the diminished scale "key" the original chord is in. **Figure 14-19** shows an Eb7b9 chord approaching an AbΔ chord in this manner, a device that Bill Evans was fond of playing. All four upper structure VI chords are derived from the same diminished scale.

Figure 14-20 shows upper structure #IV minor chords moving in minor thirds.

Figure 14-16

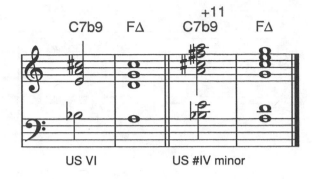

US VI   US #IV minor

Figure 14-17

US bIII

Figure 14-18

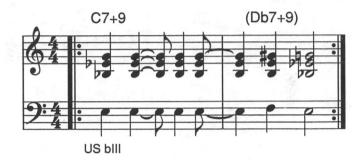

US I minor

Figure 14-19

(C7b9 A7b9 Gb7b9 Eb7b9)
all upper structure VI

Figure 14-20

US #IV minor...

123

Figure 14-21

Figure 14-22

You can use this idea when voicing melodies that move in minor thirds over V chords, as in **figure 14-21**, bar 6 of Jimmy Van Heusen's "Here's That Rainy Day." The three chords on beats 2-4 of the second bar are upper structure VI chords moving in minor thirds. Another opportunity is in bar 18 of Benny Golson's "Along Came Betty," as shown in **figure 14-22**. The F7b9 chord is derived from diminished scale harmony, and the first five notes of the melody line move up in minor thirds, voiced with upper structure VI chords. The last three melody notes in the bar move chromatically, as do the upper structure VI chords.

Practice tips Go around the cycle of fifths with each upper structure. Think of all the chords from each melodic minor key as a group, so you can play upper structures on more than just V chords. Do the same with the upper structures from each diminished scale.

Suggested tunes to work on

Stella By Starlight	Blue In Green
Up Jumped Spring	I Thought About You
Peace	In Your Own Sweet Way
Along Came Betty	Here's That Rainy Day
Search For Peace	Killer Joe
Chelsea Bridge	Rapture
Someday My Prince Will Come	Wave
Quiet Now	Soul Eyes

Play just the melody in **figure 15-1**, the pretty Johnny Mandel-Dave Frishberg ballad, "You Are There."[1] Most of the melody consists of a single pentatonic scale. Now play it with the chords. The lush chord changes effectively mask the almost nursery-rhyme effect that pentatonic scales can create. Until the F on the fourth beat of bar 7 in the second ending, every note in the melody is from the C pentatonic scale. The C pentatonic scale returns on the third beat of the last bar of the bridge (right before the D.S.), and continues to the end of the tune.

Figure 15-1

---

[1] Irene Kral, *Gentle Rain*, Choice 1020, a duo album with Alan Broadbent on piano.

Figure 15-2

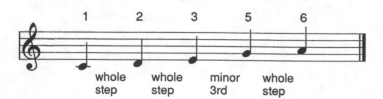

Although there are many five-note scales, the term "pentatonic scale" usually refers to the type of scale shown in **figure 15-2**. An easy way to think of it is I-2-3-5-6 of the major scale. Or, you can think of it as the major scale minus the fourth and seventh notes of the scale. Or, you can think of it intervalically as "whole-step, whole-step, minor third, whole-step."

Like any other scale, the pentatonic scale has modes, as shown in **figure 15-3.** The fifth mode is played so often that it has acquired its own name: the *minor pentatonic*. A good way to practice pentatonic scales is by breaking them into modes, as in the exercise in **figure 15-4**. Most of the music we play is in 4/4 time, so the five-note pentatonic scale in this exercise is broken into four-note groupings. The lick shown in **figure 15-5** is often the first pentatonic pattern that jazz musicians learn to play. Countless rock 'n roll tenor players have borrowed this lick, so use it sparingly, please.

Figure 15-3

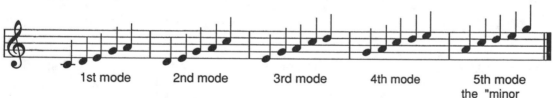

Figure 15-4

Figure 15-5

How many pentatonic scales occur naturally in the key of C? If you said three, you're right. The C, F, and G pentatonic scales are all found in the key of C major **(figure 15-6)**. I'll call them the I, IV, and V pentatonic scales. These terms are only meant to help you learn their position relative to the major key they are derived from. They are *not* common usage terms like "D-7," "tritone substitution," or "II-V-I." If you say to a musician friend "I'm playing on the IV pentatonic," they'll either think you're a genius or crazy—probably the latter.

Figure 15-6

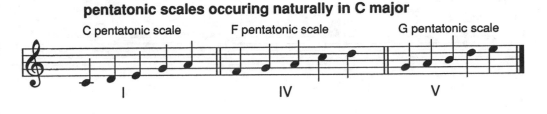

pentatonic scales occuring naturally in C major

C pentatonic scale   F pentatonic scale   G pentatonic scale

I   IV   V

Play each pentatonic scale—I, IV, and V—with your right hand while playing the left-hand voicings for II-V-I in the key of C. Over D-7, the II chord, all three pentatonic scales will sound good **(figure 15-7)**. The V pentatonic scale, based on G, is a bit more interesting than the other two because it contains both B and E—the sixth and ninth of the D-7 chord.

Figure 15-7

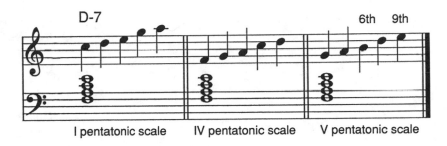

I pentatonic scale   IV pentatonic scale   V pentatonic scale

Over G7, the V chord, both the I and IV pentatonic scales have C, an "avoid" note on a G7 chord **(figure 15-8)**. While this doesn't mean that you can't play them, it restricts their use quite a bit. If you play the V pentatonic scale over G7, however, there is no "avoid" note. The V pentatonic also sounds good because it contains both A and E—the ninth and thirteenth of a G7 chord.

Figure 15-8

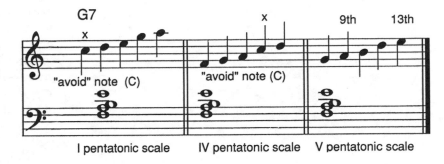

I pentatonic scale   IV pentatonic scale   V pentatonic scale

Over CΔ, the I chord, the IV pentatonic scale has F, an "avoid" note on a CΔ chord **(figure 15-9)**. Both the I and V pentatonic scales sound fine on a CΔ chord, neither having F, the "avoid" note. The V pentatonic scale sounds richer because it has both B and D—the major seventh and ninth of a CΔ chord.

Figure 15-9

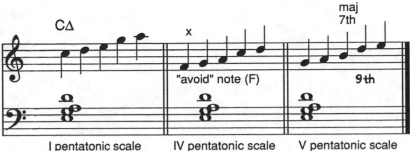

I pentatonic scale   IV pentatonic scale   V pentatonic scale

Notice the greater sense of space when you play pentatonic scales. Pentatonic scales are unique because, constructed of whole steps and minor thirds only, they lack the chromaticism of the half steps found in major and melodic minor scales. The ear enjoys hearing more air, space, and light in this larger-interval scale.

Figure 15-10

In case you haven't noticed, the V pentatonic scale works on all three chords: II, V, and I. This can simplify playing on a II-V-I considerably. Try improvising on the II-V-I in C playing just the V pentatonic scale, the one based on G, as shown in the example in **figure 15-10**. Practice this example in all twelve keys until you can automatically play on the V pentatonic scale in any key.

Look at **figure 15-11**, the changes to John Coltrane's "Giant Steps,"[2] a tune that has the reputation of being difficult to play. "Giant Steps" is a challenging tune, but it's not quite as tough as you think. In its sixteen bars are 26 chord changes. At a moderately fast tempo, that's a lot of chords to play. How many keys does it go through? The first chord is BΔ. The next two chords, D7 and GΔ, are the V-I in the key of G. The next chord, Bb7, is the V chord in the key of Eb. That's three keys in just the first four chords! *Every single chord in the tune, however, is from those three keys—B major, G major, and Eb major.* And, because you can play a V pentatonic scale over a II-V-I, you can play "Giant Steps" using just three pentatonic scales.

Above the staff in **figure 15-11** are the chord changes to "Giant Steps." Below the staff are the key changes, with the V pentatonic scale of each key shown directly below the key. Notice how less often key changes occur than chord changes. If you play an entire solo using nothing but pentatonic scales, it might be pretty boring. Mixed in with more conventional "playing the changes," however, pentatonic scales will give your playing structure, and a feeling of increased space.

---

[2] John Coltrane, *Giant Steps*, Atlantic SD-l3ll.

Figure 15-11

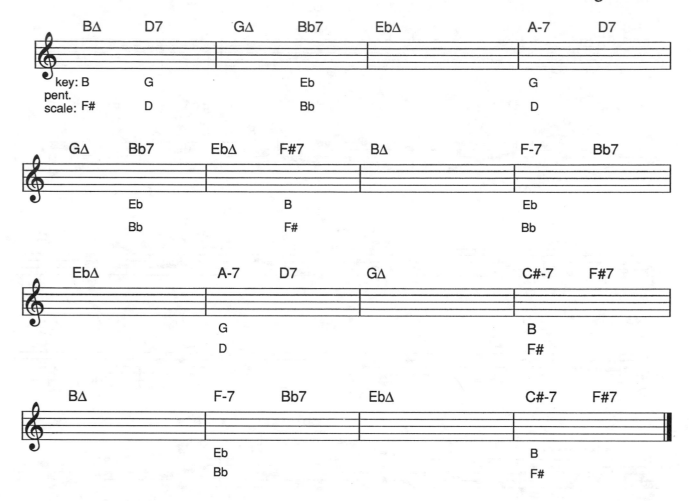

key: B G Eb G
pent.
scale: F# D Bb D

Figures **15-12a**, **15-12b**, and **15-12c** show a pentatonic solo on the changes to "Giant Steps." **Figure 15-12a** is the solo with chord symbols only. **Figure 15-12b** is the same solo with easy half-note chords in the left hand. **Figure 15-12c** is the same solo again, this time with more rhythmic left-hand accompaniment.

Figure 15-12a

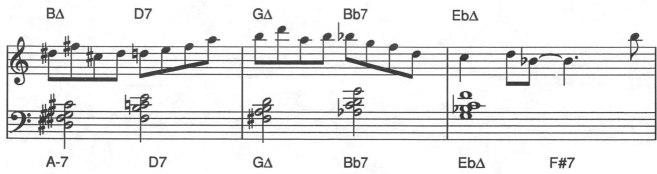

Figure 15-12c

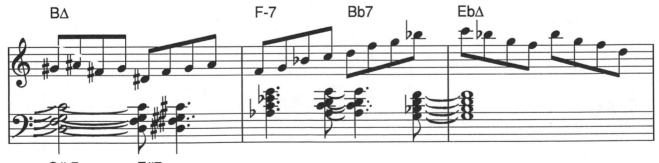

"Giant Steps" is not the easiest tune to start playing pentatonic scales on, but it demonstrates how using the V pentatonic scale can make a challenging tune more accessible. Try playing V pentatonic scales on simpler tunes like "Just Friends" or "Tune-up."

There's another way to look at playing the V pentatonic scale over II-V-I. What are the "avoid" notes on the II-V-I chords in the key of C?

- On a D-7 chord there is no "avoid" note.
- On a G7 chord the "avoid" note is C.
- On a CΔ chord, the "avoid" note is F.

Figure 15-13

The "avoid" notes on the II-V-I in the key of C are C and F. If you remove C and F from the C major scale, you'll have five notes left over, as shown in **figure 15-13.** Those five notes are the G pentatonic scale. *The V pentatonic scale is the major scale without the "avoid" notes.*

the C major scale, minus C and F, the two "avoid" notes = G pentatonic scale

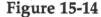

Figure 15-14

There is another pentatonic scale that is often played on a I chord. Play a left-hand voicing for CΔ, as in **figure 15-14**, and improvise on a D pentatonic scale with your right hand. The F# changes the chord to CΔ+4, or C Lydian. This pentatonic scale is built on the second note of the major scale, so I'll call it the II pentatonic scale.

Figure 15-15

In melodic minor harmony, there is only a single naturally occurring pentatonic scale. It is built off of the fourth note of the melodic minor scale **(figure 15-15).** Playing a line from this IV pentatonic scale over a melodic minor voicing may sound weird or "out" if you're not used to it **(figure 15-16).** This is because pentatonic scales sound resoundingly "major," and when you play them over the very exotic and decidedly "un-major" sound of a melodic minor chord, strange (and beautiful) things happen. If your ear doesn't accept this yet, don't worry about it, it's all a matter of individual taste, and tastes change.

Pentatonic scales occuring naturally in C melodic minor

C melodic minor scale   F pentatonic scale

IV

Figure 15-16

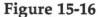

No pentatonic scales occur naturally in diminished or whole-tone harmony.

There are many five-note scales other than the pentatonic scale. Two in particular are played by many jazz musicians. The Japanese *in-sen*[3] scale is shown in **figure 15-17**. Play it up and down a few octaves while holding the sustain pedal down, and you'll be transported many miles to the East. The unusual pattern of intervals is "half step, major third, whole step, minor third." The half step on the bottom gives this scale a very un-pentatonic flavor, even though it is a five-note scale.

Figure 15-17

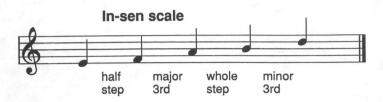

In-sen scale

half step / major 3rd / whole step / minor 3rd

Figure 15-18

C major scale   D melodic minor scale   E In-sen scale

III of C major and
II of D melodic minor

The in-sen scale can be derived from both the major and melodic minor scales **(figure 15-18)**. It is built off of the third note of the major scale, and the second note of the melodic minor scale. Although you can play it on all the chords derived from either major or melodic minor harmony, musicians like John Coltrane and McCoy Tyner have played it mainly on altered dominant and Phrygian chords, as in the two examples using the E in-sen scale in **figure 15-19**. *When playing an alt chord, use the in-sen scale built off of the second note of the melodic minor key. When playing a Phrygian chord,* use *the in-sen scale built off of the third note of the major key.*

Figure 15-19

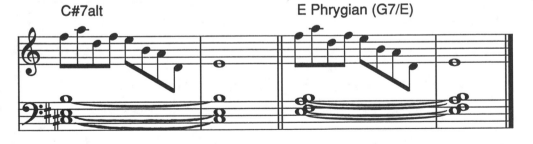

C#7alt   E Phrygian (G7/E)

---

[3] Erroneously called the *Kumoi* scale in one jazz theory book. The Kumoi scale based on E has the notes E, F, A, B, C. The in-sen scale could also be called a variant of the *hira-joshi* tuning for the *koto*, a Japanese stringed instrument. The use of these terms in connection with jazz theory is tenuous at best—Japanese theory doesn't translate easily into Western theory. And no, the in-sen scale is not derived from Antonio Carlos Jobim's tune "How *In-sen*-sitive."

Figure 15-20 shows another five-note scale. This scale doesn't have a commonly accepted name, but I've heard it called the "altered pentatonic" scale. The interval pattern is "half step, major third, whole step, whole step." Unlike the in-sen scale, which can be derived from both the major and melodic minor scales, the altered pentatonic is derived from the melodic minor scale only, and is built off of the second note of the melodic minor scale (shown to the right). **Figure 15-21** shows an E altered pentatonic phrase over a C#7alt chord. *When playing a chord from melodic minor harmony, play the altered pentatonic scale built off of the second note of the melodic minor key.*

Figure 15-20

E "altered" pentatonic scale   D melodic minor scale

II of D melodic minor

Figure 15-21

The blues scale is largely interchangeable with the fifth mode of the pentatonic scale, also known as the minor pentatonic scale. **Figure 15-22** shows both a C minor pentatonic scale and a C blues scale (the octave is doubled here in both scales). They are almost identical, the only difference being the chromatic passing note between F and G in the blues scale. **Figure 15-23** shows two similar phrases over a C7+9 chord. The notes in the first phrase are derived from the C minor pentatonic scale. The notes in the second phrase are from the C blues scale.

Figure 15-22

C minor pentatonic scale   C blues scale

Figure 15-23

C minor pentatonic scale.............................   C blues scale..

There are many other five-note scales, but the three covered in this chapter—the pentatonic, the in-sen, and the altered pentatonic—are among the ones most played by jazz musicians today. Although pentatonic scales have been in common use only since the early 1960s, Bud Powell was playing them in the late 1940s in his tune "So Sorry Please,"[4] a fragment of which was shown in Chapter Thirteen **(figure 13-1)**.

Summary

- On the II chord you can play the I, IV, and V pentatonic scales.
- On the V chord you can play the V pentatonic scale.
- On the I chord, you can play the I, II, and V pentatonic scales.
- *On a II-V-I, you can play the V pentatonic scale.*
- On all major scale-derived chords you can play the in-sen scale based on the third note of the key.
- On melodic minor chords you can play the pentatonic scale based on the fourth note of the melodic minor scale.
- On melodic minor chords you can play the in-sen scale based on the second note of the melodic minor scale.
- On melodic minor chords you can play the altered pentatonic scale based on the second note of the melodic minor scale.

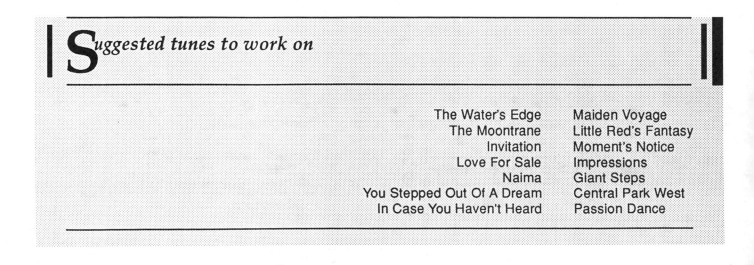

Suggested tunes to work on

The Water's Edge	Maiden Voyage
The Moontrane	Little Red's Fantasy
Invitation	Moment's Notice
Love For Sale	Impressions
Naima	Giant Steps
You Stepped Out Of A Dream	Central Park West
In Case You Haven't Heard	Passion Dance

---

[4] Bud Powell, *The Genius Of Bud Powell*, Verve 821690.

CHAPTER SIXTEEN ≣
Voicings, Voicings, Voicings

This chapter shows how you can combine So What, fourth, and upper structure voicings in II-V-I progressions. It also introduces lots of new voicings. Wherever possible, I'll identify the pianist who plays a particular voicing. It's important for you as a jazz pianist to have a wide variety of voicings in your repertoire. As an accompanist, you'll need to provide a magic carpet of sound behind a soloist, one that expresses a broad range of emotion and texture. Consonance and dissonance, transparency and opaqueness, strength and tenderness, happiness and sadness—all must be at your fingertips.

Play **figure 16-1**. This II-V-I uses a So What voicing for the D-7 chord, an upper structure VI for the G7b9 chord, and a fourth voicing for the CΔ chord. Combining voicings like this produces very smooth voice leading as well as nice sounding chords. When you're 'comping, these combinations of voicings provide the soloist with a smooth, rich harmonic background.

Figure 16-2 shows a G7 upper structure resolving to a CΔ fourth voicing on the first two chords of Bob Haggart's "What's New?" Notice how the first voicing expands chromatically in the top and bottom voices into the second chord.

Figure 16-3 shows a more transparent II-V-I than the one in **figure 16-1**. The root of the D-7 chord has been omitted, so it now sounds like Gsus. The G7b9 chord has no doubled note, as in **figure 16-1**. The result is a II-V-I with three four-note chords, each voice resolving downward. Notice that the top three notes on the D-7 voicing form an F major triad in second inversion, resolving chromatically down to an E major triad in second inversion on the G7b9 chord.

In the II-V-I progression in **figure 16-4**, D-7 is voiced as a So What chord with its root omitted, sounding like Gsus. The G7alt chord is voiced as an upper structure bVI. The CΔ chord uses a So What voicing. Notice the contrary motion in the top and bottom voices. Also note the expansion from four- to five-note chords.

Figure 16-1

Figure 16-2

Figure 16-3

Figure 16-4

Figure 16-5

orig. chords: F-7   Bb7   Eb△

SW   SW   US II   US VI   4th
      inverted   B7+11   Bb7b9

Figure 16-6

D-7   G7b9

Gsus   US #IV minor.......

Figure 16-7

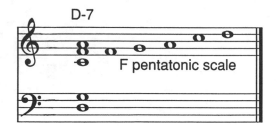

D-7

F pentatonic scale

Figure 16-5 shows the last phrase of Cole Porter's "All Of You," voiced with two inverted So What chords, two upper structures, and a fourth chord. Note the reharmonization.

Figure 16-6 shows something you might play on a II-V progression. The So What voicing for the D-7 chord is inverted—the root (D) is on top instead of on the bottom, resulting in a Gsus chord. It resolves to a G7b9 upper structure #IV minor voicing. The upper structure voicing then goes up and down a minor third. G7b9 is a diminished scale chord and—remember—you can always move around in minor thirds in diminished scale harmony. In this example, the G7b9 chord symbol on the third beat is anticipated by a beat and a half, the chord being played on the "and of one." You can play with the time like this pretty freely when soloing, but be careful of anticipating chords by more than a half-beat when 'comping, or what you play might clash with the soloist. That doesn't mean you shouldn't do it, but use caution.

Incidentally, the five notes of a So What chord form a pentatonic scale **(figure 16-7)**.

Figure 16-8 expands on the idea of moving around by minor thirds on diminished scale chords. The voicing shown is one that Duke Ellington often used when arranging for his sax section. Its distinctive sound comes largely from the half step interval on the bottom. **Figure 16-9** shows how this voicing can be used on the first bar of Duke's "Melancholia."[1] Melba Liston also used this voicing on the arrangement of her tune "Len Sirrah," on Blue Mitchell's album *Heads Up!*[2]

Figure 16-10 shows another example of moving by minor thirds on a diminished scale chord. These are *double diminished chords*. The right hand plays one diminished seventh chord, the left hand another, and the two chords together contain all the notes of the diminished scale **(figure 16-11)**. An easy way to find this voicing on a D7b9 chord is to think of your right hand playing a diminished seventh chord with the root—D—on top, while your left hand plays a diminished seventh chord with the third—F#—on the bottom.

Figure 16-8

E7b9 (or G7b9, Bb7b9, Db7b9)

Figure 16-9

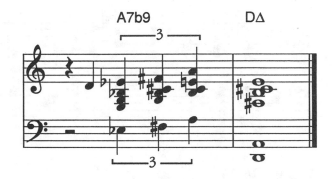

Figure 16-10

D7b9 (or B7b9, Ab7b9, F7b9)

Figure 16-11

---

[1] Duke Ellington, *Piano Reflections*, Capitol M-11058.
[2] Blue Note BST 84272, with some great playing by McCoy Tyner.

Figure 16-12

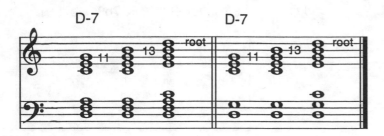

Figure 16-12 shows two new ways to voice a minor seventh chord. In the first bar, thirds are stacked on top of each other on a D-7 chord. The three variations shown have the eleventh, thirteenth, or root on top. You played the one with the eleventh on top in the last two bars of "Mirror, Mirror" in Chapter Fourteen **(figure 14-8)**. In the second bar, thirds are stacked over a fourth on the bottom, the three variations again with the 11th, 13th, or root on top. To hear how the voicings sound in context, play the two examples in **figure 16-13**. When voicing melodies with these chords, look for minor seventh chords with the eleventh, thirteenth, or root in the melody.

Figure 16-13

Figure 16-14

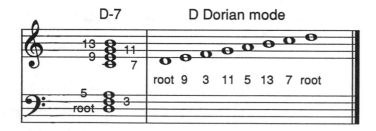

Let's go back to the second example in the first bar of **figure 16-12**. This voicing, as shown in **figure 16-14**, contains all the notes in the D Dorian scale (shown on the right).

Figure 16-15

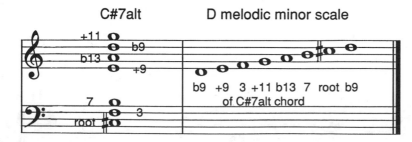

Another voicing that uses all the notes of the scale from which it is derived is the lush voicing for C#7alt shown in **figure 16-15**. You need big hands to play this one, because it has a span of a minor tenth in the right hand. This seven-note chord has all the notes of the D melodic minor scale. What's the "key signature" for D melodic minor? Melodic minor scales are not usually thought of as having key signatures, but melodic minor harmony is much easier to master if you note what accidentals occur in each scale, and think of that as a key signature. To the right of the voicing in **figure 16-15** is the D melodic minor scale, which would have a key signature of one sharp (C#). G melodic minor is the most unusual example, with a key signature of F# and Bb **(figure 16-16)**. Although it's rare for a composer to use melodic minor key signatures, Béla Bartók did so in his *Mikrokosmos*, Volume II, number #41.[3] The piece has a key signature of one sharp (C#), or D melodic minor. A complete chart of melodic minor key signatures appears in the appendix as "Appendix I."

Figure 16-16

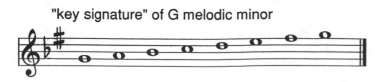

"key signature" of G melodic minor

---

[3] Béla Bartók, *Mikrokosmos*, Boosey And Hawkes 1940.

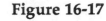

Figure 16-17 shows two voicings for an F-7 chord. The first one has a floating quality. You can hear Herbie Hancock play it as the final chord of the intro to Wayne Shorter's "Fee Fi Fo Fum."[4] When voicing melodies with this chord, look for minor seventh chords with the ninth in the melody.

The second one is a Kenny Barron voicing. You can hear him arpeggiating this voicing on his version of the traditional song "Hush-a-Bye,"[5] and also on his tune "Spiral."[6] Notice the symmetrical nature of this voicing: Each hand plays the same structure, which consists of two perfect fifths spanning a ninth. The interval between your thumbs is a half step—be aware of what the voicing *looks* and *feels* like. When voicing melodies with this chord, look for minor seventh chords with the eleventh in the melody, as in **figure 16-18**, the A-7 chord in bar 17 of "All The Things You Are." Other tunes where you could use it are the first chord in "I Didn't Know What Time It Was," "Tune-Up," "It's You Or No One," "Pent-Up House," the minor seventh chord in the second bar of "Yardbird Suite," and the A-7 chord four bars from the end of "Just Friends."

Figure 16-17

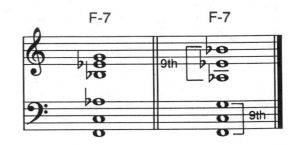

Figure 16-18

[4] Wayne Shorter, *Speak No Evil*, Blue Note 4194, an album with several of Wayne's best tunes.
[5] Kenny Barron, *Landscape*, Limetree MLP 0020.
[6] *Sphere On Tour*, Red Record 123191.

Figure 16-19 shows three examples of a triad outside the key on a major chord. The first one, with a D triad, is a voicing for CΔ+4, a C Lydian chord. You might also see this chord notated D/C. The second one, with an E triad, is a voicing for CΔ+5, and might be notated E/C. Chords notated in this manner are called *slash chords*. The note to the left or above the slash represents a triad and the note to the right or below the slash represents a bass note, or, as in the next example, another triad. This last example shows a B triad over a C triad, usually notated B/C. This chord has both a major third and a major seventh, suggesting a CΔ chord. Notating it other than as a slash chord would yield something like CΔ+4,+9, which is too confusing. Most musicians prefer the symbol B/C. This chord is derived from the B whole step/half step diminished scale, and enables you to improvise using the diminished scale on a major chord. The first use of this chord by a jazz pianist was probably the Gb/G chord on the first beat of the fourth bar of Bud Powell's "Glass Enclosure."[7] Red Garland often played this chord as a reharmonization of the final I chord in a tune, as on the last chord of Miles Davis' "Four."[8] Another example is the last chord in Red's trio version of Frank Loesser's "If I Were A Bell."[9]

Figure 16-19

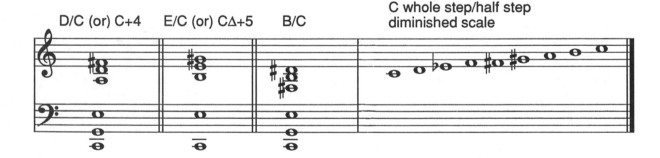

Figure 16-20

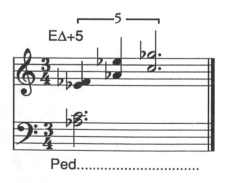

Play the second example in **figure 16-19** again, the CΔ+5 Lydian augmented chord. Contrast it with the feathery voicing that Herbie Hancock plays on the EΔ+5 chord on the sixteenth bar of the head on Wayne Shorter's "502 Blues,"[10] as shown in **figure 16-20**.

[7] *The Amazing Bud Powell, Vol. 2,* Blue Note l504.

[8] Miles Davis, *Workin',* Fantasy/OJC OJC-296.

[9] Red Garland, *Red Garland's Piano,* Fantasy/OJC OJC-073.

[10] Wayne Shorter, *Adam's Apple,* Blue Note 84232 (one of Herbie's best albums).

Figure 16-21 shows the last four bars of the bridge of Tadd Dameron's "Our Delight."[ll] Each V chord is preceded by another V chord a half-step above (see reharmonization below bass staff). This is called *chromatic approach*. All the V chords except the last Eb7 are upper structure II voicings. Notice how each group of two chords expands, the top and bottom voices moving away from each other in contrary motion.

Figure 16-21

In Chapter Eight, you learned left-hand voicings for alt chords. Starting with a left-hand voicing for a V chord, you raised the ninth and flatted the thirteenth, as in the B7 chord in **figure 16-22**. If you played this B7alt voicing just as Herbie Hancock walked through your front door, and you asked him "What chord am I playing, Herbie?" He'd probably say "F7." It looks like F7 and sounds like F7, so it must be F7. Your hip voicing for B7alt turns out to be F7, an *unaltered tritone substitution*. To play a left-hand voicing for an alt chord that can't be mistaken for an unaltered tritone substitution, play either of two combinations: the third, fifth, seventh, and ninth of the melodic minor *key* the alt chord is derived from; or the root, third, fifth, and seventh of the melodic minor key. B7alt is derived from the C melodic minor scale. The 3-5-7-9 and I-3-5-7 of C melodic minor are shown in **figure 16-23**. These four notes are not found in any other melodic minor key, nor any major key, diminished scale, or whole-tone scale. *They are characteristic of C melodic minor only.*

Either of these voicings will work for almost any chord in C melodic minor: C-Δ, Dsusb9, EbΔ+5, F7+ll, Aø, and B7alt. I said *almost* any chord in C melodic minor. The I-3-5-7 combination doesn't work too well for EbΔ+5, because most musicians like the pure sound of a G major triad over an Eb for an EbΔ+5 chord.

Figure 16-22

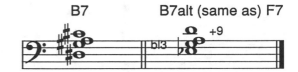

Figure 16-23

B7alt, also C-Δ, Dsusb9, EbΔ+5, F7+11, Aø (all the chords in C melodic minor)

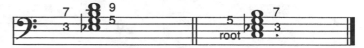

ll Philly Joe Jones and Dameronia, *Look, Stop, And Listen*, Uptown 27.l5.

You can invert these 3-5-7-9 and l-3-5-7 melodic minor voicings, as in **figure 16-24**.

Whether you play these "characteristic" melodic minor voicings is a matter of personal taste. Bill Evans usually played the B7alt voicing that was shown in **figure 16-22**.

Figure 16-24

3-5-7-9 of C melodic minor   1-3-5-7 of C melodic minor

Figure 16-25

Eø   A7alt

In Chapter Ten, you learned that on a llø, V7alt progression you can move the left-hand voicing for the ø chord up a minor third and it becomes the alt chord (**figure 10-11**). The same thing works with upper structures, as in **figure 16-25**. The Eø chord moves up a minor third and becomes an A7alt chord. Eø is from G melodic minor. A7alt is from Bb melodic minor. The melodic minor "key" of the alt chord is a minor third above the melodic minor "key" of the ø chord. This is another example of parallelism, identical chords repeated at a different pitch.

Figure 16-26

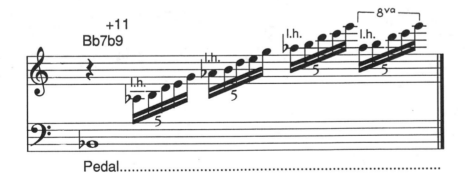

Pedal...

In classical music, most *arpeggios* outline triads, and are played with the right hand. Many arpeggios played by jazz pianists are much more complex, involving five-, six-, and even seven-note chords. One way to play them is to use both hands, as shown in **figure 16-26**. After playing the low Bb with your left hand, play the first Ab of each five-note group with the thumb of your left hand, your right hand playing the other four notes of each group of five notes. Don't let the sight of five-note groups intimidate you. You don't have to "count" when playing this. The groups of five are just written that way so the total of all the notes in the bar will add up to four beats.

Reversing direction in the middle of arpeggios can be very effective, as shown in **figure 16-27**. This is much easier to play than it looks. After playing the low Bb with your left hand, play the first Ab of each five-note group with the thumb of your left hand. Your right hand plays the other four notes of each group. The first note in your right hand in each group is a minor third lower than the Ab you played with your left hand. **Figure 16-28** shows another arpeggio that reverses direction, this time on a minor-major chord.

Many pianists favor a more open sound in the left hand, and play three-note left-hand voicings, unlike the four-note voicings covered in Chapters Seven and Eight. **Figure 16-29** shows a II-V-I in the key of D with three-note instead of four-note chords.

Figure 16-27

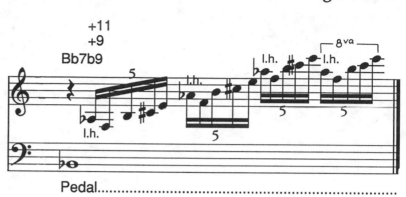

Pedal..

Figure 16-28

Pedal..

Figure 16-29

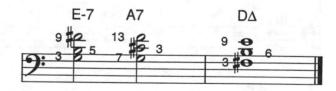

A common way to voice a sus chord with three notes is to play the root, fourth, and seventh. **Figure 16-30** shows a phrase with these sus voicings in the left hand. The right-hand line is based on the V pentatonic scale of the key of each sus chord. As an example, the right-hand line in the first bar is based on the C pentatonic scale, the V pentatonic scale in the key of F, the same key that the Csus chord is derived from. The last four eighth notes in the third bar, from the A pentatonic scale, can be heard two different ways: They anticipate the Asus chord in the next bar, or they are derived from the V pentatonic scale of the left-hand voicing, which, despite the F#sus chord symbol, is also the same three-note voicing used for the DΔ chord in **figure 16-29**.

You could also play **figure 16-30** if the harmony for this five bars were just a Csus chord. Using parallelism allows you to get "outside" the harmony by moving a structure (the voicing) or pattern (the pentatonic line) in a parallel fashion. You can move to another, or as in this case, to several keys before returning to home base. McCoy Tyner and trumpeter Woody Shaw are two acknowledged masters of this technique.

Figure 16-30

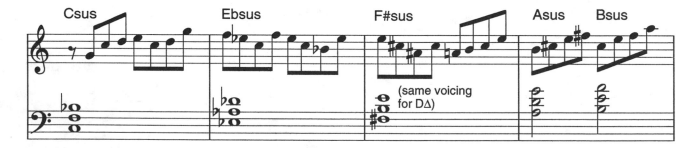

There is another type of three-note voicing, often played by Thelonious Monk,[12] one with a lot of "bite" in it because it has a half step interval on the bottom. **Figure 16-31** shows four of these voicings. To use them you'll need to remember the following:

- On a major seventh chord, play the seventh, root, and third of the *chord*.
- On any other chord from major scale harmony—II, V, sus, Phrygian, Lydian—play the third, fourth, and sixth of the *key*.
- On any melodic minor chord, play the second, third, and fifth of the melodic minor *key*.
- On a dominant seventh b9 chord, play any one of four combinations, each consisting of a half step and a minor third, and built on either the root, +9, +II, or thirteenth of the *chord*. These four voicings, like everything in diminished scale harmony, are a minor third apart from each other.

Notice that the intervalic pattern is half-step/major third on all of these three-note voicings except the dominant seventh b9 chords, which are half-step/minor third.

Figure 16-31

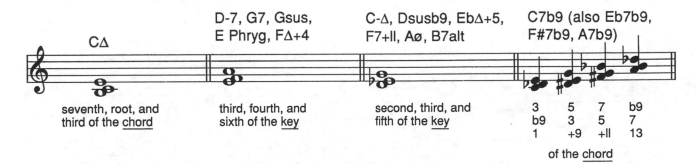

---

[12] Thelonious Monk, *Solo Monk,* Columbia 9149. Listen to Monk's use of three-note voicings on the DbΔ chords in stride sections of "Ask Me Now."

Figure 16-32 is an arrangement of John Coltrane's "Naima,"[13] using many of these three-note voicings, each played after the root of the chord is played on the first beat of the bar. All of the three-note voicings follow the rules just shown.

Figure 16-32

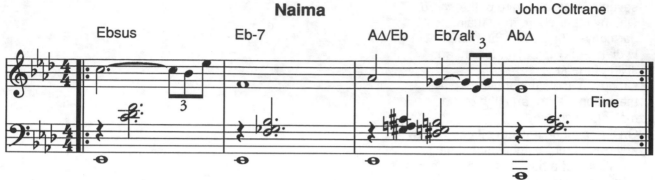

Naima

John Coltrane

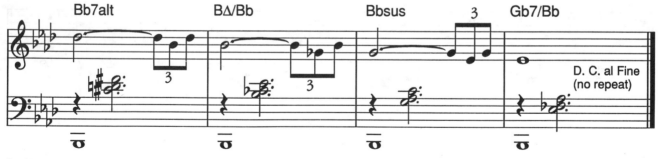

[13] John Coltrane, *Giant Steps*, Atlantic l3ll (Wynton Kelly on piano).

You can combine upper structures sequentially, as shown in the next two examples. First, on the turnaround figure on the eighth bar of Benny Carter's "When Lights Are Low" **(figure 16-33)**, the Ab and Gb triads cascading down over the tritone of a C7 chord are alternating bVI and bV upper structures. In **figure 16-34**, upper structures II, bVI, and #IV minor are combined.

You can also combine upper structures vertically, as shown in **figure 16-35**. This voicing combines a D major triad (upper structure VI), and a B minor triad (upper structure #IV minor), in a single chord: F7b9, +II.

Figure 16-36 shows a four-note left-hand voicing for an E Phrygian chord, Esusb9.

Figure 16-33

Figure 16-34

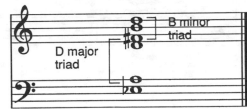

Figure 16-35

Figure 16-36

Figure 16-37 shows bars 17-20 of Donald Byrd's "I'm So Excited By You."[14] The original chords are shown above the staff. The arrangement of this four bars uses the Kenny Barron minor seventh voicing **(figure 16-17)**, fourth chords, a new sus voicing, and an upper structure VI, all flowing smoothly together.

Figure 16-37

K Barron voicing   4ths..................   Fsus   US VI   4ths   Ebsus

You can enhance left-hand voicings by adding octaves or triads in the right hand, as shown in **figure 16-38**. This adds weight and power to the chords whether you are soloing or 'comping.

Figure 16-38

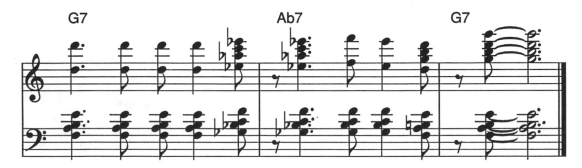

14 Donald Byrd, *Mustang*, Blue Note 4238 (one of Donald's best albums, with some great McCoy Tyner on piano).

Can you invent some new voicings of your own? Here's a method to experiment with: First select a scale, such as the F melodic minor scale **(figure 16-39)**. Choose a number of notes for a voicing—let's say six. Choose an intervalic or structural pattern, for example two minor triads, the root of the top triad a fifth higher than the top note of the bottom triad. **Figure 16-40** shows our hypothetical voicing, based on F, the root of the scale. Your left hand plays an F minor triad. A fifth above C, the top note of the triad, your right hand plays a G minor triad. A nice sounding chord results: F minor with a ninth, eleventh, and thirteenth—and no seventh.

Now the real fun begins. Walk this voicing up the F melodic minor scale. What's the "key signature" of F melodic minor? F melodic minor has two flats: Ab and Bb. Keeping that in mind will help you "see" the voicings as you go along. **Figure 16-41** shows all the new voicings going up the scale. Some are very dissonant. Some of the triads have become major, augmented, or diminished, rather than minor. The interval between your hands is no longer always a perfect fifth. On two of the voicings, it's a tritone. On another, it's a minor sixth. Some of the chords are not as easily named or analyzable as the first one was. Do you like the way they sound? They have a very Gil Evans-like quality.[15] Experiment with other scales, numbers of notes, interval combinations, inversions, and see what you come up with.

Figure 16-39

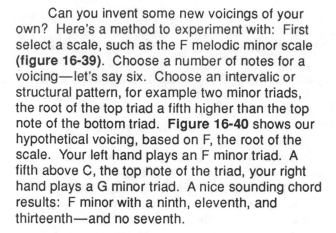

Figure 16-40

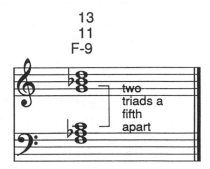

Figure 16-41

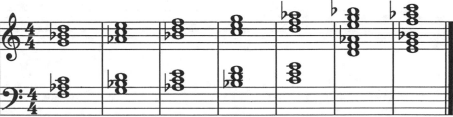

---

[15] Gil Evans worked closely with Miles Davis over a period of four decades. Their best known collaborations are: Miles Davis, *Birth Of The Cool,* Capitol 16168; Miles Davis, *Miles Ahead*, Columbia 40784; Miles Davis, *Sketches Of Spain*, Columbia 40578; Miles Davis, *Porgy & Bess*, Columbia 40647.

As you learn new voicings, you'll need to memorize what chord tone is on top. This is absolutely necessary when voicing tunes. Look at **figure 16-42**. This melody line is over a series of minor seventh chords, except for one sus chord. The first chord, Bb-7, has an Eb, the eleventh, in the melody. You could play the melody line over left-hand voicings, but let's opt for richer, two-handed voicings. How many two-handed minor seventh voicings do you know with the eleventh in the melody? **Figure 16-43** shows most of the two-handed minor seventh voicings covered so far, with the chord tone on top—the melody note—identified just to the right of the note. Each type of voicing is identified just below. So What chords, So What chords with doubled notes, a So What variation shown in Chapter Twelve **(figure 12-10)**, stacked thirds, a fourth chord voicing, and the Herbie Hancock and Kenny Barron minor seventh voicings from this chapter are all shown.

Figure 16-42

Figure 16-43

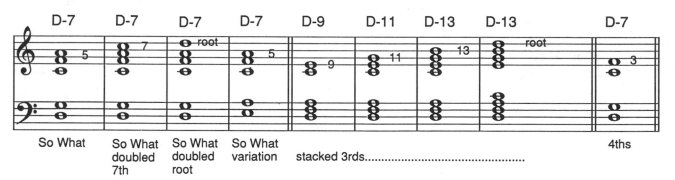

So What   So What doubled 7th   So What doubled root   So What variation   stacked 3rds...   4ths

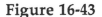

Herbie Hancock   Kenny Barron

In **figure 16-44**, our melody line has
been voiced using some of the choices shown
in **figure 16-43**. The Gsus chord, with the third in
the melody, has been voiced with a sus voicing
you learned in Chapter Four.

Figure 16-44

Kenny
Barron

So What........... sus
add 3rd

So What
doubled 7th

Herbie
Hancock

So What
variation

stacked
3rds

Red Garland

Figure 16-45

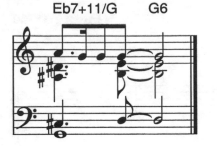

Figure 16-46

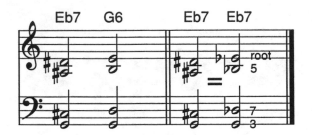

I'll end this chapter appropriately, with a cadence. **Figure 16-45** shows one that Duke Ellington often played, approaching a I chord with a dominant seventh chord a major third below, over the pedal of the tonic I chord. In classical theory this is called a *German sixth*. **Figure 16-46** shows the two chords in question, sàns the melody of the preceding figure. The curiously spelled first chord is enharmonically just Eb7.

This chapter just scratches the surface of possible voicings. One way to expand your repertoire of voicings is to transcribe them off of records. Some transcribing techniques will be covered in Chapter Twenty-Three. Remember, you can't learn to play jazz from a book alone. Listen!

CHAPTER SEVENTEEN
Stride and Bud Powell Voicings

Stride

Pre-bebop pianists played a left-hand style called *stride* (**figure 17-1**). Derived from both classical music and ragtime, stride piano provided rhythm and harmony in both solo and group playing. James P. Johnson, prominent in the 1920s, Fats Waller in the 1930s and 40s, and Art Tatum in the 1930s, 40s, and 50s were perhaps the three greatest exponents of stride playing. Duke Ellington, Willie "The Lion" Smith, Lucky Roberts,[1] Jess Stacy, and many other great pianists were adept at playing stride. As **figure 17-1** shows, in a stride left hand the pianist usually played a root or a tenth on the first and third beats of the bar, and a simple triad or dominant seventh chord on the second and fourth beats. More recently, stride has evolved to include the left-hand voicings developed by Bill Evans and Wynton Kelly in the late 1950s, as shown in **figure 17-2**.

With the arrival of bebop in the mid-1940s, the function of the pianist in the rhythm section changed radically. The new music demanded a lighter, less oom-pah left-hand style for pianists (more on this new style later in the chapter). Bud Powell and Thelonious Monk pioneered this new style, although both occasionally still used stride in their solo playing.[2] Stride was for the most part neglected by the inheritors of Bud and Monk's legacy, and is only rarely heard in the bebop pianists who matured in the 1950s and 60s. As a distinct solo style, it has made a comeback in the 1980s.

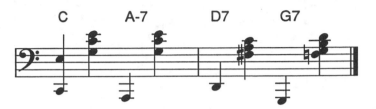

Figure 17-1

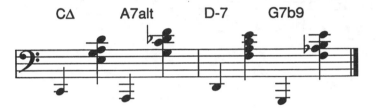

Figure 17-2

---

[1] Lucky Roberts & Willie "The Lion" Smith, *Harlem Piano*, Good Time Jazz 10035.

[2] Bud Powell plays stride on "Body And Soul," on his album *The Genius Of Bud Powell*, Verve 821690. He plays a partially stride version of Jerome Kern's "The Last Time I Saw Paris," on *The Amazing Bud Powell*, Verve 2506, that displays the generally ignored Fats Waller side of his roots. Thelonious Monk plays stride versions of "Dinah," and "I'm Confessin'," on his album *Solo Monk*, Columbia PC-9149, and stride versions of "Lulu's Back In Town," and "Nice Work If You Can Get It," on *It's Monk's Time*, Columbia 8984.

Figure 17-3 shows a modern stride version of a variation of the changes to the first four bars of Billy Strayhorn's "Daydream." The root of each chord is played on beats one and three, and, unlike the simple triads in **figure 17-1**, left-hand voicings are played on beats two and four.

Figure 17-3

Figure 17-4

Figure 17-4 shows a device known as *walking tenths*, useful when a major seventh or dominant seventh chord lasts a bar or more. Art Tatum was a master at this. If you can't reach a tenth, try "rolling" the tenth, as shown in **figure 17-5**.

In **figure 17-6**, an extra note has been added to the walking tenths. Dave McKenna (who sometimes sounds like he has three hands), incorporates three-note walking tenths into his stride style.[3] If your hand isn't big enough to reach these three-note tenths, don't force it. You could risk getting tendonitis, which is painful and has ruined a few careers.

There are inumerable walking tenths patterns, but the one shown in **figure 17-6** is perhaps the most commonly played of them all. Note the arrangement of notes in each of the four chords. The four chords are a C major triad, a D minor triad, an incomplete D# diminished seventh chord, and a C major triad with E in the bass. The analysis is as follows, each chord reading, from the bottom up:

Figure 17-5

Figure 17-6

- On the major triad: root, fifth, third
- On the minor triad: root, fifth, third
- On the diminished chord: root, seventh, third
- On the major triad on the fourth beat: third, root, fifth

[3] Dave McKenna, *My Friend The Piano*, Concord Jazz 3l3.

OK, that's the *analytical* way of looking at the walking tenths pattern in **figure 17-6.** As important, perhaps even more so, is the *visual* aspect, or how you "see" the pattern. Look first at the outer notes. The top note walks up chromatically—easy to remember. The bottom note goes up a whole step at first, and then two chromatic steps. Isn't that easier than memorizing numbers, like root-fifth-third? The middle note, if your hand is big enough to encompass all three notes, goes up a whole step, then a minor third, then repeats the previous note. A visual imprint is made in your mind's eye as you practice the pattern, and you can forget about the numbers.

Figure 17-7 shows three different ways to add some harmonic interest to a bar that has a single major seventh chord. In the first example, a left-hand voicing for a D-7 chord is played on the third beat of the bar. In the second example, a voicing for G7 is played on the third beat. In the final example, D-7 and G7 are played on the third and fourth beats.

Figure 17-7

Figure 17-8 shows the changes to John Coltrane's "Giant Steps" arranged for stride left hand. Walking tenths are played in bars 3, 7, II, and I5. The examples shown in **figure 17-7** are played in bars 9 and I3 to add harmonic interest.

Figure 17-8

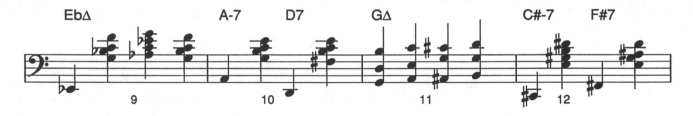

Incorporating some inner movement into stride playing can help moderate its relentless up-and-down effect. **Figure 17-9** shows the third of the Ab7 chord moving up to the +II on the third beat, and then back down again on the fourth beat. **Figure 17-10** shows how, on a dominant seventh b9 chord, you can take advantage of its diminished scale characteristics and move the voicing around in minor thirds. **Figure 17-11** reverses the normal pattern of root-chord-root-chord, making it chord-root on the third and fourth beats of the bar.[4]

It's natural to want to use the sustain pedal when playing stride, to compensate for the time lag in your left hand as it moves from root to chord and back again. Unfortunately, it's also easy to over-use the pedal and run everything together. The cure? Extreme as it may sound, you should practice stride at least part of the time *without using the pedal.* Although you may find this painfully difficult at first, it produces immediate results. The motion in your left hand from root to chord will smooth out considerably, and you'll be sustaining the roots and the chords much more with your left hand than when using the pedal. Of course it's OK to use the pedal in "real life," but practicing at least part of the time sans pedal is good for you.

Lots of good transcribed stride is available in sheet music. Jed Distler's Art Tatum transcriptions[5] and other publications are gold mines of stride techniques.

Figure 17-9

Ab7

Figure 17-10

G7b9

Figure 17-11

D-7   G7

---

[4] Jaki Byard, the most eclectic jazz pianist of all, plays great stride. His style spans everyone from James P. Johnson, whose music he has recorded, through Errol Garner, Bud Powell, Monk, and beyond, all mixed together in his own inimitable way. He plays a stride version of Gershwin's "Our Love Is Here To Stay" on his album *Parisian Solos*, Futura 05.

[5] Jed Distler, *Art Tatum*, Amsco Publications.

Figure 17-12 shows an arrangement of the first four bars of Fats Waller's "Ain't Misbehavin'," in which the left hand plays tenths with an extra note added. I've improvised on the melody on the last two beats of bar 4 to allow for a II-V progression (forgive me, Fats). Figure 17-13 shows a variation of this arrangement, with quarter notes instead of half notes in the left hand. If your hand isn't big enough to reach a tenth or put the middle note in the tenth, figure 17-14 shows a way of approximating this style. Figure 17-15 shows the same four bars, but with more modern left-hand voicings as part of the stride effect, and a chord substitution in the third bar—A7+11 in place of the G7+5 chord. Figure 17-16 shows how the early bebop pianists might have played the first four bars of "Ain't Misbehavin'." These root position left-hand voicings were first played extensively by Bud Powell.

Figure 17-12

Figure 17-13

Figure 17-14

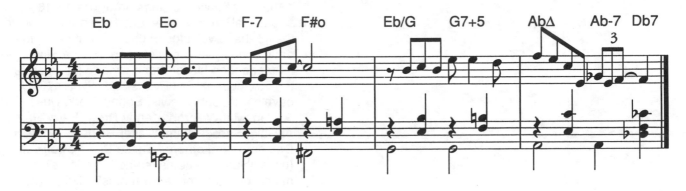

Figure 17-15

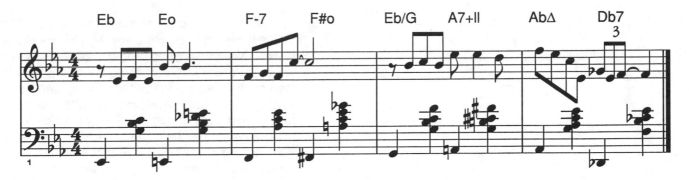

Figure 17-16

Bud Powell voicings

The Bud Powell voicings[6] in **figure 17-16**— skeletal, rudimentary, and transparent—were the left-hand voicings of choice for most of the early bebop pianists, including Horace Silver (he later changed his left hand style to incorporate the voicings that Bill Evans and Wynton Kelly developed), John Lewis, Sonny Clark, Duke Jordan, Mal Waldron, Kenny Drew, Barry Harris,[7] Al Haig, Sadik Hakim, Walter Bishop, Jr., Tadd Dameron, and others. These Bud Powell voicings (usually just two notes, sometimes three), consist mainly of roots, thirds (or tenths), sixths, and sevenths. **Figures 17-17, 17-18**, and **17-19** show three variations of Bud Powell voicings with the same bebop line in the right hand.

Most of the jazz pianists who emerged in the 1960s played the left-hand voicings Bill Evans and Wynton Kelly developed, and the use of Bud Powell voicings declined. Most young jazz pianists today start out by learning the Bill Evans-Wynton Kelly voicings, and Bud Powell voicings often seem primitive by comparison. Bud Powell voicings have some advantages, however. For one thing, they are lower on the keyboard, allowing the pianist's right hand to use the melodically very powerful octave around and below middle C. The Bill Evans-Wynton Kelly left-hand voicings restrict your right hand to a higher range of the keyboard. Many of the the best pianists today play an eclectic mix of left-hand voicings, Bud Powell voicings, upper structures, fourth chords, So What chords, block chords (covered in Chapter Nineteen), and others.[8]

---

[6] *The Amazing Bud Powell, Vol. I and Vol. II*, Blue Note 81503 and 81504, and *The Genius Of Bud Powell*, Verve 2506 (especially Bud's tune "Hallucinations").

[7] Barry Harris is perhaps the best pianist carrying on the Bud Powell tradition, as well as being a great interpreter of Monk's music. His use of Bud Powell-style left-hand voicings can be heard on his tune "Oh So Basal," from his album *Bulls-Eye!*, Prestige 7600

[8] Listen to Mulgrew Miller's left hand on his solo on the title track of his album *Wingspan*, Landmark 1515.

Figure 17-17

Figure 17-18

Figure 17-19

Figure 17-20

G7b9

Play the voicing in **figure 17-20**. By itself, this voicing sounds rather crude. In context, however, as in **figure 17-21**, the overall effect is much prettier. The notes in the right hand in bar 2 come from the second mode of the F melodic minor scale (more on this mode in Chapter Twenty-Two).

Figure 17-22 shows the changes to the first eight bars of Charlie Parker's "Confirmation" as they might have been played in stride style by a pianist influenced by Fats Waller. **Figure 17-23** shows the same eight bars as Bud Powell might have played them. **Figure 17-24** shows the the same eight bars as they might be interpreted by a solo pianist familiar with both stride and left-hand voicings.

Figure 17-21

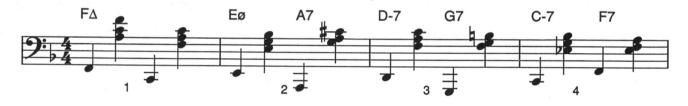

Figure 17-22

Figure 17-23

Figure 17-24

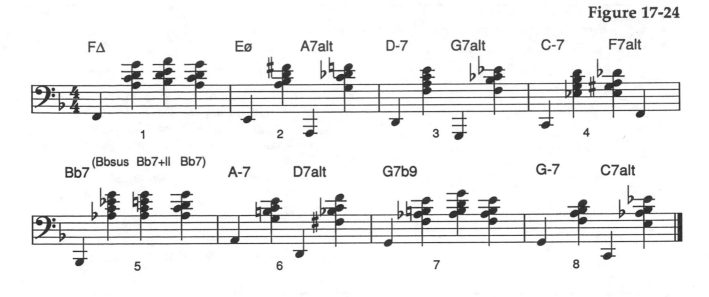

Barry Harris

Photo © by Jerry Stoll

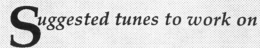

Suggested tunes to work on

Stride	Bud Powell voicings
Daydream	Confirmation
Namely You	Yardbird Suite
Honeysuckle Rose	Scrapple From The Apple
I've Got The World On A String	Dig
I'm Old Fashioned	Donna Lee
Sweet And Lovely	"Rhythm" changes
I'm Gettin' Sentimental Over You	Tune-up
Ain't Misbehavin'	Anthropology
Memories Of You	Bouncin' With Bud
When You Wish Upon A Star	Hallucinations
Giant Steps	Daahoud

Play **figure 18-1**, a line over a progression of IIø-Valt chords. The line is made up entirely of what some musicians call *minor sixth scales*, a four-note scale that outlines a minor sixth chord. **Figure 18-2** shows the minor sixth scale for each of the chords in the previous example. Each minor sixth scale outlines the root, third, fifth, and sixth of the melodic minor scale from which the chord is derived.

Figure 18-1

Figure 18-2

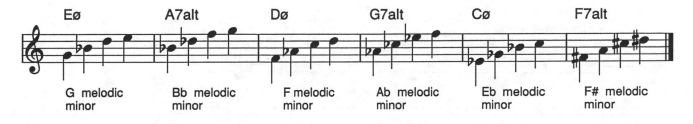

Figure 18-3

You can play these minor sixth scales rapidly around the keyboard, as in **figure 18-3**, or cascade them through a chord change, as in **figure 18-4**.

Figure 18-4

Minor sixth scales have a timeless quality. Everyone from Teddy Wilson through McCoy Tyner and Mulgrew Miller[1] has played them. **Figure 18-5** shows how a pianist in the 1930s might have played a minor sixth scale line over a C minor chord. **Figure 18-6** shows how a pianist influenced by McCoy might play the same line over a B7alt chord.

Figure 18-5

[1] Listen to Mulgrew's solo on the title track of Monty Croft's *A Higher Fire*, Columbia 45122.

Figure 18-6

B7alt

Play **figure 18-7**, a C minor sixth scale line over a C7+9 chord. The four notes of this scale—C, Eb, G, and A—are the root, +9, fifth, and sixth of a C7+9 chord. Now play **figures 18-8**, a C minor pentatonic line over a C7+9 chord, and **18-9**, a C blues scale line over the same C7+9 chord. Hear how all three scales—C minor sixth, C minor pentatonic, and C blues—have a similar bluesy sound. In today's music, the three scales are often played interchangeably. *On dominant seventh +9 chords, play the minor sixth scale based on the root of the chord.*

Figure 18-7

C7+9

C minor sixth scale

Figure 18-8

C7+9

C minor pentatonic scale

Figure 18-9

C7+9

C blues scale

Figure 18-10

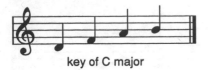

key of C major

In major scale harmony, the minor sixth scale is built off of the second note of the major scale **(figure 18-10)**. **Figure 18-11** shows a minor sixth scale line built off of D—the second note of the C major scale—played over several chords derived from C major. Notice that the line sounds good on all of the chords, except the CΔ chord itself, because the D minor sixth scale contains F, the "avoid" note on a CΔ chord. For a major seventh chord, you could play the minor sixth scale built off of the *sixth* of the key, as shown in **figure 18-12**. Playing this scale over CΔ adds an F#, changing the chord to CΔ+4, or C Lydian.

Figure 18-11

x = "avoid" note

Figure 18-12

As shown in the examples in **figures 18-1**, **18-2**, and **18-3**, the minor sixth scale from melodic minor scale harmony is built off of the first note of the melodic minor "key." **Figure 18-13** shows a line based on a C minor sixth scale played over all of the chords derived from C melodic minor.

Your ear may or may not be ready for the bitonal effect of this rather conventional minor line played over a very exotic melodic minor chord. Although there are no "avoid" notes in melodic minor harmony, the line sounds very different over each of the chords (the Dsusb9 chord, and the chord with G in the bass and no chord symbol, will both be covered in Chapter Twenty-Two).

Figure 18-13

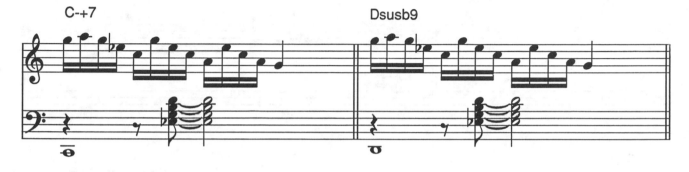

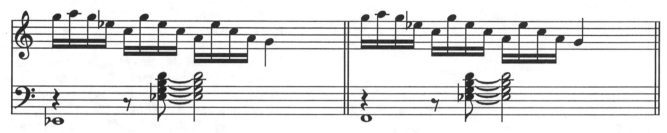

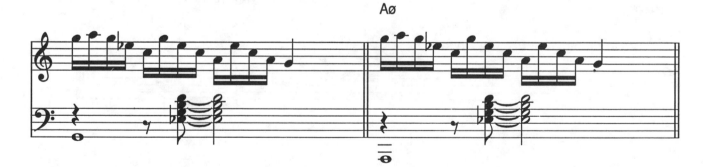

There are many four-note scales other than minor sixth scales. The symmetrical nature of diminished scale harmony offers numerous possible four-note scales. One example is shown in **figure 18-14**, followed by a line based on this scale over a C7b9 chord. Invent some of your own four-note diminished scales, but remember, *they have to sound good.*

Figure 18-14

Some four-note scales are so versatile that you can play them over many chords from many keys. Look at the scale shown in **figure 18-15**, and play the line shown in the next bar. The scale is based arbitrarily on Bb (it could just as easily start on C, Eb, or F). In how many major keys do these four notes occur? Mentally go through all the key signatures and see if you can come up with the right answer. If you said four keys, you're right. These four notes occur in the keys of Bb, Eb, Ab, and Db. You can play the line in **figure 18-15** over the major seventh chords in three of those keys: EbΔ, DbΔ, and AbΔ **(figure 18-16)**.

Figure 18-15

Figure 18-16

Now listen to the same line over a Bb△ chord **(figure 18-17)**. Despite the four Ebs (the "avoid" note on a Bb△ chord), the line sounds much more consonant than the last bar of **figure 18-11**, which also had four "avoid" notes. Listening to an avoid note is a subjective, and changeable, experience. Let your taste be your guide.

Figure 18-17

X="avoid" notes (?)

Figure 18-18

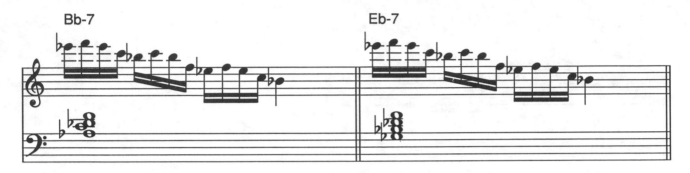

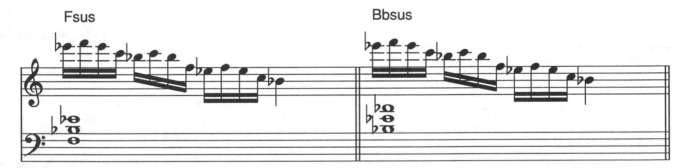

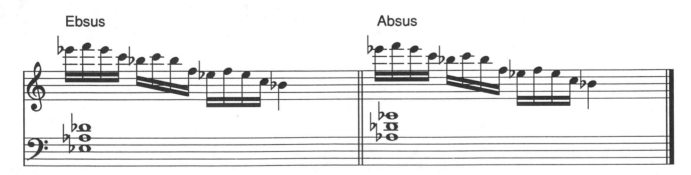

Because there are no "avoid" notes on minor seventh and sus chords, you can play the same line over the minor seventh and sus chords from the four keys just mentioned **(figure 18-18)**. You can also freely play the line over the dominant seventh chords from two of those four keys **(figure 18-19)**. But the line may not sound very good to you over the other two dominant seventh chords **(figure 18-20)** because the scale has the "avoid" note of each of those chords.

Again, listen very carefully to "avoid" notes. Dissonance can sound great out of context. Dropped into the middle of a pretty ballad, however, a dissonant note might sound like a bomb going off. On the other hand, consonance and dissonance are subjective, and you might like the "avoid" notes better than any of the other notes in the examples![2]

Figure 18-19

Figure 18-20

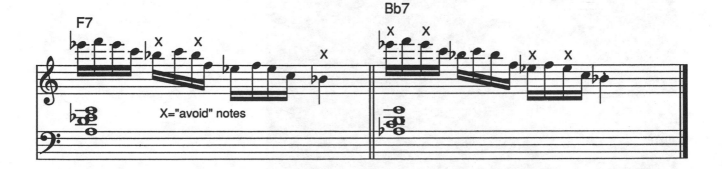

X="avoid" notes

---

[2] This is why they call it music *theory*.

Figure 18-21

You can play the same line over a GbΔ chord as well, even though the C in the four-note scale is not found in the key of Gb **(figure 18-21)**. C makes the chord GbΔ+4, or Gb Lydian.

And there's more—I hope you're not getting tired of this lick—because the same four-note scale is also found in Bb and Eb melodic minor. **Figure 18-22** shows the line (I promise this is the last example) over a voicing from each of those two tonalities. Because melodic minor chords are freely interchangeable, the line sounds good over all the chords shown.

Figure 18-22

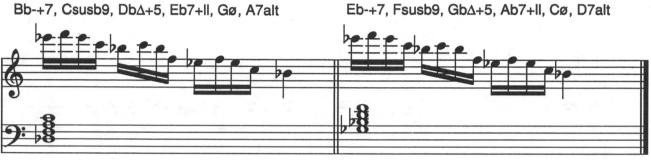

Bb-+7, Csusb9, DbΔ+5, Eb7+II, Gø, A7alt   Eb-+7, Fsusb9, GbΔ+5, Ab7+II, Cø, D7alt

(all the chords from Bb melodic minor)   (all the chords from Eb melodic minor)

Mulgrew Miller   Photo © by Lee Tanner

Two different four-note scales derived from melodic minor harmony are shown in **figure 18-23**. As was discussed in Chapter Sixteen, these four-note combinations from C melodic minor—the root, third, fifth, and seventh in the first example; the third, fifth, seventh, and ninth in the second example—are found in the "key" of C melodic minor only. They are not found in any other melodic minor scale, nor in any major, diminished, or whole-tone scale. As such, they are *characteristic* of the sound of C melodic minor. **Figure 18-24** shows a line using mostly these two four-note scales over the changes for the last eight bars of "Stella By Starlight." Except for the last Bb in the Dø bar, the first Ab in the Cø bar, and the E sharp and E natural, the last two notes, all the notes in this line are from either the I-3-5-7, or 3-5-7-9 combinations from the melodic minor scales shown below the bass clef. Why the exceptions? Why not? The line might sound too "perfect" otherwise.

Figure 18-23

four-note scales characteristic of C melodic minor

Figure 18-24

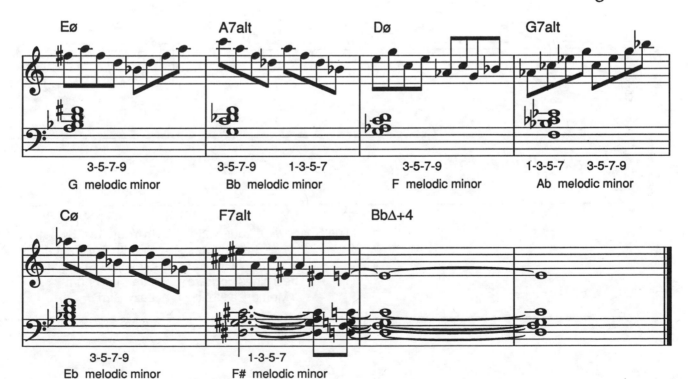

The number of theoretically possible four-note scales must be in the tens of thousands. Only a small number of them sound musical, however. Be inventive and come up with some of your own. One method of finding new scales is shown below. The notes of the C major scale are shown. The Xs underneath each note show just a few of the possible four-note combinations. Experiment by playing them over various chords from C major and see if you like any of them enough to learn and use them.

	C	D	E	F	G	A	B
1)	X	X	X	X			
2)	X	X	X		X		
3)	X	X		X	X		
4)	X	X		X		X	
5)	X			X	X		X
6)		X	X	X	X		
7)		X	X		X	X	

Let's say you like the sound of the third one shown: C, D, F, G. Practice it in each of its four modes (**figure 18-25**) and play it over various chords from C major. The one and only factor in deciding whether to use any scale is simple—*it has to sound good*.

Figure 18-25

Suggested tunes to work on

The Shadow Of Your Smile	In Your Own Sweet Way
Stablemates	Search For Peace
Invitation	Stella By Starlight
All The Things You Are	Fee Fi Fo Fum
Moment's Notice	Lazy Bird

Block chords—basic

Play **figure 19-1**, the first four bars of Kenny Dorham's classic "Blue Bossa,"[1] and **figure 19-2**, the first four bars of another classic, Miles Davis' "Solar."[2] This is the sound of *block chords*. Read the notes very carefully. Block chords, with their odd interval combinations, are often easier to "see" on the keyboard than on the written page.

Figure 19-1

Figure 19-2

[1] Joe Henderson, *Page One*, Blue Note BIIE-84140, with McCoy Tyner on piano.
[2] Miles Davis, *Walkin'*, Fantasy OJC-213.

There are many different block chord styles, and pianists such as Red Garland,[3] Wynton Kelly, Bobby Timmons, Bill Evans,[4] and George Shearing all developed their own unique ways of playing block chords. Rather than trying to cover all of them, I'll concentrate on just one approach, but one that includes techniques that pianists as diverse as Shearing, Barry Harris, Kenny Barron, and McCoy Tyner have all used.

To play block chords is to harmonize the melody or a solo line, both hands locked together and moving parallel in the same rhythm, as in the preceding examples. In fact, block-chord playing is sometimes called *locked hands*. The number of notes played varies from style to style. Bill Evans often played block chord solos with a single note in the right hand over a four note voicing in the left-hand. Red Garland played two-handed chords of seven or eight notes. George Shearing often plays four notes in the right hand, one in the left. The style covered here is much more transparent—for the most part, you'll play three notes in your right hand and one note in your left hand.

---

[3] Red's most famous block chord solo is his version of the traditional "Billy Boy," on Miles Davis' album *Milestones*, Columbia CJ-40837. Red also played block chord solos on ballads. Two good examples are his versions of Arthur Schwartz's "I See Your Face Before Me," on John Coltrane's album *Settin' The Pace*, Fantasy OJC 078, and the Richard Whiting-Newell Chase standard "My Ideal," on Coltrane's *Bahia*, Prestige 24110.

[4] Bill's lyrical block chord solo on Bronislau Kaper's "On Green Dolphin Street" is one of his best. Originally on a Miles Davis Columbia release called *Jazz Track*, this album has unfortunately been unavailable in the U.S. for many years. It is available on the French Columbia label as *Miles At Newport*, CBS 63417.

Bobby Timmons

Photo © by Lee Tanner

Figure 19-3 shows a technique called *four-way close*, which is the basis for several block-chord styles. Arrangers commonly use four-way close when writing for four saxes, four trumpets, or four of anything. On the first line, a C major scale with a chromatic passing note (G#) between G and A (the extra note will be explained soon), is voiced alternately with C6 and diminished seventh chords. Note that the chords with chord tones in the melody—the root, third, fifth, and sixth—are voiced as C6 chords. The chords with non-chord tones in the melody (D, F, G#, and B) are voiced as diminished seventh chords. All four diminished seventh chords are inversions of the same chord. Listen to how well these chords flow together.[5]

On the second line of **figure 19-3**, C-6 and diminished seventh chords alternate up a scale with the same extra chromatic passing note (G#). Again, the chords with chord tones in the melody—the root, third, fifth, and sixth—are voiced as C-6 chords. The chords with non-chord tones in the melody (D, F, G# and B) are voiced with the same diminished seventh chord, each one in a different inversion.

On the third line of **figure 19-3**, C-7 and diminished seventh chords alternate up a scale with an extra chromatic passing note (B natural). Again, chord tones in the melody (C, Eb, G, Bb) are voiced as C-7, non-chord tones (D, F, G#, B) as the same diminished seventh chord, each one in a different inversion.[6]

On the fourth line of **figure 19-3**, C7 and diminished seventh chords alternate up a scale with an extra chromatic passing note (B natural). And again, chord tones in the melody (C, E, G, Bb) are voiced as C7, non-chord tones (D, F, G#, B) as the same diminished seventh chord.

---

[5] Barry Harris refers to this scale as the "major sixth diminished scale," although he uses it in a different context (cf "Exploring the sixth diminished scale," by Fiona Bicket with Barry Harris, *The Piano Stylist and Jazz Workshop*, pp. 22-23, June-July, 1989).

[6] The four-way close C-7 scale on the third line of **figure 19-3** is actually the same as the four-way close Eb6 scale, but starting on C. Eb6 and C-7 have exactly the same notes.

Figure 19-3

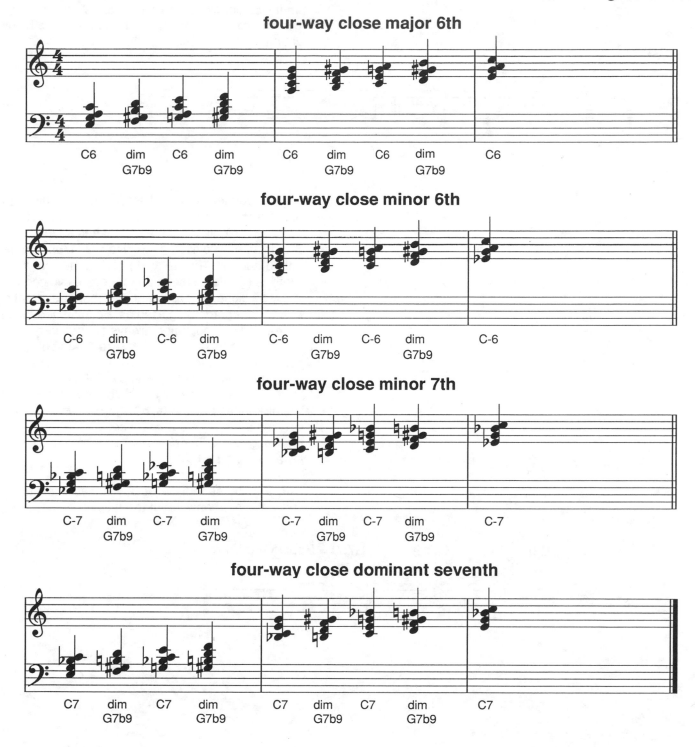

four-way close major 6th

four-way close minor 6th

four-way close minor 7th

four-way close dominant seventh

The extra chromatic passing note has been added to each scale because there would otherwise be two C6, C-6, C-7, or C7 chords in a row **(figure 19-4)**, which interrupts the smooth flow when every other chord is diminished.

Figure 19-4

As you learned in Chapter Nine, diminished seventh chords are often dominant seventh b9 chords in disguise. All the diminished seventh chords in the previous examples are G7b9 chords without the root **(figure 19-5)**. G7 is the V of any C chord, so as you play these four scales voiced in four-way close, you're hearing C chords alternating with G7b9 chords disguised as a diminished seventh chord. This combination always sounds very smooth. On the first line of **figure 19-3** you're playing alternating C6 and G7b9 chords. The second line alternates C-6 and G7b9 chords. The third line alternates C-7 and G7b9 chords. The last line alternates C7 and G7b9 chords, two dominant seventh chords. *A dominant seventh chord resolving to another dominant seventh chord a fifth lower is called a V of V.*

Play these four-way close scales a few times, first with and then without the music.

Figure 19-5

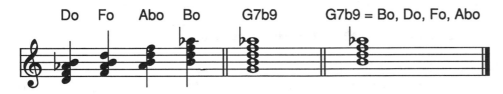

Double the melody an octave below in four-way close and you have the basis for the block-chord style that George Shearing popularized in the 1940s and 50s. **Figure 19-6** shows the C major scale (with G#, the extra note) in four-way close with the melody doubled in the left hand. **Figure 19-7** shows the first two bars of Jack Strachey and Harry Link's "These Foolish Things," arranged, except for the last chord, with Shearing-style voicings.

Figure 19-6

four-way close, double melody (George Shearing)

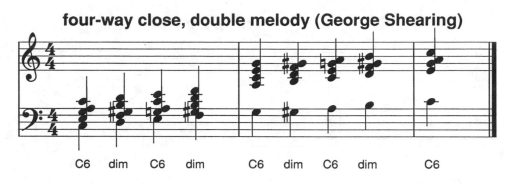

C6 dim C6 dim   C6 dim C6 dim   C6

Figure 19-7

EbΔ   F-7   Bb7b9 +11

Eb6 dim Eb6 dim Eb6............   F-7.........................

Figure 19-8 shows the same four scales with the second note from the top of each chord dropped an octave and played with your left hand. This technique is called *drop 2.* Like four-way close, drop 2 is used by arrangers when writing for four horns. Listen to how much fuller the chords sound in drop 2 than in four-way close. Play these drop 2 scales a few times, first with and then without the music.

Figure 19-8

To use this technique when voicing tunes, look for melodies that move stepwise. **Figure 19-9** shows the first bar of Duke Ellington's "What Am I Here For?" voiced in drop 2. In **figure 19-10**, drop 2 is applied to five notes in the first bar of Jimmy Van Heusen's "Polka Dots And Moonbeams." **Figure 19-11** shows the first two bars of "Blue Bossa," first in four-way close, then in drop 2. The first line shows "Blue Bossa" voiced with a C-7 chord, the second line with a C-6 chord.

Figure 19-9

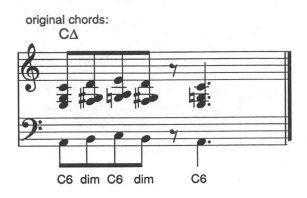

Figure 19-10

Figure 19-11

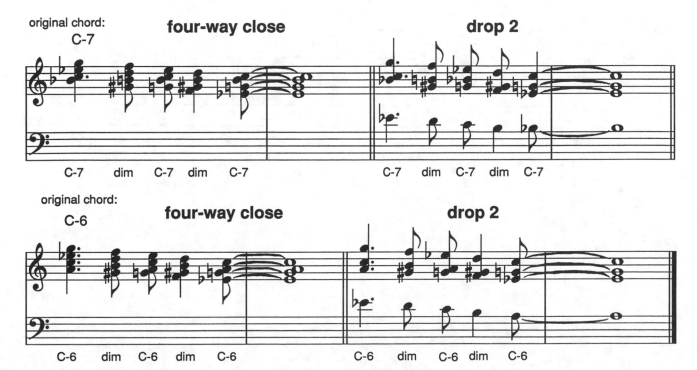

The diminished chord that's really a disguised V of V, the one used in the last line of **figure 19-3**, can also be used to connect chords other than two dominant chords. The first line of **figure 19-12** shows the first five chords of a C major scale in four-way close, then in drop 2. The second line shows the same thing, but with two additional diminished chords (the ones with D# and F# in the melody). They are really disguised D7b9 chords without the root, the V of V in C major.

Most books on classical theory call the disguised V of V diminished chord an "irregular diminished seventh." An easy way to think of this chord is that it is built off of the root of the I chord (in this case C), or minor thirds away from the root (Eb, F#, and A).

Figure 19-12

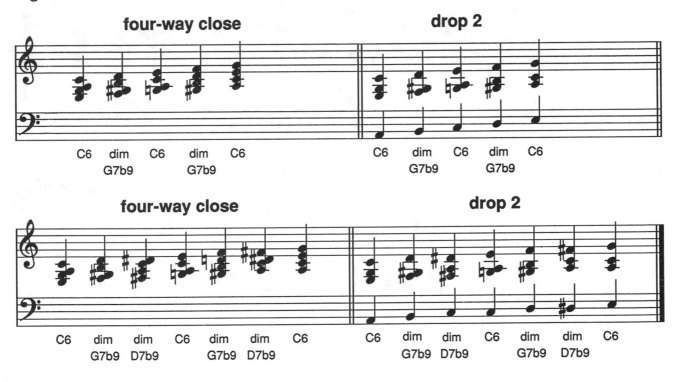

Figure 19-13 shows the first bar of Harry Warren's "Chattanooga Choo-Choo" voiced with this disguised V of V chord in drop 2. The D#o chord has the same notes as an F#o chord. The notes of an F#o chord—F#, A, C, and Eb—are the third, fifth, seventh, and b9 of D7b9, the V of V in the key of C. Barbershop quartets also use this chord a lot, as in **figure 19-14**.

Figure 19-15 shows bars 6-8 of Tadd Dameron's "Our Delight"[7] in four-way close. In this example, the Bo chords between Bb-7 and Ab△ are the same chord as Do—the third, fifth, seventh, and b9 of Bb7b9, the V of V in the key of Ab.

Figure 19-13

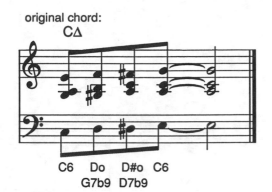

Figure 19-14

Figure 19-15

[7] Philly Joe Jones/Dameronia, *Look, Stop, & Listen*, Uptown 27.l5 (Walter Davis, Jr., the pianist).

Figure 19-16 shows a disguised V of V diminished chord connecting the Bb-7 and AbΔ chords in bars 5-8 of Ray Noble's "The Very Thought Of You," voiced in root position. The Bo chord is the same chord as Do—the third, fifth, seventh, and b9 of Bb7b9, the V of V in the key of Ab.

Figure 19-16

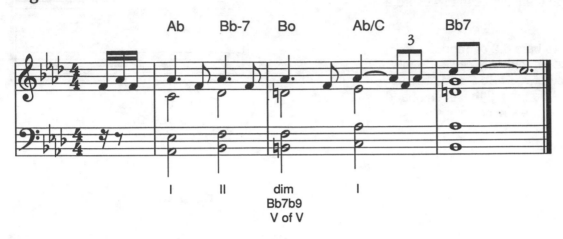

Figure 19-17 shows the melody and chord symbols for the third and fourth bars of the bridge of Arthur Johnston's "Just One More Chance." **Figure 19-18** shows how you might embellish the second bar, with two diminished chords added right before the AbΔ chord. Both are disguised Bb7b9, the V of V of AbΔ. Kenny Barron does this a great deal, and a good example is on the ninth bar of Frank Wess' solo on Harold Arlen's beautiful ballad "Ill Wind," on the Johnny Coles-Frank Wess album *Two At The Top.*[8]

Figure 19-17

Figure 19-18

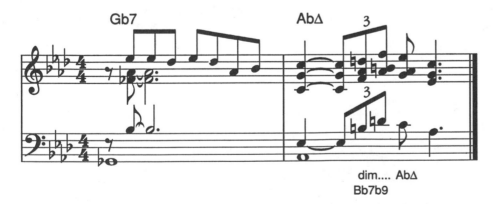

_____

[8] Uptown 27.l4 (one of Kenny's best albums, on which he plays many drop 2 voicings).

Notice the two drop 2 major seventh chords at the end of **figure 19-18**. **Figure 19-19** shows all four inversions of an AbΔ chord in drop 2, with the third, fifth, seventh, and root in the melody. The last example, with the root in the melody, has a strong dissonance because of the minor ninth interval between the root on top and the seventh on the bottom.

This doesn't mean that you can't play this voicing, however; just be careful where you use it (not when accompanying singers, for example).

Figure 19-19

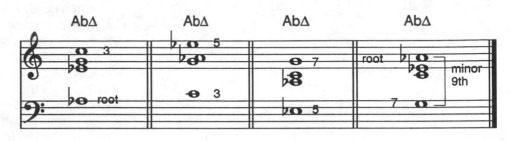

Figure 19-20 shows the first five bars of the Sigmund Romberg standard "Softly As In A Morning Sunrise," voiced in drop 2 with alternating minor sixth and diminished chords. Play this example a few times, first with the music, then without. We'll return to it later in an altered version.

Figure 19-20

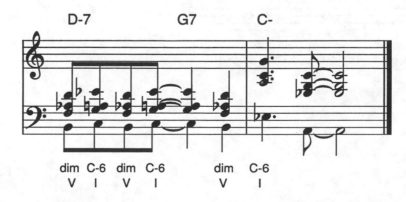

Block chords—advanced

A much richer harmonic palette can be achieved by altering drop 2 voicings. **Figure 19-21** shows a C minor scale in drop 2, with an extra chromatic passing note, B, between Bb and C. Many of the drop 2 voicings in this scale have been altered. Only the three C-6 chords are familiar drop 2 voicings. The first two diminished seventh chords—with D and F in the melody—have the third note from the top raised a whole step giving the diminished chords more "bite." **Figure 19-22** shows the conventional Bo and Do drop 2 voicings, each followed by the same voicing with its third note from the top raised a whole step.

Figure 19-21

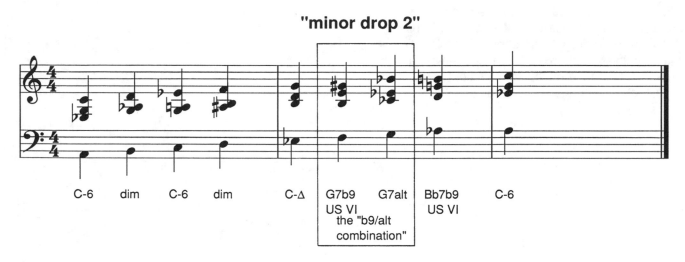

"minor drop 2"

C-6   dim   C-6   dim   C-△   G7b9   G7alt   Bb7b9   C-6
                              US VI   US VI
                              the "b9/alt
                              combination"

Figure 19-22

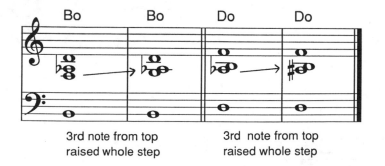

Bo   Bo   Do   Do

3rd note from top   3rd note from top
raised whole step   raised whole step

Play **Figure 19-23**—listen to the increased tension when the third note from the top of each diminished chord is raised a whole step. These are still "diminished" chords, because raising a note a whole step in a diminished chord will leave the chord in the same diminished scale, as shown in **figure 19-24**. (The two voicings are shown on the left, the diminished scale on the right.)

Figure 19-23

B whole step/half step diminished scale

Bo   Do

Figure 19-24

G half step/whole step diminished scale

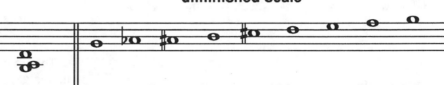

Bo

The fifth chord in **figure 19-21** is a new minor-major voicing. The sixth and eighth chords in **figure 19-21** are diminished seventh chords with the *second* note from the top raised a whole step. The two new voicings are exactly the same as upper structure VI chords for G7b9 and Bb7b9 **(figure 19-25)**. Again, by raising a note a whole step in a diminished seventh chord, you get a chord with more "bite." And again, raising a note a whole step in a diminished chord still leaves the chord in the same diminished scale.

Figure 19-25

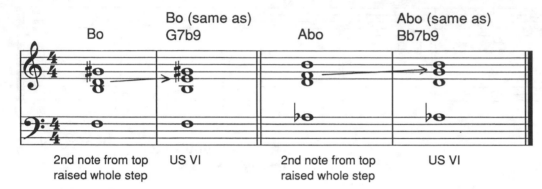

The chord between the two upper structure VI chords is a new voicing for a G7alt chord.

Since there is no commonly used name for the combination of chords grouped in the scale in **figure 19-21**, I'll refer to them as "minor drop 2."[9] Note that the G7b9 and the G7alt voicing are boxed together. I'll show several examples of how you can use them in combination, and will refer to them as "the b9/alt combination." "Minor drop 2" and "the b9/alt combination" are not common-usage terms. I've made them up just for identification purposes in this Chapter. If you tell your fellow musicians "I'm playing in minor drop 2," or "that's the b9/alt combination," they'll probably think you're either a mad genius or crazy, so *don't* use them in conversation, please. I don't believe in inventing new terms. Many of the examples in the remainder of this chapter use these new voicings. In some cases they reflect my own block chord style, and are not so much a part of the idiom in general.

---

[9] Reprinted in the appendix as "Appendix H."

Memorizing the following will help you when voicing melodies in minor drop 2:

- On the minor-major voicing, the melody note is the fifth.
- On the dominant seventh b9 upper structure voicings, the melody note is the b9.
- On the alt chord, the melody note is the +9.

Figure 19-26 is the same five bars of "Softly As In A Morning Sunrise" that appeared in **figure 19-20**, but with some of the new voicings. The B diminished chords in the fourth bar have the third note from the top raised a whole step. The second chord in the first bar and the first chord in the last bar use the new minor-major voicing. The first two chords in the second bar are the b9/alt combination, but from A minor drop 2. How is it possible to play something from A minor on a II-V in C minor? I've thought of the G7 chord in bar 2 as G7b9. G7b9 is from diminished scale harmony, where anything can be repeated at the interval of a minor third. Therefore, G7b9 = E7b9. The first melody note in the second bar, F, is the b9 of the E7b9 chord from A minor drop 2. The second melody note in the bar, G, is the +9 of the E7alt chord, also from A minor drop 2. As noted, on the b9/alt combination the melody note on the b9 chord is the b9. On the alt chord it's the +9.

Figure 19-26

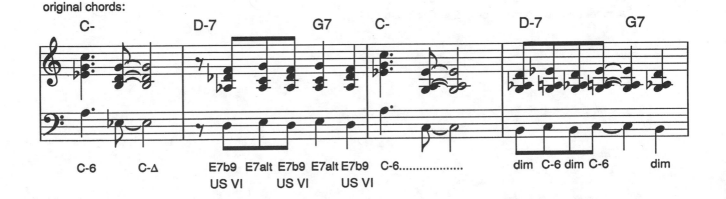

Figure **19-27** shows a line over a Dø, G7alt, C-6 progression. Now play **figure 19-28**, the same line, the first six notes voiced with the b9/alt combination but from three different keys. Read the notes carefully. There is contrary motion in the second voice from the top, and there are lots of accidentals in the bar. Look at the first six melody notes as three groups of two notes each, ascending a whole step/half step diminished scale. The first and second notes are voiced as the b9/alt combination from F# minor drop 2. The third and fourth notes are the b9/alt combination from A minor drop 2, up a minor third. The fifth and sixth notes are the b9/alt combination from C minor drop 2, up another minor third. In essence, the b9/alt combination can move sequentially at the interval of a minor third. Yes, there's a way to practice this so that you can do it easily (I'll get to it in "Practice tips" later in the chapter).

Figure 19-27

Figure 19-28

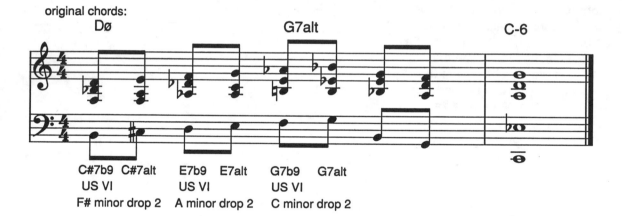

Figure 19-29 shows two examples of this idea expanded to include parallelism. The first line shows the fifth and sixth bars of Gene DePaul's "You Don't Know What Love Is" voiced in drop 2. Look at the melody notes—Db and Eb—on the chords on beats 3 and 4 of the first bar, the b9/alt combination from F minor drop 2. The two previous melody notes—Bb and C—are a minor third below, so the chords are voiced as the b9/alt combination from the "key" a minor third below, D minor drop 2. The first three chords in bar I are an example of parallelism.

The second line of **figure 19-29** shows bars 5-7 of Irving Berlin's "They Say It's Wonderful,"[10] voiced in drop 2. The first four chords in the second bar are b9 upper structure VI chords moving in parallel motion down in minor thirds, as diminished scale chords can always do. The fourth and fifth chords in the bar are the b9/alt combination from A minor drop 2.

Figure 19-29

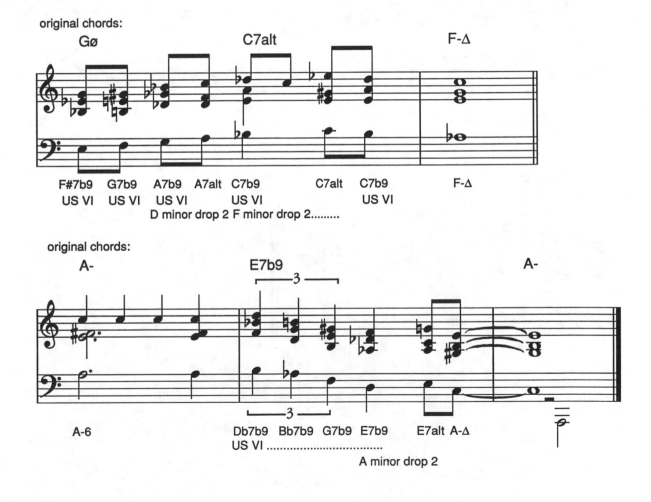

---

[10] A great version of this tune is on *John Coltrane And Johnny Hartman*, MCA/Impulse 566l (McCoy Tyner the pianist).

Look at the first four bars of "Blue Bossa," shown here as **figure 19-30**. Stepwise melodies on minor chords are ideal opportunities to use drop 2. Although the original chord symbol is C-7, the chord doesn't function as a II chord (it is not followed by F7, as in a II-V) but as a tonic minor. In addition, none of the first five notes on this C minor seventh chord is the seventh of the chord (Bb). That being the case, the C minor chords here are played as C-Δ and C-6. The diminished chords in bar I are all disguised G7b9 chords. The diminished chord on the fourth beat of the second bar is a disguised C7b9, resolving into the F-6 chord in the third bar. **Figure 19-31** shows how this diminished chord is really a disguised C7b9.

Figure 19-30

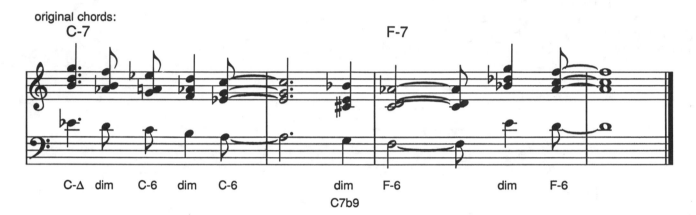

Figure 19-31

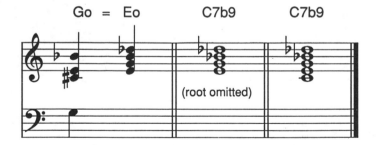

Another example of a stepwise melody over a minor chord occurs in bars 25-26 of the Rodgers and Hart ballad "Spring Is Here." **Figure 19-32** shows six notes of this line voiced in drop 2. All the diminished chords are disguised C7b9 chords. Note the voicing on the B-7 chord, a variation of the Kenny Barron voicing discussed in Chapter Sixteen.

Figure 19-32

original chords:

Another effective technique you can use when playing drop 2 is called *chromatic approach* (**figure 19-33**). This means approaching a chord with another chord from either a half-step above or a half step below. In the first bar, the C-Δ chord is approached from a half-step below by a B-Δ chord. In the second example, the C-Δ chord is approached from a half-step above with a Db-Δ chord. Chromatic approach is another example of parallelism.

Figure 19-33

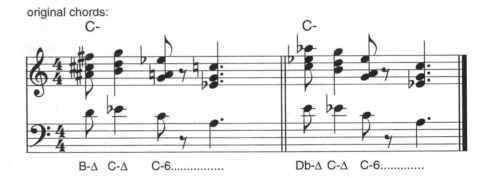

original chords:

If chords are from melodic minor harmony, think "key" rather than chord. **Figure 19-34** shows a line over a B7alt, E-Δ progression. B7alt is from C melodic minor. The first two notes in the bar are voiced as C-Δ (the I chord in C melodic minor) and C-6. The third and fourth notes in the bar are voiced with the b9/alt combination from E minor drop 2, except reversed here as alt/b9 because the melody notes—D and C—are the +9 and b9 of the B7alt chord.

Figure 19-34

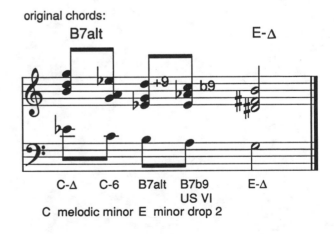

original chords:

Figure 19-35 shows a block chord solo on the first four bars of "All The Things You Are." Except for the last bar, all of the chords are voiced in drop 2. The chord on the second note in bar I is C7b9 disguised as a diminished chord, resolving to F-6. The last chord in bar I is F7b9 disguised as a diminished chord resolving to Bb-6. The third note from the top on this diminished chord has been raised a whole step, the technique shown in **figures 19-22** through **19-24**.

The first three chords in bar 2 echo the pattern in bar I, Bb-6 chords connected by F7b9 disguised as a diminished chord. The B-Δ chord is a chromatic approach to the Bb-Δ chord. The last diminished chord in bar 2 has the third note from the top raised a whole step to echo what occurs on the last chord in bar I.

The original chord symbol in bar 3 is Eb7. You can play Bb-7, Eb7—a II-V progression—in place of Eb7. The first two chords in bar 3 are Bb-6 chords, suggested by the Bb-7 part of the II-V. The Eb7 chord is then reharmonized as Eb7 alt, which is derived from E melodic minor, the source of the E-Δ and E-6 chords.

There are more than just block chords in **figure 19-35.** In bar 4 there is what is known in classical harmony as a German sixth cadence (see Chapter Sixteen) on the first two beats. The D7+II chord that follows is the tritone substitution of Ab7, the V chord of DbΔ, the chord in the next bar, which is anticipated here by one beat.

There's a lot going on in these four bars—drop 2, parallelism, tritone substitution, chromatic approach, reharmonization, diminished chords with raised notes, interchangeability of melodic minor chords, German sixth chords, anticipation.... Can you really think that fast when soloing? Yes, if you know how to practice. If you master each technique separately, you can then integrate them as you solo (more on this soon, and also in Chapter Twenty-Three).

The line your left hand plays, literally the "drop 2" voice, is a very powerful melody in itself. For the most part, this line parallels your right hand at the interval of a tenth. You can enhance the effect of this line by playing it louder than the right hand. Try really exaggerating this effect, playing the drop 2 line twice as loud as your right hand. Another way to enhance the left-hand line is to play it legato while playing all of the chords in the right hand short and staccato. And, if you really want the line to stand out, use both techniques at the same time.

A cautionary note is necessary here: When 'comping, be careful using drop 2. You can very easily bury the soloist with too rich a harmonic palette. Also, drop 2 goes well with bebop tunes and standards, but can sound totally out of place on non-II-V-I tunes like Herbie Hancock's "Maiden Voyage," or George Cables' "Think On Me."

Figure 19-35

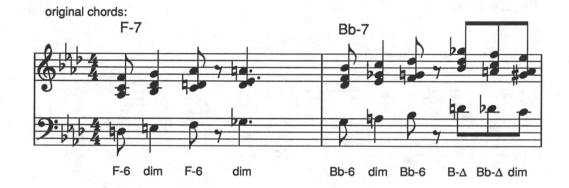

Practice
tips

Mastering drop 2 will obviously take much practice. You can reach the point where you can play the chords fluently if you know how to practice them and how to think about them as you play. First, learn where the major sixth chords are on the keyboard. **Figure 19-36** shows an exercise for this. **Figure 19-37** shows the same exercise with minor sixth chords. Practice both exercises in all keys. Also, practice the same exercise with minor seventh and dominant seventh chords.

In addition, practice the minor-major drop 2 voicing around the cycle of fifths, as in **figure 19-38**. Remember that this voicing has the fifth of the chord on top, the third on the bottom.

Practice the three different major seventh drop 2 inversions through the cycle, as shown in **figure 19-39**. I've omitted the dissonant inversion with the root on top, as shown in **figure 19-19**, but you can add it to the exercise if you like.

Figure 19-36

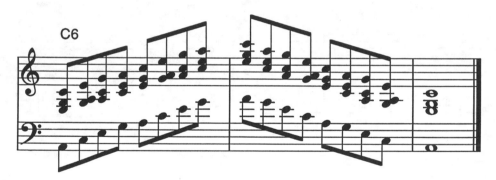

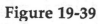

Figure 19-37

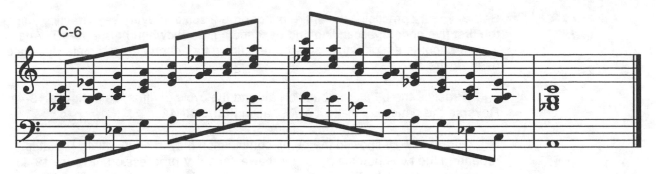

Figure 19-38

Figure 19-39

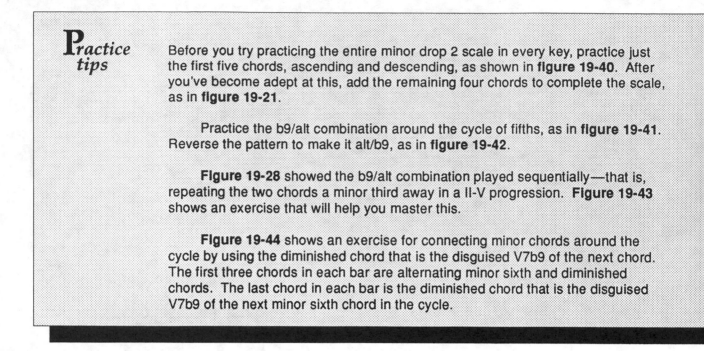

Practice **tips**

Before you try practicing the entire minor drop 2 scale in every key, practice just the first five chords, ascending and descending, as shown in **figure 19-40**. After you've become adept at this, add the remaining four chords to complete the scale, as in **figure 19-21**.

Practice the b9/alt combination around the cycle of fifths, as in **figure 19-41**. Reverse the pattern to make it alt/b9, as in **figure 19-42**.

Figure 19-28 showed the b9/alt combination played sequentially—that is, repeating the two chords a minor third away in a II-V progression. **Figure 19-43** shows an exercise that will help you master this.

Figure 19-44 shows an exercise for connecting minor chords around the cycle by using the diminished chord that is the disguised V7b9 of the next chord. The first three chords in each bar are alternating minor sixth and diminished chords. The last chord in each bar is the diminished chord that is the disguised V7b9 of the next minor sixth chord in the cycle.

Figure 19-40

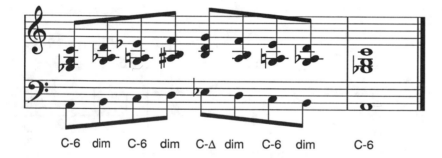

C-6   dim   C-6   dim   C-Δ   dim   C-6   dim   C-6

Figure 19-41

G7b9   alt   C7b9   alt   F7b9   alt   Bb7b9   alt

etc.

Figure 19-42

Figure 19-43

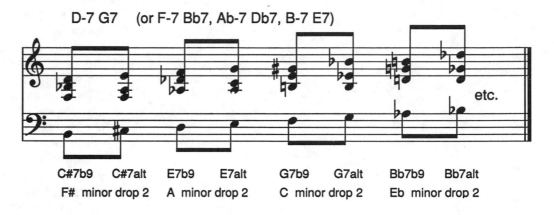

Figure 19-44

Summary: drop 2

- Look for stepwise melodies when using drop 2.
- You can voice I chords either as major sixth or major seventh chords.
- You can connect major sixth chords by two different diminished chords: one a disguised V7b9 chord, the other a disguised V7b9 of V.
- When going from a I chord to a II chord or vice versa, use diminished chords that are disguised V7b9 of V chords.
- You can think of II chords as tonic minor chords, and voice them as minor sixth, minor seventh, or minor-major chords.
- Raise the second or third note from the top on diminished chords to increase tension.
- When playing on melodic minor chords, you can substitute other chords from the same melodic minor tonality.
- When using diminished scale chords, you can use chords from diminished scales a minor third away.
- Look for half step/whole step, or whole step/half step motion on II or V chords to use the "b9/alt combination" sequentially in minor thirds.
- Parallel motion and chromatic approach are effective in drop 2.
- Accentuate the drop 2 line in the left hand.

Suggested tunes to work on

You Are Too Beautiful	It Could Happen To You
It's All Right With Me	Invitation
You Don't Know What Love Is	Polka Dots And Moonbeams
The Shadow Of Your Smile	Along Came Betty
Daydream	Darn That Dream
Lover Come Back To Me	The Way You Look Tonight
The Man I Love	

Play **figures 20-1** and **20-2**[1], and listen to the sound of *salsa*. These are *montunos*, also called *guajeos*, the repeated ostinato-like figure that pianists play in salsa music.

Figure 20-1

North Americans tend to use the terms "salsa" and "Latin music" rather loosely. Latin America is a vast area, and its music is incredibly varied. Salsa is but one small part of a musical mosaic that includes calypso (Trinidad), reggae (Jamaica), bossa nova and samba (Brazil), mariachi (Mexico), cumbia (Columbia), jorópo (Venezuela), tango (Argentina), meréngue (Dominican Republic), and altiplano music (the countries of the Andes). Tito Puente is salsa; Astor Piazzolla is not. "Salsa" is actually a term coined by music promoters in New York. *Afro-Cuban* music is the foundation of "salsa."

Figure 20-2

Drums, rhythmic patterns, and vocal call-and-response patterns were brought to Cuba by African slaves, and the admixture of Spanish harmony, melody, and song and dance forms evolved into Afro-Cuban music. From the 1930s on, Afro-Cuban music has also been highly influenced by jazz. The proximity of Cuba and the United States, especially the ease with which radio broadcasts from Miami can be heard in Havana, facilitated this influence. The cultural interchange went both ways. Before the Cuban revolution, bands frequently travelled back and forth between the two countries. From its earliest days, jazz has had a "Spanish tinge" as it was once called, due to the trade between New Orleans and other Caribbean ports. The popularity in the U.S. of Latin bands such as Xavier Cugat in the 1940s paved the way for Machito, Tito Puente, Tito Rodriguez, and others in the 1950s.

---

[1] Eddie Palmieri, "Mi Corazon Te Llama," from Eddie's album *Echando Pa'lante*, Tico III3.

Puerto Rico, a possession of the United States, adapted Afro-Cuban music to its own traditions and produced its own brand of salsa. From the 1950s on, a tremendous number of Puerto Ricans have migrated to the United States, including thousands of musicians who settled in Nueva York. Salsa today is largely on a New York-Miami-Havana-San Juan axis. Salsa is also popular in other Spanish-speaking countries with large black populations, such as the Dominican Republic, Panama, Nicaragua, Columbia, and Venezuela.

The single most unique aspect of salsa is its strict adherence to a rhythmic pattern known as *Son clave*, or just *clave* (pronounced "clah-vay"). Clave is a two-bar rhythmic pattern that occurs in two forms: forward clave, also known as 3 & 2 **(figure 20-3)**, and reverse clave, also known as 2 & 3 **(figure 20-4)**. In 3 & 2, or forward clave, the accents fall on beats one, the and of two, and four of the first bar, and beats two and three of the second bar. In 2 & 3, or reverse clave, the pattern is reversed. There is also another clave, called the *Rumba clave*, sometimes called *African clave* **(figure 20-5)**. The last note in the "3" bar in the African clave is delayed a half-beat and played on the and of four. Every component of salsa—drum patterns, piano montuno, bass tumbao, phrasing of the melody, horn lines—has to be in gear with the clave.

Virtually all salsa music (son montunos, mambos, cha-chas, guajiras, guarachas, guaguancos, danzons, congas, Mozambique, and so on), is written and played in either forward or reverse clave (an exception is the *bomba*, from Puerto Rico, which has a one-bar pattern). **Figure 20-6** shows the first few bars of "Ave Maria Morena," a traditional Cuban song written in forward clave, or 3 & 2 (the first three notes are a pickup to the first bar of the song). The rhythm of the melody states the clave pattern clearly (the clave pattern is shown in the bass clef and is not meant to be played by your left hand).

Figure 20-3

Forward clave (also known as) 3 & 2

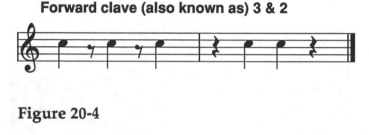

Figure 20-4

Reverse clave (also known as) 2 & 3

Figure 20-5

African (or "Rumba") clave

Figure 20-6

When adapting jazz tunes to salsa, you have to decide whether the song should be played in forward or reverse clave. Often the rhythm of the melody makes the choice obvious, as in the 2 & 3 pattern of **figure 20-7**, the first four bars of the introduction to Freddie Hubbard's "Birdlike,"[2] or the 2 & 3 pattern on the introduction to Cedar Walton's "Ojos De Rojo,"[3] as shown in **figure 20-8**.

Figure 20-7

Figure 20-8

Since jazz composers don't usually concern themselves with clave, most jazz tunes are partly in 2 & 3, partly in 3 & 2, and mostly in no particular clave. Such tunes may be difficult to adapt to salsa unless you're willing to alter the tune by adding or subtracting bars, or changing the rhythm of the melody. That's why many attempts ("hey, let's play 'Inner Urge' as a mambo") at playing jazz tunes in a salsa style often don't work too well. A song has to feel right in either forward or reverse clave to be successfully adapted.

---

[2] Freddie Hubbard, *Ready For Freddie*, Blue Note 84085.
[3] Cedar Walton, *Eastern Rebellion 2*, Timeless l06.

Figure 20-9 shows the first two bars of Thelonious Monk's "Bye-Ya,"[4] which suggests a 2 & 3 pattern. However, the melody in the eighth bar—three quarter notes—doesn't lay very well with the "3" bar of a 2 & 3 pattern, as shown in the first two bars of **figure 20-10**. If you rewrite the rhythm of the melody in bar 8 as two dotted quarter notes followed by a quarter note, it will fit the 2 & 3 clave. Both the original and the rewritten version are shown in **figure 20-10**. You don't have to rewrite the melodic rhythm of every note that doesn't fit clave in a jazz tune, only one or two here and there, to make the tune lay better against salsa rhythms. Purists who object to changing Monk's music should remember that jazz is improvised music. It's meant to be changed. If Coltrane had stopped to worry about whether or not it was right to alter the original version of a tune, the world would never have been enriched by his unique versions of Richard Rodgers' "My Favorite Things," and Mongo Santamaria's "Afro Blue." So far as I know, neither Richard nor Mongo has complained about 'Trane's alterations to their tunes.

Figure 20-9

Figure 20-10

---

[4] Thelonious Monk, *Monk's Dream*, Columbia 40786.

Figure 20-11 shows a typical montuno. This montuno is in reverse clave, or 2 & 3. Montunos are usually two, sometimes four, occasionally even eight bars long. The one shown here is a two-bar montuno for a C major chord. Because so many notes are played off the beat in Latin music, ties are often dispensed with, so you might see this same montuno written as it appears in **figure 20-12.** The montuno in **figure 20-11** has twelve notes and three ties—fifteen "bits" of information for your eyes and brain to process. The same montuno as written in **figure 20-12** has ten notes and one tie—eleven "bits."

Notice the "I 2 & & & & & &" shown below the montuno. The first two notes ("I 2") of the montuno are *on* the beat. Every note after that is on the "and," or *off* the beat. Notice that "& I" occurs going into the third, or odd-numbered bar. Tap your foot in quarter notes while saying aloud "I 2 & & & & & &." Now play the montuno with both hands either one or two octaves apart, as in **figure 20-13.** Play the figure rhythmically, but don't chop the notes short. Accent the note C slightly each time you play it. Set your metronome or drum machine to quarter notes at first. After you get comfortable with the montuno, reset the drum machine to the pattern shown in **figure 20-14**, a typical 2 & 3 pattern called *cáscara*, played on the sides of the drums and on the cymbal.

Figure 20-11

Figure 20-12

Figure 20-13

Figure 20-14

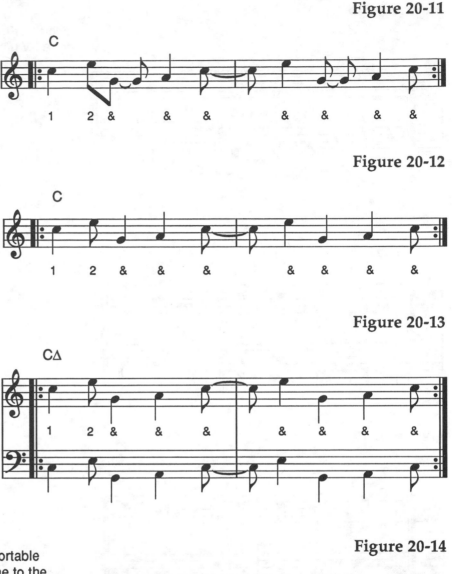

Figure 20-15

Figures 20-15, **20-16**, and **20-17** show the same montuno pattern for C-6, C-7, and C7 chords. **Figure 20-18** shows a montuno pattern for a I-V progression.

Figure 20-16

Figure 20-17

Figure 20-18

Figure 20-19 shows a four-bar montuno for a I-V-V-I progression. The rhythmic pattern is still the same as in the previous examples. Notice that you still play "& I" going into the third bar. You will continue to play "& I" going into the fifth, seventh, ninth, and each odd-numbered bar.

Figure 20-19

All of the montunos shown so far are in reverse clave, or 2 & 3. A 3 & 2 forward clave montuno is shown in **figure 20-20**. The very first note in the first bar in the example starts right on "one," but that will be the only time that you play on "one" in an odd-numbered bar—after that, "one" on odd-numbered bars will always be tied over from the previous bar. The third and fourth bars, repeated over and over, becomes the montuno. Note also that the "& I" occurs going into the *second* bar of the montuno, and will continue going into each *even*-numbered bar thereafter, unlike reverse, or 2 & 3, clave. The downbeat of the montuno always occurs on the "2" bar of the clave; the syncopated, tied-over-the-bar-line note always occurs on the "3" bar of the clave.

Figure 20-20

forward clave (3 & 2)

Figure 20-21

Figure 20-22

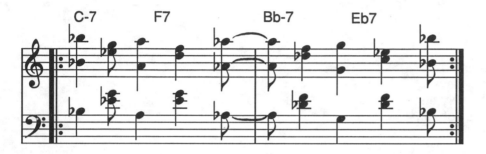

Many Latin tunes have very simple harmony, in some cases only one or two chords. II-V progressions are popular in salsa, as in the example shown in **figure 20-21**. As in most other II-V progressions, the seventh of the II chord resolves down a half-step to become the third of the V chord. A montuno for a III-VI-II-V progression (the first two bars of Clare Fischer's pretty cha-cha "Morning")[5] is shown in **figure 20-22**. A variation of this montuno is shown in **figure 20-23**.

Figure 20-23

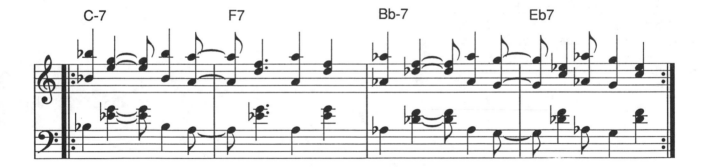

[5] Cal Tjader, *Soul Burst*, Verve 8637.

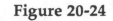

Montunos can be played in tenths instead of octaves. **Figure 20-2** at the beginning of the chapter is a good example. **Figure 20-24** shows a montuno in tenths on a I-IV-V-IV progression. A variation is shown in **figure 20-25.**

In general, once you've started a montuno, you should not change it until a new section of the tune begins. Although the masters of the genre occasionally alter the montuno in places, the importance of establishing a groove is paramount in Latin music, and changing the montuno breaks the groove. Remember, salsa is primarily dance music—you should play "in the pocket."

Figure 20-24

Figure 20-25

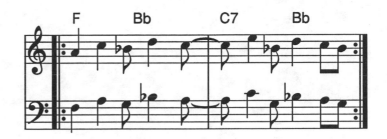

In a salsa band, each rhythm instrument—piano, bass, timbales, congas, bongos, güiro, cowbell—plays a different rhythm, and they all fit together nicely like pieces in a jigsaw puzzle. The bass player's pattern is called a *tumbao*. Most tumbaos accent the fourth beat of each bar, reinforcing the conga drum pattern. A great way to practice is to play the bass line, or tumbao, with your left hand while you play the montuno with your right hand, as in **figure 20-26**. In real life you probably wouldn't do this except for a special effect, any more than you would play a walking bass line in a rhythm section that already has a bass player. For practice, however, this is an invaluable exercise. If you can master it, you'll probably feel a lot more comfortable in a salsa rhythm section. You should "lock in" with the bass player as much as possible since the two of you (unless there is a guitarist) are the only harmony instruments in the rhythm section.

Notice in **figure 20-26** that, except for the first beat in the very first bar, the only point where your right hand (the pianist) and your left hand (the bass player) coincide is on the "and of two" in each bar (see arrows). It may take you some time to master this exercise, but when you do, your feeling for the music and your sense of place in the rhythm section will improve dramatically.

Figure 20-26

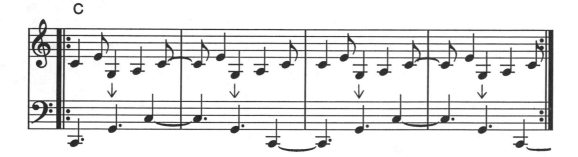

Once you're able to play this exercise, try playing **figure 20-27.** Rhythmically it's the same as **figure 20-26.** Notice that the note your left hand (the bassist) plays on the fourth beat of each bar anticipates the chord in the next bar. **Figure 20-28** shows a montuno (right hand) and a tumbao (left hand) on a I-IV-V-IV progression in a minor key.

Figure 20-27

Figure 20-28

You might want to try some more challenging examples of montunos and tumbaos combined. Here are two of my own invention. **Figure 20-29** is the montuno and tumbao for "Shoshana."[6] **Figure 20-30** shows the montuno and tumbao for "Keeper Of The Flame."[7] Remember, except as an occasional effect, you don't want to play the tumbao with your left hand—unless you want the bass player glaring at you, or worse.

Figure 20-29

[6] Cal Tjader, *Gozame! Pero Ya*, Concord Picante l33.
[7] As played by Charlie Otwell on Poncho Sanchez' album *Bien Sabroso!*, Concord 239.

Figure 20-30

Figure 20-31

Piano solos in a salsa band should be more rhythmic than melodic, with lots of octaves and big chords. The sheer volume and density of a salsa rhythm section will probably drown you out if you try to play a single-note line bebop solo. **Figure 20-31** shows a two-bar chordal solo fragment on a C7 chord. **Figure 20-32** shows a solo fragment in octaves over C7. Again, salsa is primarily dance music, and even when it's for listening only, the rhythmic aspect is more important than harmony and melody. Use *lots of octaves* during your solos, and play rhythmically.

Figure 20-32

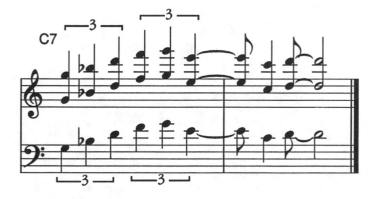

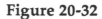

One of the first great Afro-Cuban pianists was Pedro Justiz, better known as "Peruchín." He mixed jazz and Afro-Cuban music in what was for its time (the 1940s and 50s) an utterly original style, one which was echoed later on by Noro Morales. In the early 1960s Eddie Palmieri arrived on the scene, and since then he has been the greatest influence on salsa piano. Any of his early recordings and many of his more recent ones are gems.

Some other great salsa pianists to listen to include: Papo Lucca of Orquesta Sonora Ponceña; "Lilín" (Luis Martinez Griñan), who played with the legendary Arsenio Rodriguez; Jésus Perez, who played with the charanga band Arcaño; Orestes Lopez, who recorded with the great bassist Israel Lopez, better known as "Cachao"; Sonny Bravo; Larry Harlow; Rafael Ithier of El Gran Combo; Charlie Palmieri (Eddie's brother); Eddie Martínez; Oscar Hernández, who has played with everybody from Ruben Blades to Ray Barretto, Tipica 73, and the Fania All Stars; Chucho Valdez of Irakere; Lino Frias of the great Sonora Matancera; and René Hernández. Check out the "Listen/Salsa and Latin Jazz" section in the back of the book for a list of suggested records.

Not too many jazz pianists have studied and absorbed clave into their playing, although that has changed somewhat in recent years. The few that have include Bud Powell,[8] Chick Corea,[9] Herbie Hancock,[10] and Hilton Ruiz.[11] Many of Thelonious Monk's tunes strongly imply clave, although there is no evidence that he ever studied Afro-Cuban music. I once worked with a band that played Monk's "Straight, No Chaser" as a mambo in reverse clave. Every so often we'd play it in forward clave without changing anything else, and it worked either way. Monk's tune "Evidence," has been recorded by Jerry Gonzalez.[12]

---

[8] Listen to Bud's "Un Poco Loco," on *The Amazing Bud Powell*, Blue Note 1504.

[9] Listen to Chick's montunos and solos on "Descarga Cubana," from Cal Tjader's album *Soul Burst*, Verve 8637; on "Viva Peraza," from Armando Peraza's album *Wild Thing*, Skye G923, unfortunately out-of-print for many years; and on Joe Henderson's "Ya Todavia La Quiero," on Joe's album *Relaxin' At Camarillo*, Contemporary 14006.

[10] Listen to Herbie's album *Succotash*, Blue Note LA152-F, originally released as *Inventions And Dimensions*.

[11] Listen to Hilton's version of "I Love Lucy," from Jerry Gonzalez' album *Ya Yo Me Cure*, Pangaea 6242.

[12] ibid.

There have been some great Latin jazz bands. Mongo Santamaria, still active in his 70s, and the late Cal Tjader and Willie Bobo were leaders of three of the best. Tito Puente[13] switched from a big band to a Latin jazz sextet format in the 1980s, and he, Poncho Sanchez, and Manny Oquendo's Libre[14] are the most popular Latin jazz groups today.

Most Latin jazz bands involve a compromise. The jazz musicians in a Latin jazz group grow up playing and listening to jazz, and their knowledge of Latin music is often minimal. The same thing in reverse is true of the Latin musicians. A small group of musicians, most of them from New York, have grown up with both idioms, and are comfortable playing both kinds of music. Trombonist Barry Rogers (who did much of the arranging for Eddie Palmieri's bands), saxophonist Mario Rivera (with Tito Puente's band for the past few years), pianist Hilton Ruiz, and trumpeter/percussionist Jerry Gonzalez are all exceptional musicians adept at playing both kinds of music. All of them except Barry appear on an album that Jerry produced called *Ya Yo Me Curé*,[15] which is a great introduction to Latin jazz, besides being a sensational album. Another great Latin jazz album to start your listening with is the Eddie Palmieri-Cal Tjader album *El Sonido Nuevo*.[16]

For a more in-depth study of clave, with considerable history of the music, and lots of montuno examples, I highly recommend *Afro Cuban/Salsa Workshop Guidebook*, by Rebeca Mauleón,[17] the pianist with San Francisco's best salsa band, The Machete Ensemble.[18]

---

[13] Tito Puente, *El Rey*, Concord 250 (Jorge Dalto on piano).
[14] Manny Oquendo's Libre, *Con Salsa, Con Ritmo, Vol. I*, Salsoul 4109 (Oscar Hernández on piano)
[15] Pangaea 6242.
[16] Verve 8651.
[17] Available for $15.00 from Rebeca Mauleón, 1563 Treat Ave., San Francisco, CA 94110.
[18] The Machete Ensemble, *Africa, Vol. I*, Machete M-102.

Suggested tunes to work on

Morning	Nica's Dream
Bye-ya	Linda Chicana
Moment's Notice	It's You Or No One
Tune-up	Sabor
Philadelphia Mambo	A Night In Tunisia
Blue Bossa	Record-A-Me
Invitation	On Green Dolphin Street
Ojos De Rojo	Cubano Chant
Soul Sauce	I Love Lucy
Cuban Fantasy	Lotus Blossom

'Comping, short for accompanying (or complementing), is what the pianist does behind the soloist, and during ensemble sections. The 'comper's job description is to stimulate the soloist harmonically and rhythmically, to accentuate turnarounds, bridges, and so on, to strengthen the form of the tune, *and to stay out of the soloist's way*. It's possible to do this while playing lots of notes (Art Tatum, McCoy Tyner) or with a minimum of notes (Count Basie, Gil Evans). Many pianists play too busily and bury the soloist, while others play too timidly and provide no inspiration for the soloist. How do you achieve a balance? The first rule is to LISTEN to the soloist. That's so easy to say, yet so hard to do. It's not unusual to get caught up in your own little world while 'comping and forget that your basic job is to play second fiddle. Try to find that midpoint between boldness and restraint. Alternate 'comping aggressively with staying more in the background, until both extremes start to pull toward the center, achieving a synthesis.

A singer once told me (she was unhappy because I was 'comping too busily behind her), "Play when I don't sing, and don't play when I sing." Although that's an exaggeration of what an accompanist is supposed to do, there's more than a grain of truth to it. Count Basie basically played when the horns didn't, and didn't play when the horns did. Some pianists seem telepathic in being able to tell precisely when the soloist is going to breathe, especially Wynton Kelly[1] and Herbie Hancock.

---

[1] A great example is Wynton's 'comping behind soloists Miles Davis, Hank Mobley, and John Coltrane on the title track of Miles' lp *Someday My Prince Will Come*, Columbia 8456.

Figure 21-1

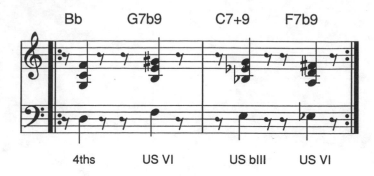

Figure 21-2

Many beginning pianists tend to 'comp too much behind the beat, as in **figure 21-1**. The chords change on beats one and three in this I-VI-II-V progression, but in the 'comping pattern shown here, the chords are played on the "and" of one and three, a half beat behind. While there's nothing wrong with playing a chord a half beat behind, too much of this drags the time down. Fortunately, this fault is easily corrected. **Figure 21-2** shows the same set of changes, but with the chords anticipated by a half beat instead of played a half beat behind. Turn on your metronome or drum machine and play each phrase several times. You'll hear much more energy coming from **figure 21-2** (the type of voicing is identified beneath the bass staff).

The same thing holds true for your left hand when you're soloing with your right hand. **Figure 21-3** shows a I-VI-II-V progression with the left hand playing a behind-the-beat pattern. **Figure 21-4** shows the same changes with the left hand now anticipating each chord by a half beat. Again, check this out with your metronome or drum machine and feel the extra energy coming from **figure 21-4**.

Figure 21-3

Figure 21-4

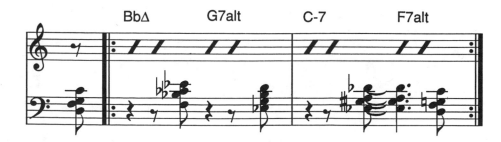

Hank Jones   Photo ©1981 Brian McMillen

The short, stabbing chord style in the previous examples is only one 'comping approach. It works very well when the rhythm section is playing "in two." A more sustained type of 'comping is shown in **figure 21-5**, a chorus of the changes to Joe Henderson's "Serenity."[2] This is an imaginary 'comp, because the soloist you're supposed to be listening to is missing, but it's a good approximation of this style.

Our imaginary 'comper has added a b9 and a +11 to the A7 and Bb7 chords, and a +11 to the Db7 and Gb7 chords. The EΔ and EbΔ chords have been changed to E Lydian and Eb Lydian. These alterations are shown below the bass staff. How much chord altering and reharmonization can you get away with when 'comping? A conservative amount is usually OK—chances are the substitute chords won't conflict, or the soloist will make many of the same alterations anyway. If the substitute chords do conflict, back off and play more "straight" the next go-round, listening very carefully to see whether you can pick up on the soloist's harmonic style. Here are some general guidelines (not rules) for altering chords when 'comping:

- On II chords that aren't part of a II-V progression—that is, when the II chord is acting like a tonic minor—it's often OK to play minor-major (-Δ).
- On V chords, it's often OK to use tritone substitution.
- On V chords that are part of a II-V progression or resolve downward a fifth, it's often OK to play b9 or alt—the soloist frequently makes those alterations anyway. Listen carefully.
- On V chords that are *not* part of a II-V progression and *don't* resolve downward a fifth, Lydian dominant (+11) is usually a safe alteration. Lydian dominant chords usually don't resolve down a fifth.
- On I chords, it's almost always OK to play a Lydian (Δ+4) chord.
- On I chords, it *may* be OK to play a Lydian augmented (Δ+5) chord. Listen carefully to see if you are stimulating or clashing with the soloist.
- On VI chords—as in a I-VI-II-V progression—it's OK to substitute a V chord, making it the V of the following II chord.

---

[2] Joe Henderson, *In 'N Out*, Blue Note 4166, McCoy Tyner on piano (the 'comp shown in the example is not what McCoy plays on the record).

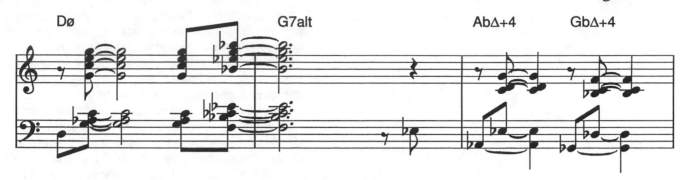

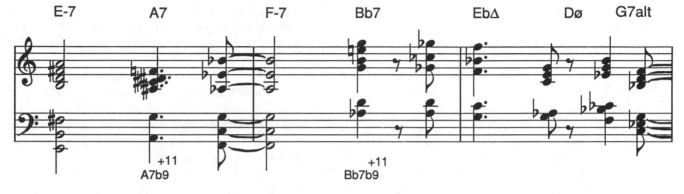

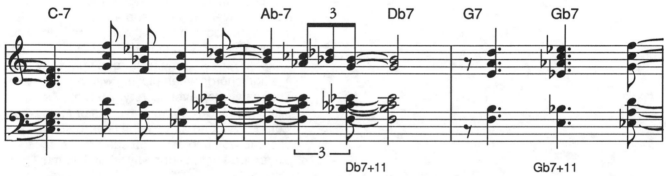

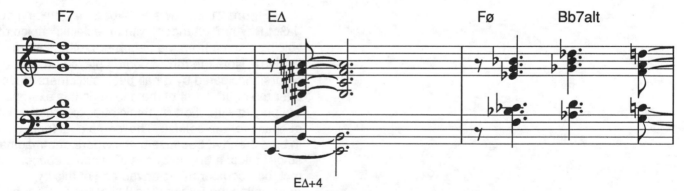

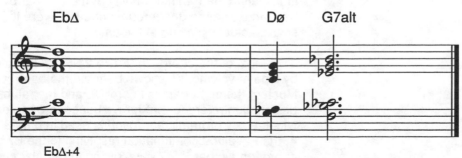

Remember, these are guidelines, not rules. There are plenty of exceptions. Any alterations further out than those just listed (substituting sus or Phrygian for V chords, for example) may endanger your continued employment, *unless*—and this is a big unless—you are 'comping for a great improviser who may already be making such alterations, and will want you to be creative and stimulating as you 'comp for them. Herbie Hancock, Chick Corea, and McCoy Tyner are all daring 'compers—they sometimes lead the soloist as much as follow. This is a very subjective area, involving a great deal of nonverbal communication. Indeed, the only communication may be musical. Listen; be supportive; be open; be imaginative; and listen some more.

Figure 21-5 has several root position chords in bars 3-5. Once again, we've entered a subjective area. How much root position should you play when you're playing with a bass player? Since Bill Evans and Wynton Kelly started using left-hand voicings in the late 1950s, the trend has been away from using root position voicings. Prior to that, Bud Powell, Horace Silver, Red Garland and other pianists played the roots most of the time, as in the Bud Powell voicings you learned in Chapter Seventeen. An often repeated myth is: "don't play any root position chords when playing with a bass player." The reality, however, is very different. As an example, McCoy Tyner plays lots of roots when he 'comps. As long as you don't overdo it, most bassists won't object. You can always ask the bass player "do I get in your way when I 'comp?"

Figure 21-6 shows eight bars of 'comping on "I Got Rhythm" changes, with an eclectic choice of voicings, some from the bebop era, others more modern. Note the mix of chords played on the beat, others anticipated by a half beat, still others played after the beat. Most of the chords in this example are played with short rhythmic attacks, creating lots of space for the soloist. The 'comp gets fairly busy in bars 3 and 4, because that's where our imaginary soloist takes a breath and leaves some space. In fact, our 'comper takes advantage of this by anticipating the F minor tonality of the fifth bar by a beat-and-a-half, a dangerous maneuver were the soloist actually playing at the time.

Most of the chords in **figure 21-6** are identified by type of voicing, as shown beneath the bass staff. Much of the eight bars is in drop 2, and the "alt/b9" designation refers to that term's usage in Chapter Nineteen. Chromatic approach is used in bars 3 and 4, the F#7alt/b9 combination resolving to the F7 chord, and in bar 6, A7+II resolving to the Ab7 chord.

Figure 21-6

4ths   G7alt/b9   Fsus   US #IV minor SW   G7b9   alt/b9   F#7alt

F#7b9 F7alt   F-6 dim F-6   US #IV minor   4ths   US II US II
                                                        A7+11 Ab7+11

US VI   US VI   US VI
G7b9   F#7b9   F7b9

Cedar Walton and Curtis Fuller

Photo © by Jerry Stoll

Be aware of the range of each solo instrument, and be careful not to 'comp too much in the same register as the soloist. If you 'comp high up on the keyboard during a soprano sax solo, for example, you'll just get in the soloist's way.

Many pianists 'comp timidly behind bass solos. Bass players often complain about the band "losing energy" behind their solos. Although you should play less behind a bass solo, what you *do* play should be rhythmically and harmonically just as strong as on a horn solo. Another common fault is to 'comp behind bass solos exclusively in the upper register, à la Count Basie. Experiment with using the middle register, and even below that, especially if the bassist is soloing in his or her upper register.

If you're playing an unfamiliar tune for the first time and your part has no melody, just chord symbols, 'comp very simply the first few times through. Listen for where the space in the tune occurs, so that when you know the tune better you can fill in all the right places.

When 'comping for an unfamiliar soloist for the first time, use the same approach. 'Comp with restraint and listen to their style. Do they play a lot of notes or do they use a lot of space? Are they a harmonically complex player, or a melodically simple player? Are they somewhere in between these extremes? I once had a gig with two well-known San Francisco saxophonists. One was a Charlie Parker disciple, the other took his cue from Coltrane, circa 1960. With two such different styles to 'comp for, I had to adjust for what notes to alter on dominant seventh chords. For the Bird-influenced altoist, I played b9 voicings most of the time on the V chords. For the 'Trane devotee, I played mostly alt voicings on the V chords. Of course I listened to both soloists carefully as I 'comped, and adjusted accordingly, but just playing in the harmonically appropriate style behind the soloist gives you a head start.

Accompanying singers presents special problems. Normally, you can't be quite as harmonically adventurous as when accompanying a horn player. Unlike instrumentalists, singers have no valves or keys to push down, and no strings to pluck. The pitch of each note sung is thus ever so much more fragile and dependent on what you play behind them. Also, singers often are not as well prepared as instrumentalists in giving you musical direction as to key, tempo, intros, endings, and so on. Why this is so would take too much space to go into here. Be sensitive to their needs. See the "Listen/Vocal" section of this book for a list of great vocal accompaniment albums.

Figure 21-7

Figure 21-8

Figure 21-9

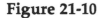

Figure 21-10

Bossa nova

Brazilian music, although rhythmically based on a two-bar clave (**figure 21-7**), doesn't have the rigid rules about clave that salsa does. Pianists play both one- and two-bar patterns, but with much more freedom than a pianist in a salsa band. **Figures 21-8** through **21-11** are loosely based on what Cedar Walton plays as he 'comps during Walter Booker's great bossa nova "Book's Bossa," on Donald Byrd's album *Slow Drag*.[3] Few jazz pianists play bossas as forcefully and "in the pocket" as Cedar. The chords in these examples are arbitrary—you can, and should, practice the patterns on a variety of chords. The repeat signs are just for the purpose of practice. In Brazilian music, you don't have to repeat the same two-bar pattern over and over again as in salsa. **Figure 21-12** is based on a pattern that Cedar plays on Freddie Hubbard's arrangement of Clare Fischer's "Pensativa," on Art Blakey's album *Free For All*.[4]

One-bar patterns are also played on bossa novas, and eight different patterns are grouped together as an eight-bar vamp, in **figure 21-13**.

Most jazz pianists solo on bossa novas as they would on jazz tunes, except sometimes playing with a "straight-eighth" rather than a swing feeling (Cedar Walton's solo on the aforementioned "Pensativa" is played with a swing feeling throughout). Probably the best-loved piano solo on a bossa nova is Herbie Hancock's lyrical solo on Lee Morgan's "Ceora."[5]

---

[3] Blue Note 84292.
[4] Blue Note 4l70.
[5] Lee Morgan, *Cornbread*, Blue Note 4222.

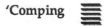

Figure 21-11

Figure 21-12

Figure 21-13

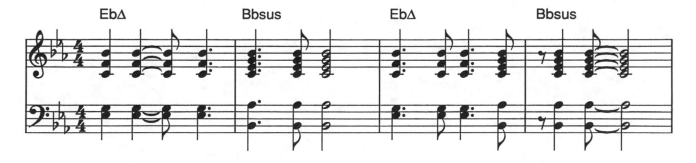

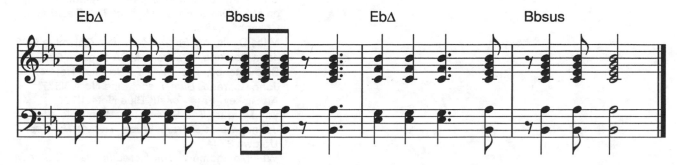

Listen

The best thing you can do to improve your 'comping is to listen to the pianists who are the best 'compers. Wynton Kelly is Number One on the all-time 'comp parade.[6] He played with an amazingly buoyant feeling, and always seemed to be harmonically in the right place at the right time. Herbie Hancock[7] is an exquisite 'comper. McCoy Tyner[8] is very aggressive, often playing powerful hypnotic vamps. Chick Corea[9] is harmonically very inventive, rhythmically very precise. Kenny Drew,[10] Cedar Walton,[11] Barry Harris,[12] Kenny Barron,[13] Tommy Flanagan,[14] Hank Jones,[15] Mulgrew Miller,[16] and Sonny Clark[17]—all have unique styles of 'comping, and all *swing*.

---

[6] One of my favorite examples is Wynton's 'comping on Miles Davis' *Friday Night at The Blackhawk*, Columbia 44257.

[7] Miles Davis, *My Funny Valentine*, Columbia 9l06.

[8] John Coltrane, *Crescent*, MCA/Impulse 5889.

[9] Blue Mitchell, *The Thing To Do*, Blue Note 4l78.

[10] John Coltrane, *Blue Trane*, Blue Note 8l577.

[11] Art Blakey, *Free For All*, Blue Note 4l70.

[12] Lee Morgan, *The Sidewinder*, Blue Note 4l57.

[13] Johnny Coles & Frank Wess, *Two At The Top*, Uptown 27.l4.

[14] Wes Montgomery, *The Incredible Jazz Guitar Of Wes Montgomery*, Riverside 320.

[15] Cannonball Adderly, *Somethin' Else*, Blue Note l595.

[16] Marvin "Smitty" Smith, *Keeper Of The Drums*, Concord Jazz 325.

[17] Tina Brooks, *The Complete Tina Brooks*, Mosaic MR4-l06.

CHAPTER TWENTY-TWO ☰
Loose Ends

This chapter covers subjects that have been omitted from previous chapters for various reasons, but aren't big enough to merit chapters of their own. Hence: "Loose Ends."

Sus, Phrygian, and the second mode of melodic minor

Play **figure 22-1** and listen to the sound of three different types of sus chords.

Sus and Phrygian chords were covered in Chapter Four. However, the final chord in **figure 22-1** is another type of sus chord that was not covered in Chapter Four. It is derived from the second mode of the melodic minor scale. All three sus chords function as V chords, and resolve smoothly to the CΔ chord a fifth below **(figure 22-2)**.

Figure 22-1

Gsus

Gsusb9 (or) GPhryg

Gsusb9 (or) Dø/G (or) F-Δ/G

Figure 22-2

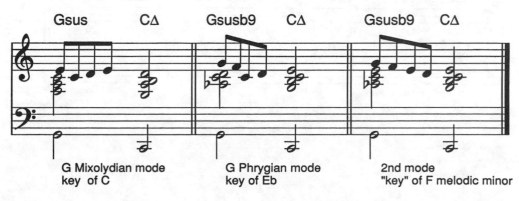

Gsus   CΔ   Gsusb9   CΔ   Gsusb9   CΔ

G Mixolydian mode   G Phrygian mode   2nd mode
key of C   key of Eb   "key" of F melodic minor

Figure 22-3 shows the scales for all three chords, each based on G (reprinted in appendix as "Appendix G"). Play each scale over the left-hand voicing shown. A good definition of a sus chord would be "a V chord in which the fourth doesn't act like an 'avoid' note." All three chords fit this definition. Play the fourth of each scale by itself over each left-hand voicing, and you'll hear that none of the fourths sound like an "avoid" note. In fact, the fourth of each scale (C) appears in the left-hand voicing shown for each chord.

The first scale shown in figure 22-3, for the Gsus chord, is the Mixolydian mode of the C major scale. The second scale shown, for a Gsusb9 chord, is the Phrygian mode of the Eb major scale. The third scale shown, with the same Gsusb9 chord symbol, is the second mode of the F melodic minor scale.

Figure 22-3

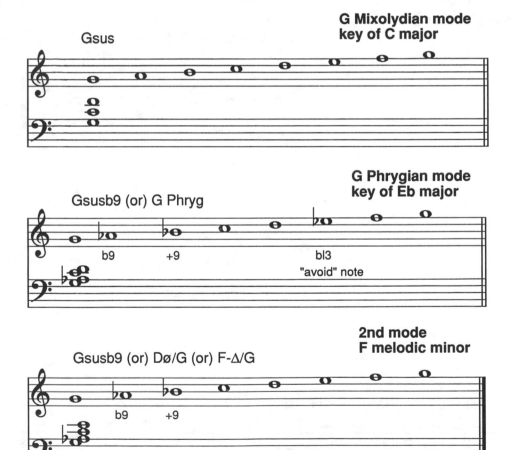

Why the same chord symbol for two different chords? Unfortunately, neither chord has a single generally accepted chord symbol. Susb9 is a commonly used symbol for a Phrygian chord, although some musicians write out the full "G Phrygian," or a shorthand "G Phryg." The sus chord derived from the second mode of the melodic minor scale is not used enough for jazz musicians to have agreed on a chord symbol, but more often than not "Gsusb9" is used, the same symbol for a G Phrygian chord. Occasionally someone will notate the second mode melodic minor chord as F-Δ/G or Dø/G, both of which reflect its derivation from F melodic minor.

Comparing the two susb9 scales, you can see that they differ by one note. G Phrygian has an Eb, or a bl3. This note sounds like an "avoid" note if played over a Phrygian chord, as you can hear when playing the first chord shown in **figure 22-4.** The bl3 is usually played as a passing note only, and is not voiced with the chord. In case your reaction to this chord was "hey, that sounds interesting," remember that "avoid" notes often sound very "interesting" when played out of context. The same note might sound pretty jarring in the middle of a pretty ballad. The second chord shown in **figure 22-4**, from F melodic minor, has an E natural—a natural thirteenth—which sounds consonant.

One solution to the notation problem would be to call the Phrygian chord Gsusb9, bl3 and the melodic minor chord Gsusb9, l3. Neither of these symbols is commonly used, so if you notate them like this for other musicians, be prepared for some blank looks. Jazz musicians only started to play susb9 chords in the mid-1960s, but more and more musicians are becoming adept at playing them, and maybe in five or ten years definitive chord symbols will emerge.

Figure 22-4

Gsusb9 — Eb major
Gsusb9 — F melodic minor

Figure 22-5

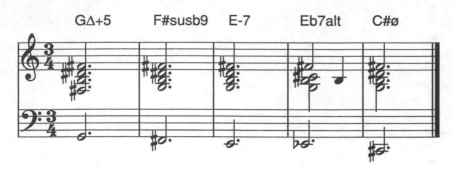

Figure 22-6

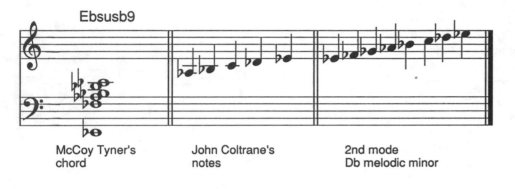

McCoy Tyner's chord   John Coltrane's notes   2nd mode Db melodic minor

A great example of the melodic minor sus chord is the F#susb9 chord found in Wayne Shorter's mysterious and haunting "Dance Cadaverous."[1] **Figure 22-5** shows bars 45-49, with an F#susb9 chord in the second bar. The bass line walks down an E melodic minor scale. All of the chords except for the E-7 chord are derived from the E melodic minor scale.

Another beautiful use of melodic minor sus harmony is found on the last chord just before the third "A" section of John Coltrane's "After The Rain."[2] McCoy Tyner freely plays an Eb Phrygian chord out of time, as Coltrane plays a line made up of the first five notes of the Ab major scale. Four of those notes—Ab, Bb, Db, and Eb—are in the Eb Phrygian mode. The other note that Coltrane plays—C—transforms McCoy's chord into the second mode of Db melodic minor **(figure 22-6)**.

Another example of a melodic minor sus chord is played by Herbie Hancock right after the two octave Bbs at the beginning of Miles Davis' recording of "All Of You."[3]

[1] Wayne Shorter, *Speak No Evil*, Blue Note 84194, Herbie Hancock on piano.

[2] John Coltrane, *Impressions*, MCA/Impulse 5887, McCoy Tyner on piano.

[3] Miles Davis, *My Funny Valentine*, Columbia 9106.

You can use the second mode melodic minor sus chord to reharmonize II chords. **Figure 22-7** shows the first four bars of "Tune-Up." The original II chord (E-7), is replaced by an Asusb9 chord, the second mode of G melodic minor. **Figure 22-8** shows the first four bars of "Stella By Starlight." The original Eø chord in the first bar has been reharmonized as Asusb9, the second mode of G melodic minor. Because this chord is taking the place of an Eø chord, you could also notate it as Eø/A. The original C-7 chord in the third bar has been reharmonized as Fsusb9, the second mode of Eb melodic minor.

Figure 22-7

Figure 22-8

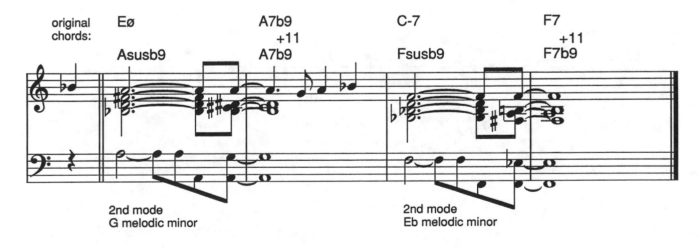

Aeolian harmony

Aeolian is the sixth mode of the major scale. The bridge of Miles Davis' "Milestones,"[4] consists of a single chord—A Aeolian (although Paul Chambers plays the fifth, E, so often that you could almost say the bridge is in E Phrygian). Aeolian chords are rarely specifically called for, and there is some confusion over exactly what constitutes an Aeolian chord and when to use an Aeolian scale. Some jazz theory books tell you to play the Aeolian scale over the VI chord in a I-VI-II-V progression **(figure 22-9)**. In most cases, however, the VI chord in a I-VI-II-V is a *dominant* chord, as in the first four bars of "Rhythm" changes **(figure 22-10)**. In classical theory, this would be expressed as I-V/II-II-V.

Figure 22-9

G Aeolian mode
key of Bb

Figure 22-10

G Mixolydian mode
Key of C

---

[4] Columbia 40837.

The Aeolian mode is a possible choice if the VI chord is a minor seventh rather than a dominant chord, as in **figure 22-9**. Listening to the evidence, however (recordings), you hear many of the great jazz musicians playing G Dorian, or even G minor-major, on the G-7 chord in this progression. Playing the Eb from the G Aeolian mode on a G-7 chord works fine as a passing note, but held against the chord it sounds like an "avoid" note. You'll hear this if you play the voicing for G-7 in **figure 22-11** while holding down the sustain pedal, and then play the Eb shown. If you play G-7 as the "VI" chord in a I-VI-II-V, and the soloist accentuates an Eb, they are probably thinking of the VI chord as G7alt rather than G-7 (Eb is the b13 of G7alt). Like any good 'comper, you should then switch to G7alt. One reason often given to play the Aeolian scale on a VI chord is that it allows you to stay in the same key over all four chords of a I-VI-II-V. This is a lazy musician's approach, and lacks the melodic possibilities available when you use chords from different keys in the same progression.

When the fifth of a minor chord moves up chromatically to a b6 **(figure 22-12)**, the resulting minor b6 chord is a very effective place to play the Aeolian mode. **Figure 22-13** shows how Kenny Barron uses this idea in the second and fourth bars of his tune "Sunshower."[5] Another place you could play Aeolian harmony is on the C-b6 chord on the second bar of the bridge of Fats Waller's "Ain't Misbehavin'."

Figure 22-11

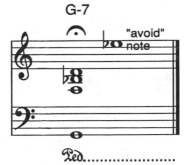

Figure 22-12

Figure 22-13

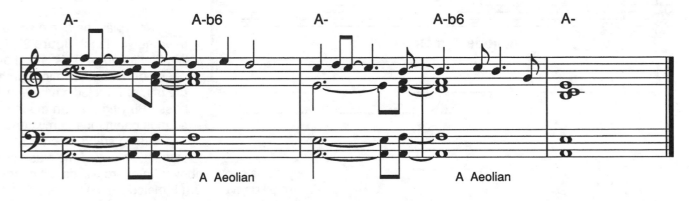

[5] Various artists, *One Night Stand: A Keyboard Event*, Columbia KC2 37100.

The fifth mode of melodic minor

The chord based on the fifth mode of the melodic minor scale is rarely used. Analyzing this mode in the traditional way can be misleading. **Figure 22-14** reveals a scale with a major third and a minor seventh, suggesting a dominant seventh chord. The Ab would be the b13 of the chord. Voicing the chord as C7b13 while playing the scale over it creates all sorts of problems, however. Both F and G—the fourth and fifth—may sound like "avoid" notes if held against the C7b13 voicing. Do they sound like "avoid" notes to you? Again, "avoid" notes are subjective. Played out of context, almost anything will sound at least "interesting." Here is one way you can judge whether or not a note is dissonant enough to restrict its use on a chord: The King has offered you half of his kingdom plus his daughter, the princess (or son, the prince), in marriage. All you have to do is play the chord in **figure 22-14** with your left hand, while playing one note in the right hand. Would you dare play F or G, or would you play some other note? If the King doesn't like your choice of note, off with your head! (P.S.: The King likes Herbie Hancock.)

Figure 22-14

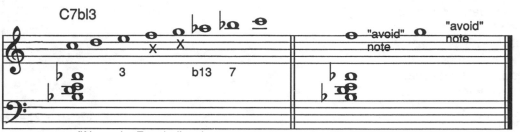

fifth mode, F melodic minor

Figure 22-15

any of the chord symbols below:

F-Δ/C   Gsusb9/C   AbΔ+5/C   Bb7+11/C   Dø/C   E7alt/C

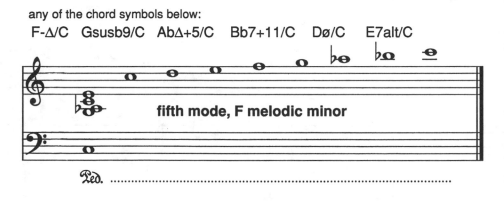

fifth mode, F melodic minor

Now play the same scale over the voicing in **figure 22-15**. Ah, that's better. This is a chord based on F melodic minor, with C, the fifth of F melodic minor, in the bass. Playing the fifth mode here sounds beautiful and mysterious. There is no standard chord symbol, so any of the slash chord symbols shown above the chord will do, since they are all derived from F melodic minor. You get half the kingdom, plus the princess (or the prince). To be truthful, many innovative musicians who were ahead of their time (Monk, Bird, Coltrane, Cecil Taylor) might have lost their heads.

Coltrane changes

John Coltrane created a harmonic revolution with the chord changes on his composition "Giant Steps."[6] At first, nobody but 'Trane could even play them (Tommy Flanagan struggled with them on the original recording, but in fairness to Tommy, probably nobody else at the time could have done any better). **Figure 22-16** shows the changes to "Giant Steps." Although this tune is challenging, its 26 chords go through only three keys—B, G, and Eb.

Figure 22-16

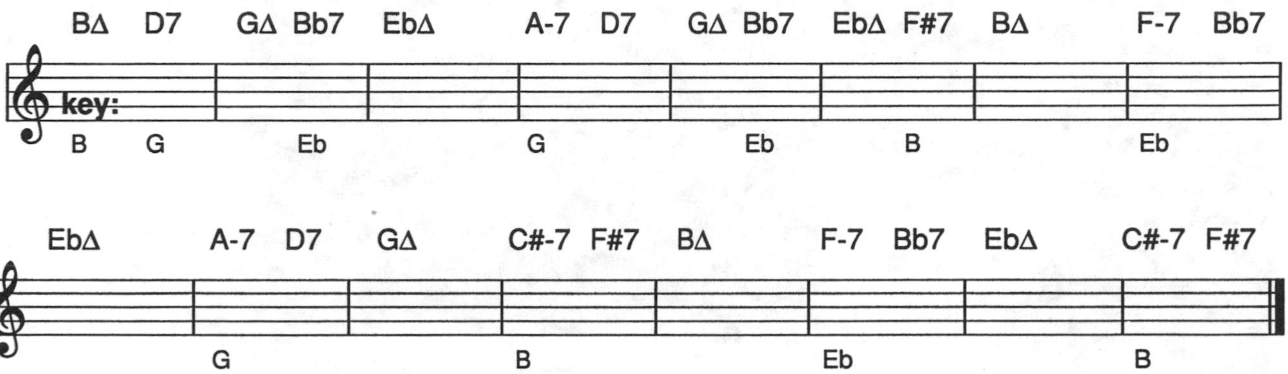

BΔ	D7	GΔ	Bb7	EbΔ	A-7	D7	GΔ	Bb7	EbΔ	F#7	BΔ	F-7	Bb7
B	G		Eb		G			Eb			B	Eb	

key:

EbΔ	A-7	D7	GΔ	C#-7	F#7	BΔ	F-7	Bb7	EbΔ	C#-7	F#7
	G			B			Eb			B	

Look at the "key" designations below the staff in **figure 22-16**. Each new key, or *tonal center*, is a major third away from the preceding key, whether moving up or down. **Figure 22-17** shows this movement more graphically, the whole notes representing the tonal centers in "Giant Steps." When you move around by major thirds (B-G-Eb-B), the octave is divided into three equal parts. Although Coltrane was the first jazz musician to use this concept extensively, he may have gotten the idea from the changes on the bridge of Richard Rodgers' "Have You Met Miss Jones" **(figure 22-18)**, which uses the same movement of tonal centers by major thirds.

Figure 22-17

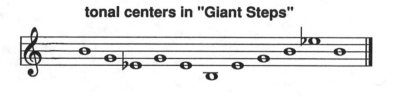

tonal centers in "Giant Steps"

Figure 22-18

BbΔ	Ab-7	Db7	GbΔ	E-7	A7	DΔ	Ab-7	Db7	GbΔ	G-7	C7
Bb	Gb					D	Gb				

Key:

---

[6] John Coltrane, *Giant Steps*, Atlantic 1311.

Tommy Flanagan   Photo ©1989 Brian McMillen

I can think of three other early examples of tonal centers moving by major thirds: Duke Ellington's "In A Sentimental Mood," where the tonality on the "A" section—F major—moves down a major third to Db major on the bridge; Ellington's "Melancholia," where a similar shift occurs on the bridge, from D major up to Gb major; and Billy Strayhorn's "Chelsea Bridge," which modulates from C major to E major—again, at the beginning of the bridge. "Giant Steps" is the first example of an entire tune built around this concept. A year or two before he recorded "Giant Steps," Coltrane ended Arthur Schwartz's "If There Is Someone Lovelier Than You,"[7] with four major seventh chords—CΔ, AbΔ, EΔ, CΔ—moving down by major thirds and dividing the octave into three equal parts.

---

[7] John Coltrane, *Settin' The Pace*, Fantasy/OJC 078, Red Garland on piano.

Coltrane also used this idea on "Countdown," also from the *Giant Steps* album. The changes to "Countdown" are a reharmonization of Miles Davis' "Tune-Up."[8] **Figure 22-19** shows the changes to the first four bars of "Tune-Up," a II-V-I in the key of D. In his reharmonization, Coltrane leaves unchanged the first chord, E-7—the II chord in D major. Then he moves the tonal center down a major third from D in the first bar to a Bb∆ chord in the second bar, down another major third to a Gb∆ chord in the third bar, and down another major third to a D∆ chord in the fourth bar. The tonal centers of these reharmonized four bars are shown in **figure 22-20**. Each "new" I chord—Bb∆, Gb∆, and D∆—is preceded by its V chord, and the result is the changes to the first four bars of "Countdown" (**figure 22-21**).

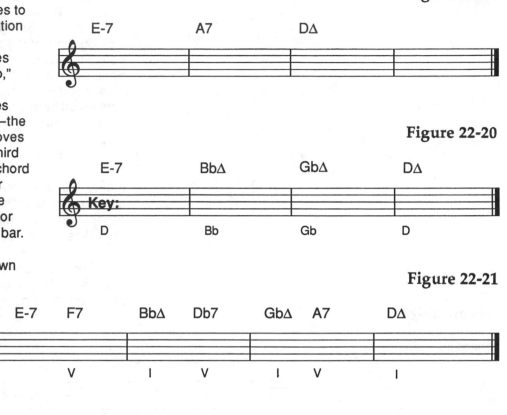

Figure 22-19

Figure 22-20

Figure 22-21

Figure 22-22 shows the changes to both tunes, "Tune-Up" above the staff and "Countdown" below the staff. As you can see, the second and third four-bar phrases of "Tune-Up" are similarly reharmonized on "Countdown." Coltrane left the last four bars of "Countdown" the same as "Tune-Up," the more conventional changes providing a four-bar relief from the very unconventional movement of the first 12 bars.

Figure 22-22

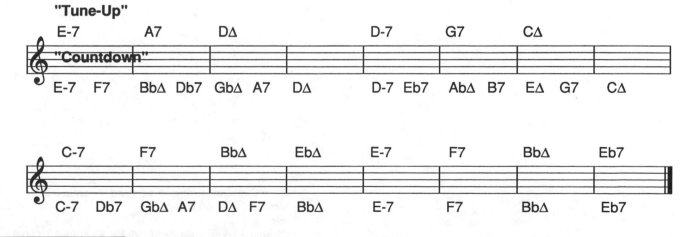

---

[8] Miles Davis, *Relaxin'*, Fantasy/OJC l90, Red Garland on piano.

Another example of this same kind of reharmonization takes place on Coltrane's version of Johnny Green's "Body And Soul."[9] **Figure 22-23** shows a commonly played set of changes for the first four bars of the bridge of "Body And Soul" above the staff, and Coltrane's reharmonization of bars 3 and 4 below the staff. Once again, the octave is divided into three equal parts, the tonal centers on bars 3 and 4 moving down in major thirds: D, Bb, Gb, D.

Using this same idea, Coltrane wrote several originals by reharmonizing the changes to existing tunes. Morgan Lewis' "How High The Moon" became "Satellite."[10] Charlie Parker's "Confirmation"[11] became "26-2."[12] Another Coltrane original, "Central Park West,"[13] also uses "Giant Steps" style changes.

Try your hand at reharmonizing some standard tunes as Coltrane did. Pick tunes with lots of II-V-I progressions and see what you can come up with.

Figure 22-23

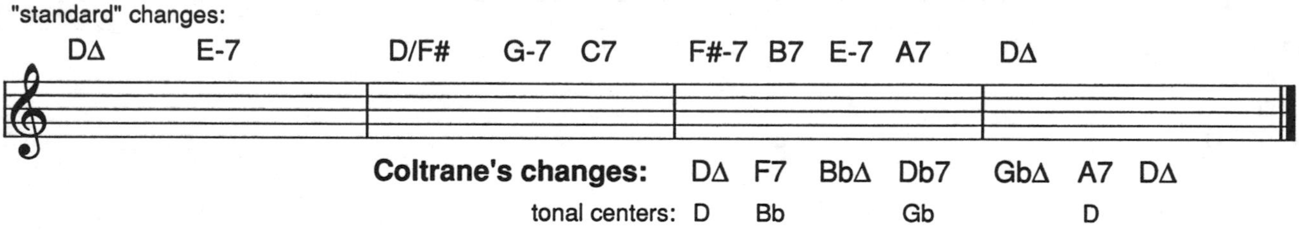

"standard" changes:

DΔ	E-7		D/F#	G-7	C7	F#-7	B7	E-7	A7	DΔ

Coltrane's changes: DΔ F7 BbΔ Db7 GbΔ A7 DΔ

tonal centers: D Bb Gb D

[9] John Coltrane, *Coltrane's Sound*, Atlantic 1419, McCoy Tyner on piano.

[10] ibid.

[11] Charlie Parker, *Bird At St. Nick's*, Fantasy/OJC 041.

[12] John Coltrane, *The Coltrane Legacy*, Atlantic 1553.

[13] John Coltrane, *Coltrane's Sound*, Atlantic 1311.

Jaki Byard

Photo © by Lee Tanner

"Rolling octaves"

Play **figure 22-24**. I think it was Jaki Byard who called this soloing technique "rolling octaves," and that's a good description of it. Your left hand plays the bottom note of each triplet, sustaining the note rather than playing it staccato, the thumb and little finger on your right hand playing the second and third notes of the triplet. They were a favorite device of Red Garland.[14] Herbie Hancock also plays them on his "Watch It,"[15] Wynton Kelly on his "Another Blues,"[16] and Art Tatum near the end of his solo on Richard Rodgers' "This Can't Be Love,"[17] and also near the end of his solo on "How High The Moon."[18]

Figure 22-24

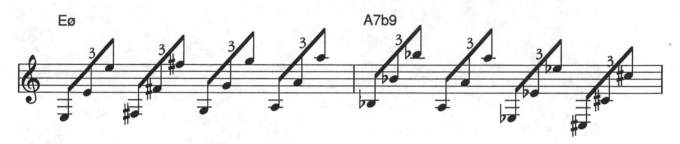

(play bottom note of each triplet with left hand, top two notes with right hand)

---

[14] Red Garland, *All Morning Long*, Prestige 7l30.
[15] *The Herbie Hancock Trio*, Sony CBS (Japan) 65 AP 650.
[16] Wynton Kelly, *Blues On Purpose*, Xanadu l98.
[17] Art Tatum, Lionel Hampton, and Buddy Rich, *Tatum/Hampton/Rich...Again!*, Pablo 23l0-775.
[18] Art Tatum, Lionel Hampton, and Buddy Rich, *Tatum/Rich/Hampton*, Pablo 23l0-720.

The harmonic major scale

Figure 22-25

Play the chord in **figure 22-25**. Herbie Hancock plays this mysterious and brooding chord (but in a different key) on bar 36 of his "Dolphin Dance."[19] You can use this chord to alter ordinary major seventh chords. When improvising on this chord, a good scale to play is the *harmonic major scale*, which is shown to the chord's right. The hybrid chord symbol is not in standard use, so be prepared for some puzzled reactions if you write it. It reflects the fact that this CΔ chord has both a fifth and a b6. The harmonic major scale is similar to the *harmonic minor scale* (**figure 22-26**), except that it has a major third.

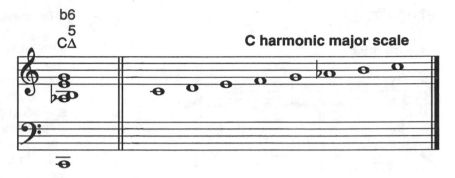

Figure 22-26

C harmonic minor scale

Figure 22-27 shows bars 9-10 of the Harry Warren-Mack Gordon standard "There Will Never Be Another You," with the original AbΔ chord changed to our new harmonic major chord, and resolving back to AbΔ on the third beat of the bar. **Figure 22-28** shows the first bar of the Sam Coslow-Arthur Johnston standard "Just One More Chance," with the original AbΔ chord changed to the harmonic major chord. You can hear Kenny Werner play this chord (although in a different key) on bar 10 of his tune "Compensation."[20] An alternate symbol you might see for this chord is C7+9/Ab.

Figure 22-27

The key element in all of the preceding examples is that the fifth is in the melody. Play through lots of tunes, looking for major seventh chords with the fifth in the melody, and see if you like the sound of them reharmonized as above. Some possibilities occur in the following tunes: "They Say That Falling In Love Is Wonderful," "Naima," "Moment's Notice," "You Are There," and "Body And Soul."

Figure 22-28

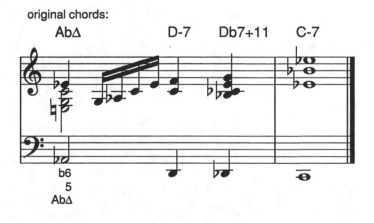

[19] Herbie Hancock, *Maiden Voyage*, Blue Note 84195.
[20] Joe Lovano, *Tones Shapes, And Colors*, Soul Note 1132.

Figure 22-29

Eb7b9/F

There's a reason they call it music theory

Play the chord in **figure 22-29**. Herbie Hancock played this dark, rich, chord in the first bar of the intro on Wayne Shorter's "Fee-Fi-Fo-Fum."[21] The chord symbol is a hybrid, reflecting that the top five notes look and sound like a voicing for Eb7b9, played over an F in the bass. F is not in the scale that goes with Eb7b9 (the Eb half step/whole step diminished scale). The chord shown contains Eb, E natural, and F, three consecutive chromatic notes in a row, something that doesn't occur in "conventional" scales, except for the chromatic scale. What to play over this chord? Try using the Eb half step/whole step diminished scale, as the chord symbol suggests. As long as you keep F in the bass, the three chromatic notes won't clash with each other. We're bending some of the rules, but that's OK. Remember, the rules come from the music, not the other way around.

This chord and the suggestion of how to play over it serves as a reminder that *theory* is only an intellectual game that we play with the music, attempting to objectively and rationally explain what is essentially a subjective, nonrational experience. Let theory be a guide for you, not a straightjacket. Above all, listen, sing through your instrument, and open your soul to the music.

[21] Wayne Shorter, *Speak No Evil*, Blue Note 4194.

Every successful musician has developed an efficient practice routine. Sitting at the piano for eight hours every day may not make you a better musician if you're not practicing the right things. As an example, I once discovered a method book of strange intervalic exercises. It was rumored that "Coltrane practiced out of this book," much as it was rumored that "Bird practiced out of Nicolas Slonimsky's *Thesaurus Of Scales*"[1] in the 1940s and 50s. It took me about six hours to go through the book the first day, but after a week I was going through the book about six times a day, driving my neighbors bananas I'm sure. Finally, someone walking past my door shouted "for Pete's sake, play a bossa nova," and I realized that my *playing* wasn't getting any better, only my ability to play through the book. Those exercises just weren't very musical because they were unrelated to anything I would play in real life. The moral of the story is: Tailor your practicing to the songs that are part of the standard jazz repertoire, and make your practicing efficient. What follows are a few suggestions on how to do just that.

Practice everything in every key

You should practice everything in every key. That includes everything—voicings, licks, styles, patterns, and tunes. *Especially* tunes. It may be difficult at first, but nothing makes you get better faster than practicing tunes in all keys. Taking a voicing through all twelve keys is a good start, but you'll learn it in the "hard" keys a lot faster and retain it better by playing it in the context of a tune, in all the keys.

---

[1] Nicolas Slonimsky, *Thesaurus Of Scales And Melodic Patterns*, Coleman-Ross Co., Inc., New York, 1947.

Some pianists learn each new tune in every key right from the start. An approach that works for me is to periodically go through my repertoire of tunes, pick out one that has evolved into an arrangement, and then play it through all keys, playing exactly the same arrangement—intro, voicings, licks, ending, and so on. I soon discover what needs to be practiced in which keys. I'll then settle on an "alternate" key other than the original, and make it a point to play the tune in the new key first on solo gigs, then with my trio. Some advantages to this approach are:

- Your ability to play in the so-called "difficult" keys improves.
- You become adept at transposing, an invaluable skill when accompanying singers.
- You can easily enhance your performance of a tune by taking the final chorus up a half- or-whole- step, an old cliché that still works like a charm.
- You discover that the original key of some tunes is not the best key for the piano. As an example, I used to be dissatisfied every time I played J. J. Johnson's "Lament," until I took it through all the keys and discovered that it sounds much better as a piano piece when played in a higher key than originally written.

Practice to your weaknesses

Suppose you are practicing a voicing around the cycle of fifths. Make note of what keys give you the most trouble. Then go back and practice the voicing again in those keys. How many seconds does it take you to play an upper structure I minor voicing on F#7+9? Can you play it as fast as you can on C7+9? Equalize your *reaction time*. Monitor your practicing so that you are aware of the keys that you need to spend more time on. By pinpointing your weaknesses like this, you'll know exactly what you need to practice most, even if you only have limited practice time. It then even becomes productive to practice in that odd five or ten minutes while you're waiting for the microwave or the start of the Giants' game on TV, because *you know exactly what you need to practice.*

Practice more than one thing at the same time

Left-hand/right-hand coordination is one of the biggest challenges in playing the piano. After you find yourself playing both a right-hand pattern and a left-hand voicing pretty well, practice them together around the cycle of fifths. In **figure 23-1**, your right hand sequences four-note minor sixth scales upward while your left hand plays V chords in a stride style around the cycle of fifths. In **figure 23-2**, your right hand sequences a four-note pattern, while your left-hand plays the same voicing moving up a minor third from each ø chord to the next alt chord. Start out slowly. *Speed comes from accuracy.* If you play accurately, speed will follow naturally. If you ever feel that your playing—on a voicing, phrase, chord progression, or the entire tune—is not quite in control, *play it slower.* You'll notice an immediate improvement.

Figure 23-1

Figure 23-2

OK, hold on to your hat. In the two-bar pattern shown in **figure 23-3**, *four* things are practiced at the same time. While your right hand plays a line including an Ab four-note minor sixth scale, your left hand plays stride for a bar, then walking tenths for a bar. The stride pattern includes three-note left-hand voicings. Here's your practice sequence:

1) Practice each idea separately at first.
2) Put all four ideas together, as in **figure 23-3**.
3) Practice **figure 23-3** in all keys.
4) Play through several tunes, playing the entire pattern every time there's a two bar II-V-I progression.

Figure 23-3

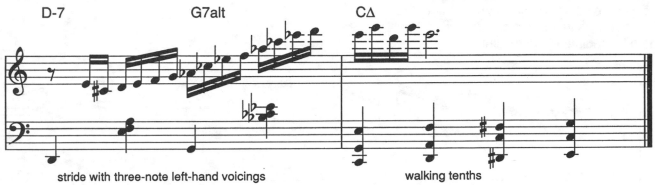

stride with three-note left-hand voicings   walking tenths

Practice within the context of tunes

As stated, a very efficient way to practice is to put everything within the context of a tune. After you've practiced that lick, voicing, or pattern, though the cycle of fifths a few times, play through a tune, dropping in your new-found gem wherever possible. The next few examples show how to do so with various techniques you've learned from this book, all on the first five bars of Gene DePaul and Don Raye's "Star Eyes."

Figure 23-4 shows the first five bars of "Star Eyes" with three-note voicings. Tritone substitutions have been used in **23-5**. Three-note voicings with added notes are shown in **23-6**. Left-hand voicings are played in **23-7**. In **figure 23-8**, b9 and +11 left-hand voicings are played on the V chords.

Figure 23-4

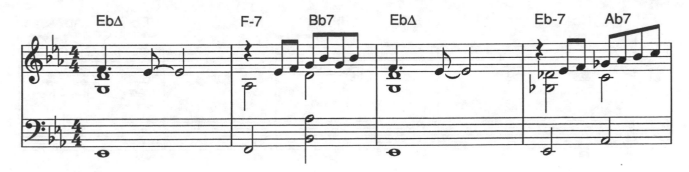

Figure 23-5

Figure 23-6

Figure 23-7

Figure 23-8

Figure 23-9 shows a four-note motíf sequencing over left-hand voicings. **Figure 23-10** shows the use of fourth, So What, and upper structure voicings. **Figure 23-11** shows a Duke Ellington-like German sixth cadence and a Kenny Barron voicing. Pentatonic scales, the in-sen scale, and displaced rhythms are shown in **23-12**. Pentatonic and four-note minor sixth scales are shown in figure **23-13**. Stride and walking tenths are shown in **23-14**, and Bud Powell voicings in **23-15**.

Figure 23-9

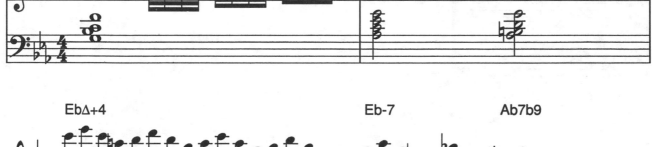

Figure 23-10

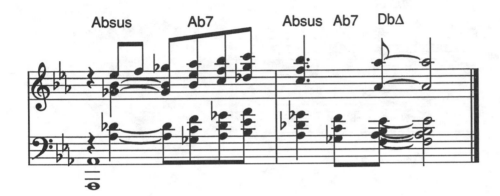

Figure 23-11

Figure 23-12

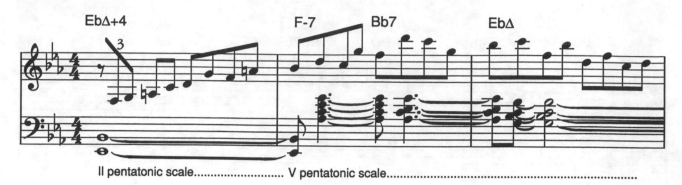

Figure 23-13

Figure 23-14

Figure 23-15

Figure 23-16

You can use the same approach when practicing "licks," phrases, motifs, and so on. **Figure 23-16** shows two short phrases, the first one to be played on major seventh chords, the second one over minor seventh chords. You can use one to "echo" the other, because they resemble each other in shape but have a slightly different rhythmic configuration for variety's sake. Notice that each phrase starts on the fifth of the chord. **Figure 23-17** shows how you might play the first five bars of "Star Eyes" using these two licks over left-hand voicings.

Figure 23-17

Figure 23-18

Figure 23-18 shows the same two motifs, but with a difference. The first one now starts on the ninth of the major seventh chord. The eighth note on the third beat falls on the +4, creating a Lydian chord. The second of the two examples uses tritone substitution. D-7, G7 has been replaced by Ab-7, Db7, but the lick still starts on the fifth of the II chord, in this case Ab-7 in place of D-7. The first five bars of "Star Eyes," using these two variations, are shown in **figure 23-19**. Play **figures 23-17** and **23-19** and hear the difference. **Figure 23-19** sounds more modern and has smoother voice leading. That doesn't make it better, but perhaps more interesting. In the first, third, and fifth bars of **figure 23-19**, your right thumb plays a note on the "and of three" that your left thumb is already playing. Lift your left thumb out of the way just before your right thumb plays the note.

Figure 23-19

Take each technique all the way through "Star Eyes." Remember, you should first practice each device separately through the cycle of fifths. Then apply the devices to a tune. This approach trains you to be able to use any technique in almost any situation.

A philosophical statement about practicing licks is timely here. Practicing patterns and licks should be used to get the fingers, brain, and eyes all in gear with each other, so that you are comfortable in as wide a range of musical situations as possible. They should become part of your musical unconscious, kind of like an inner library for you to draw upon—but they should not take the place of your main musical ideas.

Licks and patterns will always be played more on uptempo tunes, because the mind doesn't have as much time to think and the fingers will rely on what is known and secure. Use licks and patterns to get to know your instrument, but try not to use them as your entire solo repertoire.

A complete version of "Star Eyes," using a variety of techniques, appears in its entirety in **figure 23-20**. I've taken some liberties with the original chords (shown above in italics) and melodic phrasing in this example. Remember, this is jazz: you're allowed to make changes (as long as they sound good). A German sixth cadence is played in bars I and 3. Sus and Phrygian susb9 chords are

Figure 23-20

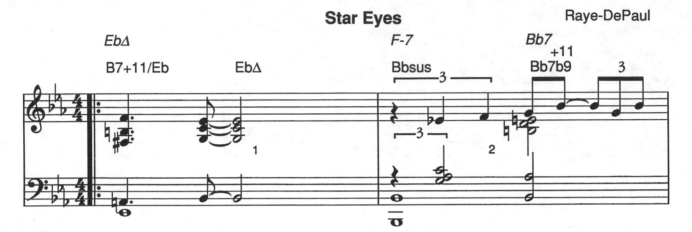

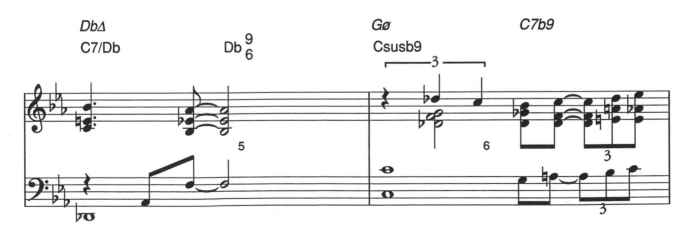

used as substitutes for II and V chords in bars 2, 4, 6, 8, 9, 17, and 19-21. Drop 2 block chords appear in bar 6, fourth chords in bars 7, 10, 14, and 15. The improvised line in bar 13 is derived from the Japanese in-sen scale. A Kenny Barron-style voicing is used on the F-7 chords in bar 16. A Gbsus chord substitutes for the final Eb△ chord.

Figure 23-20 (Continued)

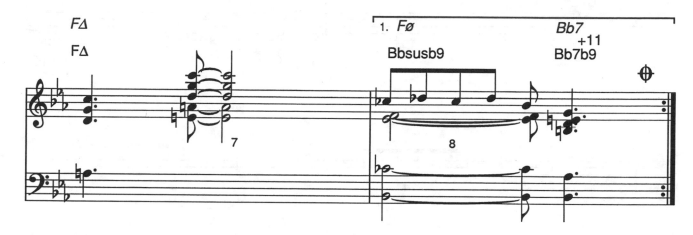

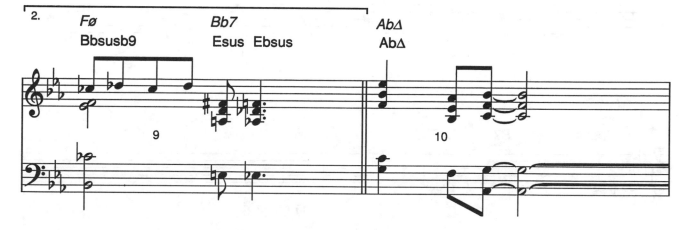

Figure 23-20 (Continued)

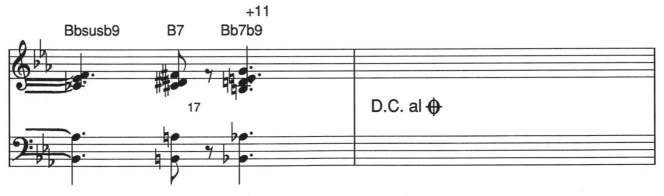

D.C. al $\oplus$

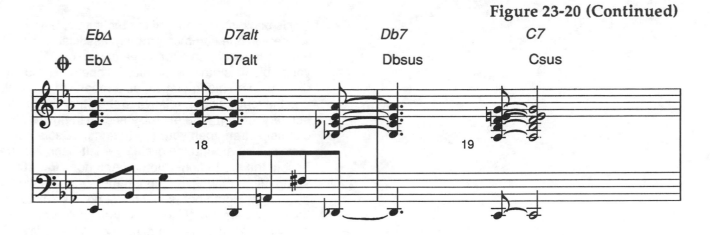

Figure 23-20 (Continued)

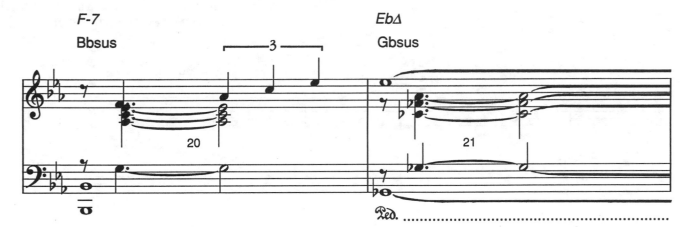

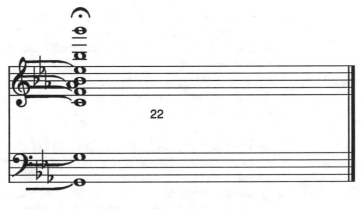

Technique

This book is not about piano technique, but there is one common problem associated with technique that I can offer some advice on. Many young pianists have weak fourth fingers. Evolution didn't plan on piano playing as a means of survival, and the fourth finger, relative to the other fingers, is not very strong. The exercise shown in **figure 23-21** can help strengthen your fourth finger. Sequence the exercise around the cycle over left-hand voicings. Accent the fourth finger notes. And don't forget to swing the phrase, even though the notes are written as straight eighth notes. If you've got a weak fourth finger problem, practicing this exercise ten minutes every day should make a difference within a few days. Plus, you're learning a new lick and practicing your left-hand voicings at the same time!

Figure 23-21

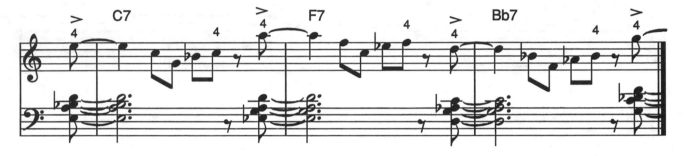

Be aware of any unnecessary muscle tension as you play. I often see pianists unknowingly hold their breath as they stretch out on a long phrase. Breathe normally and deeply. It may sound nutty, but smiling when you play can help relieve tension. Drummer Billy Higgins always smiles when he plays—does he know something we all should know?

Do you tap your foot when you play? There are more theories about how to do this correctly than you can count. Some pianists tap their toe. Jaki Byard taught me to tap my heel, because it gives your playing a sense of forward motion. Some pianists tap on all four beats; some just on one and three, or on two and four; some don't tap at all. Whatever feels natural is OK, as long as it doesn't get in the way of your playing, and isn't so loud that it distracts your fellow musicians.

Listen, listen, listen

Whether you live in a big city or a small town, jazz is probably played somewhere nearby. Listen to as much live jazz as possible. Records are not enough. Apprentice yourself to whomever seems to be the best jazz pianist in your neck of the woods. Ask them to show you some of their secrets, or if you can study with them.

Be aware of rhythm sections, not just pianists. Do the pianist, bassist, and drummer play well together? Are their styles compatible? Do they communicate well? How do they communicate? Look for eye contact or other body language. How do they let each other know when to take fours, bass or drum solos, take the tune out, and so on. You can learn almost as much by watching as by listening to the music.

If a pianist and guitar player are playing together in the same rhythm section, how do they handle the problem of each one's chords clashing with the other? Does one "lay out" while the other one 'comps? If they both 'comp at the same time, does one play more sparingly than the other? Usually the pianist takes the more dominant role, but not always. The most compatible piano/guitar combination ever was probably Wes Montgomery and Wynton Kelly. They never got in each other's way. Listen to any of their records (see the "Listen/Miscellaneous" section right after this chapter).

Transcribing

Transcribing solos and tunes off of records is an essential skill. The best way to learn a tune is by taking it off the record. Unlike reading a lead sheet, you'll hear everything—intro, melody, chords, solos, bass lines, drum hits, form, vamps, interludes, ending—so you can decide how much you need to know about the tune. To transcribe quickly and efficiently, you need the right equipment:

- A hand held Walkman-type stereo cassette player, with pitch control (called "speed control" on some machines) and a pause button. Some machines come with octave pitch control, which lets you slow things down to half speed.
- A good set of stereo headphones.

Start by transcribing the melody line. Transcribe the bass line next, or at least the note the bassist plays on each new chord change. Next, do the chord changes, using the bass line as a guide. If you're unsure whether the Eb chord in bar 6 is major or minor, play it over while striking first G, the major third, and then Gb, the minor third, on the piano Which one sounds right? If you're still unsure, try the same procedure when the chord in question comes around on the next chorus. Don't get bogged down on one chord. Go on to the next chord, and return later to work on the one that caused you problems. By then you may have solved the problem anyway, because you'll have heard how it's played on subsequent choruses.

Billy Strayhorn and Duke Ellington   Photo © by Jerry Stoll

Play along with records

Although horn players use play-along records far more than pianists do, some pianists find them a great help. The Jamey Aebersold series, large and still growing, offers three basic types of records:

1) Records of tunes by a particular songwriter, including Wayne Shorter, Horace Silver, Miles Davis, John Coltrane, Sonny Rollins, Duke Ellington, Charlie Parker, and so on.
2) Collections of standard tunes, like "Body And Soul," "Stella By Starlight," and so forth.
3) Records that deal with specific areas of study, such as II-V-I progressions, the Blues, and so on. Two especially good ones in the latter category are Vol. 16, *Turnarounds, Cycles & II/V7's*, and Vol. 21, *Gettin' It Together*.

Tape the play-along record, use your headphones, adjust the pitch control, turn off the piano channel (although some pianists like to leave it on), and you're ready to go. Your rhythm section partners on some of the Aebersold records include bassists Ron Carter, Rufus Reid, Stafford James, and Sam Jones. Your drummer may be Ben Riley, Billy Hart, Al Foster, or Louis Hayes. And if you want to 'cop some voicings from the piano track, turn the piano channel back on. World-class players like Kenny Barron[2] and Ronny Matthews[3] play on some of the records.

Play along with the real thing also. Put on a Miles Davis record and play along with Red Garland, Wynton Kelly, or Herbie Hancock. Even if you can't hear the voicings, try to play the same rhythmic patterns. Try to get into the same groove at the same energy level as the players on the record. If your record player is not in tune with your piano, tape the record, put on your headphones, adjust the pitch control, and you're in business.

---

[2] Vol. 6, *All Bird*; Vol. 11, *Herbie Hancock*; Vol. 12, *Duke Ellington*; Vol. 15, *Payin' Dues*; and Vol. 17 and 18, *Horace Silver*.
[3] Vol. 9, *Woody Shaw*, and Vol. 13, *Cannonball Adderly*.

Criticism

As a student, you willingly open yourself up to criticism and advice from your teachers. Accept all criticism, however, with at least a grain of salt. Teachers are not infallible, no matter how good they play or how well they teach. One teacher may tell you that your time is good, another that you rush or drag the time. Advice and criticism are free. That doesn't make either necessarily right. Your best critic is yourself. Tape yourself often and listen with a critical ear.

It's not a bad idea to totally ignore some forms of criticism entirely, such as reviews. The standard of professional criticism in jazz is, to put it charitably, uneven. Chick Corea's album *Now He Sings, Now He Sobs*,[4] one of the best trio albums ever recorded, was given the lowest possible rating by a leading jazz magazine. A famous jazz critic said of John Coltrane, "He often blows his tenor saxophone as though he were determined to blow it apart but his desperate attacks almost invariably lead nowhere." Another critic, reviewing Miles Davis' great album *'Round About Midnight*,[5] referred to John Coltrane as an "out-of-tune tenor player," and Red Garland as a "cocktail piano player." If they said that about *them*, what are they going to say about *you*?

Although as an artist you should strive for perfection, don't let your mistakes get you down. Improvised music, by its very nature, is full of mistakes. Listen to Joe Henderson's false entrance on the out chorus to McCoy Tyner's "Four By Five."[6] Everybody plays so great on that tune, on the whole album for that matter, that nobody cares too much about Joe's "mistake." Although it sounds like a cliché, a positive way of dealing with playing a bad note is "the next note is the first note of the rest of your solo."

Practice, listen, and live the music to the fullest, adding your contribution to America's premier art form: **Jazz!**

---

[4] Solid State l8039. Also available on a CD, Blue Note 90055.

[5] Columbia 406l0.

[6] McCoy Tyner, *The Real McCoy*, Blue Note 4264.

Listen/Intro

This sizeable-looking jazz piano discography represents, at most, perhaps 1/10 of one percent of all the jazz records made since 1945. My attempt here is to list the *best* records. This discography is personal and subjective—the selections represent the personal tastes of the author. I apologize to anyone for omitting any of their favorite albums.

If pianists such as Bud Powell, Herbie Hancock, McCoy Tyner, Barry Harris, Art Tatum, Kenny Barron, Jaki Byard, Tommy Flanagan, Red Garland, Wynton Kelly, Cedar Walton, and Mulgrew Miller seem over-represented, it's because they were, and are, the best. In many cases, particular records are recommended for the presence of musicians other than the pianist—it's hard *not* to recommend a record with Coltrane, Miles, Joe Henderson, or Wayne Shorter on it.

Be aware of *rhythm sections*, not just pianists. It may not just be Wynton Kelly that sounds great, but the combination of Wynton with Paul Chambers and Philly Joe Jones. Below is a list of some of the great rhythm sections:

- Bud Powell, Curly Russell, and Max Roach.
- Thelonious Monk, Oscar Pettiford, and Kenny Clarke.
- Red Garland, Paul Chambers, and Philly Joe Jones.
- Red Garland, Paul Chambers, and Arthur Taylor.
- Wynton Kelly, Paul Chambers, and Philly Joe Jones.
- Wynton Kelly, Paul Chambers, and Jimmy Cobb.
- Wynton Kelly, Sam Jones, and Louis Hayes.
- Barry Harris, Sam Jones, and Louis Hayes.
- Bill Evans, Scott LaFaro, and Paul Motian.
- Herbie Hancock, Ron Carter, and Tony Williams.
- Cedar Walton, Jymie Merritt, and Art Blakey.
- McCoy Tyner, Reggie Workman, and Elvin Jones.
- McCoy Tyner, Jimmy Garrison, and Elvin Jones.
- Mulgrew Miller, Ron Carter, and Al Foster.

There are many other great bassists to be aware of, including Charles Mingus, Doug Watkins, Wilbur Ware, Cecil McBee, George Mraz, Miroslav Vitous, Bob Cranshaw, Ray Drummond, Eddie Gomez, Rufus Reid, Lonnie Plaxico, Charnett Moffett, and Dave Holland.

There are many other great drummers to be aware of, including Roy Haynes, Joe Chambers, Pete LaRoca, Charlie Persip, Jack DeJohnette, Eddie Moore, Freddie Waits, Jeff "Tain" Watts, Marvin "Smitty" Smith, and Victor Lewis.

Record numbers can be very unreliable. Many companies renumber albums when they are reissued, and often a change of label number from, say, "BH-4234" to "BHV-84234," may reflect nothing more than a price change. In addition, many albums are retitled (Herbie Hancock's great Latin jazz album *Inventions and Dimensions* has become *Succotash*), issued as two-fers, or changed in other ways.

Many of the albums listed are currently out of print. To put together a good record collection, you need to haunt used record stores *regularly.* The San Francisco Bay area has several good record stores that sell used albums. The best ones are Jazz Quarter in San Francisco (owner Tom Madden is a walking discography), Village Music in Marin County, Logos in Santa Cruz (unfortunately destroyed in the big earthquake of October, 1989), and Berrigan's in Oakland.

Listen/Solo

Playing solo is a lot like playing naked, with no bass player or drummer to clothe one's mistakes. This very demanding genre has had many practitioners, but few masters. If Art Tatum seems over-represented, it's because he specialized in playing solo, and is the universally acknowledged supreme solo pianist.

Kenny Barron
- *Scratch*, Enja 4092. Listen to Kenny's "Song For Abdullah."
- *What If?*, Enja 5013. A single great solo track, Monk's "Trinkle, Tinkle," on an album that contains duo, trio, and quintet tracks.

Joe Bonner
- *The Lifesaver,* Muse 5065.

Jaki Byard
- *Parisian Solos*, Futura 05. Listen to Jaki's version of Gershwin's "Our Love Is Here To Stay," and "Bugle Call Rag."
- *Blues For Smoke*, Candid 6212.
- *Solo Piano*, Prestige 7686.
- *There'll Be Some Changes Made*, Muse 5007.

Abdullah Ibrahim   Photo ©1989 K. Gypsy Zaboroskie

Chick Corea
- *Piano Improvisations, Vol. I and II,* ECM 811979, and 829190. Listen to Chick's version of Thelonious Monk's "Trinkle, Tinkle."

Stanley Cowell
- *Musa Ancestral Streams,* Strata East 19743.

Kenny Drew
- *It Might As Well Be Spring,* Soulnote 1040.

Bill Evans
- *Conversations With Myself,* Verve 821984, Bill's album of multi-tracked solos.

Red Garland
- *Red Alone,* Moodsville 3.

Errol Garner
- *Soliloquy,* Columbia 1060.
- *Afternoon Of An Elf,* Mercury 20090.

John Hicks
- *John Hicks,* Theresa 119. Listen to John's "Steadfast." The album also has some trio tracks, with Bobby Hutcherson on vibes and Walter Booker on bass.

Abdullah Ibrahim
- *African Dawn,* Enja 4030. Listen to Abdullah's version of Billy Strayhorn's "A Flower Is A Lovesome Thing."

Hank Jones
- *Tiptoe Tapdance,* Galaxy 5108. Listen to Hank's version of Johnny Mandel's "Emily."

Kirk Lightsey
- *Lightsey I,* Sunnyside 1002. Listen to Kirk's version of Thelonious Monk's "Trinkle, Tinkle."

Dave McKenna
- *My Friend The Piano,* Concord Jazz 313.

Thelonious Monk
- *Solo Monk,* Columbia 9149.
- *Pure Monk,* Trip 5022.

Tete Montoliu
- *Yellow Dolphin Street,* Timeless 107. Listen to Tete's "Napoleon," and his walking bass line on "I Hate You."

Horace Parlan
- *Musically Yours,* SteepleChase 1141.

Bud Powell
- *The Amazing Bud Powell,* Verve 2506. Eight tracks on this otherwise trio album feature Bud playing solo. Listen to his partially stride version of Jerome Kern's "The Last Time I Saw Paris," and the left-hand voicings on "Hallucinations" discussed in Chapter Seventeen.

George Shearing
- *My Ship,* Verve/MPS 821664-1. Listen to George's version of Milton Ager's "Happy Days Are Here Again."

≣ **LISTEN**

Art Tatum
- *The Tatum Solo Masterpieces Set*, Pablo 2310-723, 13 albums.
- *Get Happy*, Jazzman 5030.
- *This Is Art Tatum*, 20th Century Fox 4162.
- *Piano Starts Here*, Columbia 9655. One of Art's most muscular albums, with a blazing "I Know That You Know" that at times sounds like the tape is on fast forward.
- *Gene Norman Presents Art Tatum, Vol. I*, GNP
- *The Complete Art Tatum Discoveries*, 20th Century Fox 607.
- *The Genius Of Art Tatum*, Vol. III, Clef 614.
- *The Art Of Tatum*, Decca 8715.
- *Capitol Jazz Classics, Vol. III*, Capitol 11028.
- *The Genius*, Black Lion 158.
- *20th Century Piano Genius*, EmArcy 826-129, recorded at a party in 1955.

Lennie Tristano
- *Lennie Tristano*, Atlantic 1224, also rereleased as half of a two-fer, *Requiem,* Atlantic 7003. Listen to Lennie's "Turkish Mambo."

McCoy Tyner
- *Echoes Of A Friend,* Milestone 9055.
- *Revelations*, Blue Note 91651. One of the best solo albums of the 1980s. Listen to McCoy play stride on parts of Jimmy McHugh's "Don't Blame Me."

Randy Weston
- *Blues To Africa*, Arista Freedom 1014. Listen to Randy's "Kasbah Kids."

Listen/Duo

Unless otherwise noted, each record is a piano-bass duo.

Kenny Barron
- Kenny Barron, *I + I + I,* Blackhawk 50601, with Ron Carter or Michael Moore.
- Kenny Barron, *What If?,* Enja 5013, with Victor Lewis. A single great piano-drums duo track, Bird's "Dexterity," on an otherwise mixed solo/trio/quintet album.

Joe Chambers
- Joe Chambers, *Double Exposure,* Muse Mr 5165, with Larry Young. Joe Chambers, one of the greatest jazz drummers, plays piano with Larry Young on organ on most of this album, which also features Joe on one solo piano track, and Larry on organ with Joe on drums on two tracks.

Chick Corea and Herbie Hancock
- *Corea/Hancock,* Polydor 6238. Jazz piano duos, no matter how good the players, usually sound clunky. The harmonic density of too many notes being played at the same time is usually blamed, but more often than not it's the juxtaposition of two different time feelings. Solo pianists, with no bassist or drummer to lean on, have to swing with no support other than whatever time feeling they generate on their own. Put two pianists together, and the differences in their respective time feelings are magnified, often by the tentativeness they bring to this often cumbersome form. Piano duo is best approached aggressively. Chick and Herbie are probably the two best in the genre.

Duke Ellington
- Duke Ellington and Ray Brown, *This One's For Blanton*, Pablo 2310-721.
- Duke Ellington and Jimmy Blanton, *Duke Ellington 1938-1940, an Explosion Of Genius*, The Smithsonian Collection P615079, four duo tracks on a six-album set.

Kenny Drew
- Kenny Drew, *Duo,* Inner City 2002, with Niels Henning Ørsted Pedersen.

Bill Evans
- Bill Evans, *Intuition,* Fantasy 9475, with Eddie Gomez.

Tommy Flanagan
- Tommy Flanagan, *Ballads & Blues*, Inner City 3029, with George Mraz.

Tommy Flanagan and Hank Jones
- Tommy Flanagan and Hank Jones, *Our Delights,* Galaxy 5113. One of the best piano duo albums ever recorded.
- Tommy Flanagan and Hank Jones, *I'm All Smiles,* Verve/MPS 817-863.

Tete Montoliu and George Coleman
- Tete Montoliu and George Coleman, *Duo,* Muse 312. One of the best horn-piano albums ever recorded.

Cecil Taylor and Max Roach
- Cecil Taylor and Max Roach, *Historic Concerts*, Soul Note 121101. An epic piano-drum duet.

Randy Weston

Photo © by Lee Tanner

Listen/Trio

Bassists and drummers, unless otherwise noted, are listed after record label and number.

Monty Alexander
- *In Tokyo*, Pablo 2310-836, with Andrew Simpkins and Frank Gant.

Kenny Barron
- *Landscape*, Limetree 0020, with Cecil McBee and Al Foster. Listen to Kenny's version of Rodgers and Hart's "Spring Is Here."
- *Autumn In New York,* Uptown 2726, with Rufus Reid and Freddie Waits. Listen to Kenny's "New York Attitude."
- *Green Chimneys*, Criss Cross 1008, with Buster Williams and Ben Riley.

Richie Beirach
- *Elm,* ECM 1142, with George Mraz and Jack DeJohnette.

Ray Bryant
- *Trio Today*, EmArcy 832589, with Rufus Reid and Freddie Waits.

Jaki Byard
- *Hi-Fly*, New Jazz 8273, with Ron Carter and Pete LaRoca. Listen to Jaki's version of James P. Johnson's "Excerpts from Yamecraw," and Jaki's "Here to Hear."
- *Here's Jaki,* Prestige 24086, with Ron Carter and Roy Haynes. Listen to "Cinco Y Cuatro," and Jaki's version of "Giant Steps."
- *Family Man*, Muse 5173, with Major Holley and J. R. Mitchell. Listen to Jaki's version of "Just Rollin' Along."

Chick Corea
- *Now He Sings, Now He Sobs*, Blue Note 90055, with Miroslav Vitous and Roy Haynes. One of the best trio albums of the 1960s.

Stanley Cowell
- *Equipoise,* Galaxy 5125, with Cecil McBee and Roy Haynes.

Kenny Drew
- *Kenny Drew Trio*, Fantasy OJC 035, with Paul Chambers and Philly Joe Jones. Listen to Kenny's version of Juan Tizol's "Caravan."
- *Introducing The Kenny Drew Trio,* Blue Note 5023, with Curly Russell and Art Blakey. Kenny's first (1953) trio date. Listen to his unusual up-tempo versions of "Be My Love," and "It Might As Well Be Spring."

Duke Ellington
- *Money Jungle*, Blue Note 85129, with Charles Mingus and Max Roach.
- *Piano Reflections*, Capitol 11058.

Bill Evans
- *Sunday At The The Village Vanguard*, Riverside 9376, with Scott LaFaro and Paul Motian.
- *Waltz For Debby,* Fantasy OJC-210 (personnel as above).
- *Spring Leaves*, Milestone 47034 (personnel as above).
- *Everybody Digs Bill Evans,* Fantasy OJC-068, with Sam Jones and Philly Joe Jones. Listen to Bill's "Peace Piece."

Tommy Flanagan
- *Eclypso*, Enja 2088, with George Mraz and Elvin Jones. Listen to Tommy's version of the title track.
- *Tommy Flanagan Plays The Music Of Harold Arlen*, Inner City 1071, with George Mraz and Connie Kay.
- *The Super Jazz Trio*, RCA (France) 45367, with Reggie Workman and Joe Chambers.

Hal Galper
- *Portrait*, Concord Jazz 383, with Ray Drummond and Billy Hart. Almost as eclectic a pianist as Jaki Byard or Chick Corea, the influences of Bud Powell, Bill Evans, Red Garland (listen to his left hand on "After You've Gone"), and Ahmad Jamal's sense of form and use of space are all blended into a passionately original style.

 **LISTEN**

Red Garland
- *Red Garland's Piano*, Fantasy OJC-073, with Paul Chambers and Arthur Taylor.
- Red Garland, *All Kinds Of Weather*, Prestige 7148 (personnel as above).
- Red Garland, *Can't See For Lookin'*, Prestige 7276 (personnel as above).
- Red Garland, *A Garland Of Red*, Prestige 7064 (personnel as above).
- Red Garland, *Groovy*, Prestige 7148 (personnel as above).
- Red Garland, *The P. C. Blues*, Prestige 7752, with Paul Chambers, Arthur Taylor, and Philly Joe Jones.
- Red Garland, *Red In Blues-ville*, Fantasy OJC 295, with Sam Jones and Arthur Taylor.
- Red Garland, *Rediscovered Masters*, Prestige P-24078, a mostly trio two-fer with Paul Chambers, Arthur Taylor, and Ray Barretto on one lp.
- Miles Davis, *Milestones*, Columbia 40837, an otherwise quintet album with one great trio track; Red's version of the traditional "Billy Boy," with Paul Chambers and Philly Joe Jones.

Errol Garner
- *Errol Garner*, Columbia 535, with Wyatt Ruther and J. C. Heard. The Elf's greatest record, with great versions of "Caravan," "Avalon," and "Will You Still Be Mine?"
- *Concert By The Sea*, Columbia 40589, with Eddie Calhoun and Denzil Best.
- *One World Concert*, Reprise 6080, with Eddie Calhoun and Kelly Martin.

Jan Hammer
- Elvin Jones, *On The Mountain,* PM 005, with Elvin and Gene Perla.

Herbie Hancock
- *Speak Like A Child*, Blue Note 84279, with Ron Carter and Mickey Roker. Listen to Herbie's trio version of Ron's "First Trip," on this mostly sextet album, one of Herbie's best.

Barry Harris
- *Barry Harris At The Jazz Workshop*, Riverside 326, with Sam Jones and Louis Hayes.
- *Barry Harris Plays Tadd Dameron*, Xanadu 113, with Gene Taylor and Leroy Williams.

Hampton Hawes
- *Live At The Montmarte,* Arista-Freedom 1020, with Henry Franklin and Michael Carvin.

Ahmad Jamal
- *Heat Wave*, Cadet 777, with Israel Crosby and Vernel Fournier. Listen to Ahmad's great version of Ralph Blane's "The Boy Next Door."

Keith Jarrett
- *Standards, Vol. I*, ECM 811966, with Gary Peacock and Jack DeJohnette.

Hank Jones
- *Love For Sale*, Inner City 6003, with Buster Williams and Tony Williams.

Wynton Kelly
- *Blues On Purpose*, Xanadu 198, with Paul Chambers and Jimmy Cobb.
- *Someday My Prince Will Come*, Vee Jay 3038 (personnel as above). Listen to Wynton play the blues on "Sassy."
- *Kelly At Midnight*, Vee Jay 3011, with Paul Chambers and Philly Joe Jones.
- *Wynton Kelly*, Riverside 254 (personnel as above).

Andy LaVerne
- *Another World*, SteepleChase 1086, with Mike Richmond and Billy Hart.

Marian McPartland
- *Ambiance,* Halcyon 103, with Michael Moore, Jimmy Madison, and Billy Hart.

Junior Mance
- Junior Mance, *The Soulful Piano Of Junior Mance*, Jazzland 930.

Mulgrew Miller
- *Work!*, Landmark 1511, with Charnett Moffett and Terri Lyne Carrington. Includes one solo track, Gershwin's "My Man's Gone Now."

Thelonious Monk
- *The Unique Thelonious Monk*, Fantasy OJC-064, with Oscar Pettiford and Art Blakey. Listen to Monk's version of Vincent Youmans' "Tea For Two."
- *Monk Plays The Music Of Duke Ellington*, Riverside 6039, with Oscar Pettiford and Kenny Clarke.

Mary Lou Williams

Phineas Newborn, Jr.
- *Back Home*, Contemporary 7648, with Ray Brown and Elvin Jones. Listen to Phineas' Errol Garner roots on "No Moon At All."
- *The Piano Artistry of Phineas Newborn, Jr.*, Atlantic 90534-1, with Oscar Pettiford and Kenny Clarke. Listen to Phineas' version of Bud Powell's "Celia."
- *A World Of Piano*, Fantasy/OJC 175, with Paul Chambers and Philly Joe Jones.

Oscar Peterson
- *Night Train*, Verve 68538, with Ray Brown and Ed Thigpen.

Bud Powell
- *The Amazing Bud Powell, Vols. I and II*, Blue Note 81503 and 81504, with Curly Russell and Max Roach. Two of the greatest trio albums ever recorded.
- *The Genius of Bud Powell*, Verve 821690, with Ray Brown, Curly Russell, Max Roach, and Buddy Rich. Among the greatest trio albums ever recorded.

Horace Silver
- *Six Pieces Of Silver*, Blue Note 1539. Two trio tracks on this album, with Doug Watkins and Ed Thigpen.
- *The Trio Sides*, Blue Note LA 474.
- *The Horace Silver Trio*, Blue Note 1520.

Art Tatum
- *Tatum/Hampton/Rich*, Pablo 2310-720, with Lionel Hampton on vibes and Buddy Rich on drums.
- *Tatum/Hampton/Rich...Again!*, Pablo 2310-775. Listen to Art on Cole Porter's "Love For Sale."
- *Art Tatum/Red Callender/Jo Jones*, Pablo 2310-735.
- *Art Tatum/Benny Carter/Louis Bellson*, Vol. I, Pablo 2310-732, with Benny Carter on alto and Louis Bellson on drums.

Bobby Timmons
- *This Here Is Bobby Timmons*, Fantasy OJC-104, with Sam Jones and Jimmy Cobb. Listen to Bobby's tunes "This Here," "Moanin'," and "Dat Dere."

McCoy Tyner
- *Inception*, MCA/Impulse 42233, with Art Davis and Elvin Jones.
- *Nights Of Ballads & Blues*, MCA/Impulse 42234, with Steve Davis and Lex Humphries.
- *Reaching Fourth*, Impulse 33, with Henry Grimes and Roy Haynes.
- *Plays Ellington,* Impulse 79, with Jimmy Garrison and Elvin Jones.
    (The above four albums, all recorded in the early 1960s, are among the greatest trio albums ever recorded.)
- *Supertrios*, Milestone 55003. A double album with Ron Carter and Tony Williams on one album, and Eddie Gomez and Jack DeJohnette on the other.

Cedar Walton
- *Firm Roots*, Muse 5069, with Sam Jones and Louis Hayes.

Mary Lou Williams
- *Free Spirits*, SteepleChase 1043, with Buster Williams and Mickey Roker.

Denny Zeitlin
- *Denny Zeitlin Trio*, Windham Hill 0112.

Listen/Vocal

Monty Alexander
- Ernestine Anderson, *Never Make Your Move Too Soon*, Concord Jazz 1479. Listen to Monty's 'comping on "Just One More Chance."

Alan Broadbent
- Irene Kral, *Gentle Rain*, Choice 1020.

Bill Evans
- *The Tony Bennett/Bill Evans Album*, Fantasy 9489, one of the best vocal albums of the 1970s.

Hank Jones
- Johnny Hartman, *I Just Dropped By To Say Hello*, Impulse 57.

Wynton Kelly
- Donna Drake, *Donna Sings Dinah*, Luxor-1.

George Shearing
- *An Evening with George Shearing and Mel Tormé,* Concord Jazz CJ-190, one of several albums they recorded together, and a Grammy winner.

McCoy Tyner
- *John Coltrane and Johnny Hartman*, MCA/Impulse 5661, one of the best vocal albums of the 1960s, with superb accompanying by McCoy.

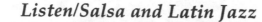

☰ LISTEN

Listen/Salsa and Latin Jazz

Sonny Bravo
- *Tipica 73*, Inca 1031.
- *Tipica 73*, Inca 1038.
- Tipica 73, *Los Dos Lados De La Tipica 73*, Inca 1053.
- Tipica 73, *Rumba Caliente*, Inca 1051.
- Tipica 73, *Into The 80s*, Fania 592.
- Tipica 73, *Intercambio Cultural*, Fania 542.
- Tito Puente, *Sensacion*, Concord 301.
- Tito Puente, *Un Poco Loco*, Concord 329.
- Tito Puente, *El Rey*, Concord 250.
- Tito Puente, *On Broadway*, Concord 207.

Gilberto Colon, Jr.
- Machito, *Live At North Sea, '82,* Timeless 168.

Chick Corea
- Cal Tjader, *Soul Burst*, Verve 8637. Listen to Chick's solo on "Descarga Cubana."
- Joe Henderson, *Relaxin' at Camarillo*, Contemporary 14006. Not a Latin album, but listen to Chick's solo on Joe's "Ya Todavia La Quiero."
- Armando Peraza, *Wild Thing*, Skye G923. Not a great album, but worth the price just for Chick's montuno and solo on "Viva Peraza."

Lino Frias
- Sonora Matancera, *Sus Grandes Exitos*, Panart 2061.
- Celia Cruz and Sonora Matancera, *Homenaje A Los Santos*, Seeco 9269.
- Conjunto Son De La Loma, *Asi Empezó La Cosa*, Montuno 514.

Luis Martinez Griñan (Lilín)
- Arsenio Rodriguez, *A Todos Los Barrios*, Cariño 5803.
- Arsenio Rodriguez, *El Sentimiento De Arsenio Rodriguez*, Cariño 5802.

Herbie Hancock
- Herbie Hancock, *Succotash*, Blue Note BN-LA152-F. Herbie's superb Latin jazz album, originally issued as *Inventions and Dimensions.*

Oscar Hernández
- Carabali, *Carabali*, Primo 418.
- Conjunto Libre, *Con Salsa, Con Ritmo, Vol. I*, Salsoul 4109.
- Conjunto Libre, *Tiene Calidad, Vol. II*, Salsoul 4114.
- Grupo Folklorico Y Experimental Nuevayorquino, *Concepts In Unity*, Salsoul 2-400.
- Grupo Folklorico Y Experimental Nuevayorquino, *Lo Dice Todo*, Salsoul 4110.
- Ray Barretto, *Ritmo De La Vida*, Fania 605.

Pedro Justiz (Peruchín)
- Peruchín, *Piano & Rhythm*, Puchito 105.
- Peruchín, *The Incendiary Piano Of Peruchín*, GNP 50.
- Cachao, *Descargas Con El Ritmo De Cachao*, Modiner 278.
- Julio Gutierrez, *Cuban Jam Session, Vol. I,* Panart 8000.
- Julio Gutierrez, *Cuban Jam Session, Vol. II,* Panart 3055.

Papo Lucca
- Papo Lucca, *Back To Work*, Inca 1083.
- *Sonora Ponceña,* Inca 1033.
- Sonora Ponceña, *Sabor Sureño*, Inca 1039.
- Sonora Ponceña, *La Orquestra De Mi Tierra*, Inca 1064.
- Fania All Stars, *Lo Que Pide La Gente*, Fania 629.

Noro Morales
- Noro Morales, *Bailemos Con Noro Morales*, Tropical 5027.
- Noro Morales, *His Piano And Rhythm*, Ansonia 1272.
- Noro Morales, *En Su Ambiente*, Marvel 98.

Charlie Palmieri
- Charlie Palmieri, *A Giant Step*, Tropical Buddah 003.
- Charlie Palmieri, Eddie Palmieri, and Cal Tjader, *Primo*, Fantasy 9422.
- Cachao, *Cachao '77*, Salsoul 4III.
- *Alégre All Stars, Vol. I*, Alégre 8I0.
- *Alégre All Stars, Vol. II*, Alégre 834.
- *Alégre All Stars, Vol. III*, Alégre 843.
- *Alégre All Stars, Vol. IV*, Alégre 844.

Eddie Palmieri
- Eddie Palmieri (with Cal Tjader), *El Sonido Nuevo*, Verve 865I, Eddie's best Latin jazz album. Listen to his solos on "Picadillo," " Unidos," and the title track.
- *Eddie Palmieri And His Conjunto La Perfecta*, Alégre 8I7, Eddie's first album (I962).
- Eddie Palmieri, *Champagne*, Tico II65.
- Eddie Palmieri, *Echando Pa'lante*, Tico III3.
- Eddie Palmieri, *Justicia*, Tico II88.
- Eddie Palmieri, *El Molestoso*, Alégre 824.
- Eddie Palmieri, *Vamonos P'al Monte* Tico I225.
- Eddie Palmieri, *Mambo + Conga = Mozambique*, Tico II26.
- Eddie Palmieri, *Sentido,* Mango I03.
- Eddie Palmieri, *Azucar Pa' Ti*, Tico II22.
- Eddie Palmieri, *Lo Que Traigo Es Sabroso,* Alégre 832.
- Eddie Palmieri, *Superimposition*, Tico II94.
- Eddie Palmieri (with Cal Tjader), *Bamboleate*, Tico II50.
- Eddie Palmieri, *The Sun Of Latin Music*, Coco I09.
- Eddie Palmieri, *Live At Sing Sing*, Tico I303.
- Eddie Palmieri, *Live At The University Of Puerto Rico,* Coco I07.
- Eddie Palmieri, *Molasses*, Tico II48.
- Eddie Palmieri, *Lucumi Macumba Voodoo,* Epic 35523.
- Eddie Palmieri, *Eddie Palmieri*, Barbaso 205.
- Eddie Palmieri, *Timeless*, Coco I63.
- Eddie Palmieri, *Solito*, Musica Latina 59.
- Eddie Palmieri, *Palo Pa Rumba*, Musica Latina 56.
- Eddie Palmieri, *La Verdad*, Fania FA 24.

Bud Powell
- *The Amazing Bud Powell, Vol. I*, Blue Note 8I503. "Un Poco Loco," was one of the first, and one of the best, Latin jazz tunes ever recorded.

Hilton Ruiz
- Jerry Gonzalez, *Ya Yo Me Curé*, Pangaea 6242. Listen to Hilton's version of "I Love Lucy" on one of the best Latin jazz albums ever recorded.

 **LISTEN**

Listen/Miscellaneous

In this section, each pianist listed appears on albums with a quartet or larger group, either as leader or sideman.

Kenny Barron
- Kenny Barron, *What If?*, Enja 5013, with Wallace Roney, John Stubblefield, Cecil McBee, and Victor Lewis. Listen to Kenny's "Phantoms."
- Johnny Coles and Frank Wess, *Two At The Top*, Uptown 27.14, with Reggie Johnson and Kenny Washington. Lots of drop 2 block chords.
- Booker Ervin, *Back From The Gig*, Blue Note LA-488. One of Kenny's best, with Woody Shaw, Jan Arnett, and Billy Higgins.
- Tom Harrell, *Moon Alley*, Criss Cross 1018, with Kenny Garrett, Ray Drummond, and Ralph Peterson. Listen to Kenny's 'comping on Tom's "Rapture," and his solo on the title track.
- Eddie Henderson, *Phantoms,* SteepleChase 1250, with Joe Locke, Wayne Dockery, and Victor Lewis. Listen to Kenny's tune "Phantoms."
- Joe Henderson, *The Kicker*, Milestone 9008, with Mike Lawrence, Grachan Moncur, Ron Carter, and Louis Hayes.
- Tyrone Washington, *Natural Essence*, Blue Note 4274, with Woody Shaw, James Spaulding, Reggie Workman, and Joe Chambers.

Walter Bishop, Jr.
- Hank Mobley, *Second Message*, Prestige 7667, with Kenny Dorham, Doug Watkins and Arthur Taylor.

Paul Bley
- Sonny Rollins and Coleman Hawkins, *Sonny Meets Hawk*, RCA 741075, with Bob Cranshaw, Henry Grimes, and Roy McCurdy. Listen to Paul's solo on Jerome Kern's "All The Things You Are."

Joanne Brackeen
- *Ancient Dynasty*, Columbia 36593, with Joe Henderson, Eddie Gomez and Jack DeJohnette.

Donald Brown
- Donald Brown, *Early Bird*, Sunnyside 1025, with Donald Harrison, Bob Hurst, Bill Mobley, Steve Nelson and Jeff Watts. Includes one solo track, Tadd Dameron's "If You Could See Me Now," and one trio track, Kurt Weill's "Speak Low."

Jaki Byard
- Sam Rivers, *Fuchsia Swing Song*, Blue Note 84184, with Ron Carter and Tony Williams.

George Cables
- Eddie Marshall, *Dance Of The Sun*, Timeless SJI 109, with Bobby Hutcherson, Manny Boyd, and James Leary.

Sonny Clark
- Tina Brooks, *The Complete Tina Brooks*, Mosaic MR4-106, with Lee Morgan, Doug Watkins, and Art Blakey.
- Dexter Gordon, *A Swinging Affair*, Blue Note 84133, with Butch Warren and Billy Higgins.
- Dexter Gordon, *Landslide*, Blue Note 1051, with Paul Chambers and Philly Joe Jones.
- Grant Green, *Born To Be Blue*, Blue Note 84432, with Sam Jones, Louis Hayes, and the great Ike Quebec on tenor.

Eddie Moore, Herbie Lewis and George Cables

Photo © by Jerry Stoll

Chick Corea
- Stan Getz, *Sweet Rain*, Verve 8l5054, with Ron Carter and Grady Tate. Listen to Chick's "Windows."
- Joe Henderson, *Mirror, Mirror*, Pausa 7075, with Ron Carter and Billy Higgins.
- Blue Mitchell, *The Thing To Do*, Blue Note 84178, with Junior Cook, Gene Taylor, and Al Foster. Listen to Chick's eclectic roots displayed in his solo on Joe Henderson's "Step Lightly."
- Donald Byrd, *The Creeper*, Blue Note LT l096, with Sonny Red, Pepper Adams, Miroslav Vitous, and Mickey Roker. Listen to Chick's solo on "Samba Yanta."

Stanley Cowell
- Bobby Hutcherson, *Spiral*, Blue Note 996, with Harold Land, Reggie Johnson, and Joe Chambers. Listen to Stanley's solos on Joe Chambers' "Ruth" and Harold Land's "Poor People's March."

Walter Davis, Jr.
- Art Blakey, *Au Théatre des Champs*, RCA (France) 3745l, with Lee Morgan, Wayne Shorter, and Jymie Merritt.
- Donald Byrd, *Byrd In Hand*, Blue Note 840l9, with Charlie Rouse, Pepper Adams, Sam Jones, and Arthur Taylor.

Kenny Drew
- *The Complete Tina Brooks*, Mosaic MR4-l06. One of Kenny's best, with Jackie McLean, Blue Mitchell, Johnny Coles, Paul Chambers, Philly Joe Jones, Arthur Taylor, and Wilber Ware.
- John Coltrane and Paul Chambers, *High Step*, Blue Note LA45l-H2-0798, with Donald Byrd, Kenny Burrell, Curtis Fuller, and Pepper Adams. Listen to Kenny's minimal but effective 'comping behind Paul Chambers' solo on "Visitation," and some great early (l955) Coltrane.
- *Paul Chambers' Music—A Jazz Delegation From The East*, Jazz: West 7, with Paul Chambers, Philly Joe Jones, John Coltrane, and Kenny Dorham.
- John Coltrane, *Blue Trane*, Blue Note 8l577. One of the best albums of the l950s, with Lee Morgan, Curtis Fuller, Paul Chambers, and Philly Joe Jones.
- Kenny Dorham, *Whistle Stop*, Blue Note 4063, with Hank Mobley, Paul Chambers, and Philly Joe Jones.
- Dexter Gordon, *Daddy Plays The Horn*, Bethlehem 68l8, with Leroy Vinnegar and Lawrence Marable.
- Jackie McLean, *Bluesnik*, Blue Note 4067, with Freddie Hubbard, Doug Watkins, and Pete La Roca.
- Sonny Rollins, *Tour De Force*, Fantasy OJC-095, with George Morrow and Max Roach. Sonny at his greatest, including "B. Quick," and "B. Swift," two of the fastest tunes ever recorded.

Duke Ellington
- Duke Ellington & John Coltrane, *Duke Ellington and John Coltrane*, MCA/Impulse 39l03, with Jimmy Garrison, Aaron Bell, Sam Woodyard, and Elvin Jones. One of the sweetest albums ever recorded.
- Duke Ellington and Billy Strayhorn, *Great Times!*, Riverside OJC l08. Includes four tracks with great Oscar Pettiford 'cello solos.

Bill Evans
- Miles Davis, *Kind Of Blue*, Columbia 40579, with John Coltrane, Cannonball Adderly, Paul Chambers, and Jimmy Cobb. One of the best and most influential albums of the l950s. First recordings of "So What," "Blue In Green," and "All Blues." Wynton Kelly plays piano on one track.
- Miles Davis, *Jazz At The Plaza*, Columbia 32470, with John Coltrane, Cannonball Adderly, Paul Chambers and Philly Joe Jones.
- Miles Davis, *Miles At Newport*, Columbia CBS (France) 634l7, with Cannonball Adderly, John Coltrane, Paul Chambers, and Jimmy Cobb. Originally released as *Jazz Track*. Listen to Bill's great block chord solo on Bronislau Kaper's "On Green Dolphin Street." Wynton Kelly plays piano on some tracks.

Tommy Flanagan

- *Paul Chambers Quintet*, Blue Note 1564, with Donald Byrd, Clifford Jordan, and Elvin Jones.
- Freddie Hubbard, *The Artistry Of Freddie Hubbard*, Jasmine 71, with Curtis Fuller, Art Davis, Louis Hayes, and some great John Gilmore.
- Wes Montgomery, *The Incredible Jazz Guitar Of Wes Montgomery*, Riverside 320, also rereleased as part of of the two-fer *While We're Young*, Milestone 47003, with Percy Heath, Ron Carter, Albert Heath, Lex Humphries, and Ray Barretto.

Red Garland

- Red Garland, *Soul Junction*, Prestige 7181, with John Coltrane, Paul Chambers, and Arthur Taylor.
- Red Garland, *Dig It*, Prestige 7229, with John Coltrane, George Joyner, Paul Chambers, and Arthur Taylor.
- Red Garland, *All Morning Long*, Fantasy OJC-293, with John Coltrane, Donald Byrd, Paul Chambers, and Arthur Taylor.
- Red Garland, *Rediscovered Masters,* Prestige 24078, with Paul Chambers, Doug Watkins, Arthur Taylor, Specs Wright, and Ray Barretto.
- John Coltrane, *Soultrane*, Fantasy OJC-021, with Paul Chambers and Arthur Taylor.
- *John Coltrane With The Red Garland Trio*, Prestige 7123 (personnel as above).
- John Coltrane, *Traneing In*, Prestige 7123 (personnel as above).
- John Coltrane, *Settin' The Pace,* Fantasy OJC-078 (personnel as above). Listen to Red's block chord solo on Arthur Schwartz's "I See Your Face Before Me."
- John Coltrane, *The Stardust Session*, Prestige 24056, with Wilbur Hardin, Paul Chambers, and Jimmy Cobb.
- John Coltrane, *Lush Life*, Fantasy OJC-131, with Donald Byrd, Earl May, Paul Chambers, Albert Heath, Arthur Taylor, and Louis Hayes.
- John Coltrane, *Black Pearls*, Prestige 7316, and *The Believer*, Prestige 7292, also reissued as the two-fer *Black Pearls & The Believer,* with Donald Byrd, Freddie Hubbard, Paul Chambers, Arthur Taylor, and Louis Hayes.
- Miles Davis, *'Round About Midnight,* Columbia 40610, with John Coltrane, Paul Chambers, and Philly Joe Jones.
- Miles Davis, *Cookin'*, Fantasy OJC-128 (personnel as above).
- Miles Davis, *Workin'*, Fantasy OJC-296 (personnel as above).
- Miles Davis, *Relaxin',* Fantasy OJC-190 (personnel as above).
- Miles Davis, *Steamin'*, Prestige 7580 (personnel as above).
- Miles Davis, *Walkin'*, Fantasy OJC-213 (personnel as above).
- Miles Davis, *The New Miles Davis Quintet*, Fantasy/OJC 006 (personnel as above). Listen to Red's block chord solo on "There Is No Greater Love."
- Miles Davis, *Milestones*, Columbia 40837 (personnel as above). Listen to Red's trio version of "Billy Boy."
    (All of the above Miles Davis recordings were among the best and most influential records of the 1950s.

Benny Green

- Benny Green, *Prelude*, Criss Cross 1036, with Terence Blanchard, Jovan Jackson, Peter Washington, and Tony Reedus. Listen to Benny's solo on Jerome Kern's "The Song Is You."
- Ralph Moore, *Images,* Landmark 1520, with Terence Blanchard, Peter Washington, and Kenny Washington. Listen to Benny's solo on Elmo Hope's "One Second, Please."

Onaje Allan Gumbs

- Woody Shaw, *Stepping Stones*, Columbia 35560, with Carter Jefferson, Clint Houston, and Victor Lewis.

Jan Hammer

- Elvin Jones, *Merry-Go-Round*, Blue Note 84414. Listen to Jan's solo on his "Lungs."

Herbie Hancock

- Herbie Hancock, *The Prisoner*, Blue Note 84321, with Joe Henderson, Johnny Coles, Garnett Brown, Buster Williams, and Albert Heath. Some of Herbie's best writing, including "I Have A Dream," and some great Joe Henderson.
- Herbie Hancock, *Speak Like A Child*, Blue Note 84279, a sextet album with Ron Carter and Mickey Roker. Great writing, and one of the best albums of the 1960s.
- Herbie Hancock, *My Point Of View*, Blue Note 84126, with Donald Byrd, Grachan Moncur, Hank Mobley, Grant Green, Chuck Israels, and Tony Williams. Listen to Herbie's solo on "King Cobra."
- Herbie Hancock, *Maiden Voyage,* Blue Note 84195, with Freddie Hubbard, George Coleman, Ron Carter, and Tony Williams.
- Herbie Hancock, *Empyrean Isles*, Blue Note 84175. One of Herbie's best, with Freddie Hubbard, Ron Carter, and Tony Williams.
- Miles Davis, *Nefertiti*, Columbia 9594, with Wayne Shorter, Ron Carter, and Tony Williams.
- Miles Davis, *Filles De Kilimanjaro*, Columbia 9750 (personnel as above).
- Miles Davis, *Miles Smiles*, Columbia 9401 (personnel as above).
- Miles Davis, *At The Plugged Nickel*, CBS Sony 25AP (personnel as above).
- Miles Davis, *Sorcerer*, Columbia 9532 (personnel as above).
- Miles Davis, *My Funny Valentine*, Columbia 9106, with George Coleman, Ron Carter, and Tony Williams. Listen to Herbie's solo on Cole Porter's "All Of You."
- Miles Davis, *Four And More*, Columbia 9253 (personnel as above).
- Miles Davis, *In Europe*, Columbia 8983 (personnel as above).
- Miles Davis, *Seven Steps To Heaven*, Columbia 8851.
- Miles Davis, *Miles In St. Louis*, VGM 0003.
- Miles Davis, *Miles in Berlin, Columbia.*
  (All of the above Miles Davis records were among the best and most influential recordings of the 1960s.)
- Kenny Dorham, *Una Mas*, Blue Note 46515, with Joe Henderson, Butch Warren, and Tony Williams.
- Joe Henderson, *Power To The People,* Milestone 9024, with Mike Lawrence, Ron Carter, and Jack DeJohnette.
- Freddie Hubbard, *Hub Tones*, Blue Note 84115, with James Spaulding, Reggie Workman, and Clifford Jarvis.
- Bobby Hutcherson, *Oblique*, Blue Note GXF-3061, with Albert Stinson and Joe Chambers. One of Herbie's (and Bobby's) best albums.
- Lee Morgan, *Cornbread*, Blue Note 84222, with Jackie McLean, Hank Mobley, Larry Ridley, and Billy Higgins. Listen to Herbie's beautiful solo on Lee's "Ceora."
- Wayne Shorter, *Etcetera*, Blue Note 1056, with Cecil McBee and Joe Chambers. Listen to Herbie's solo and 'comping on Wayne's "Barracudas," and the Phrygian chords on Wayne's "Penelope."
- Wayne Shorter, *Speak No Evil*, Blue Note 84194, with Freddie Hubbard, Ron Carter, and Elvin Jones.
- Wayne Shorter, *Adam's Apple*, Blue Note 84232, with Reggie Workman and Joe Chambers.
- Wayne Shorter, *Schizophrenia*, Blue Note 84297, with Curtis Fuller, James Spaulding, Ron Carter, and Joe Chambers.
  (The above Wayne Shorter albums were among the best and most influential recordings of the 1960s.)
- Woody Shaw, *In The Beginning*, Muse 5298, with Joe Henderson, Ron Carter, and Joe Chambers.
- *Charles Tolliver and his All Stars,* Black Lion 28 410-9, with Gary Bartz, Ron Carter, and Joe Chambers. Listen to two exceptional Charles Tolliver tunes: "Lil's Paradise," and "Household Of Saud."

Barry Harris
- Barry Harris, *Bull's Eye!*, Prestige 7600, with Kenny Dorham, Charles McPherson, Pepper Adams, Paul Chambers, and Billy Higgins.
- Benny Golson, *The Other Side Of Benny Golson*, Riverside 290, with Curtis Fuller, Jymie Merritt, and Philly Joe Jones.
- Dexter Gordon, *Clubhouse*, Blue Note LT 989, with Freddie Hubbard, Bob Cranshaw, and Billy Higgins.
- Lee Morgan, *The Sidewinder*, Blue Note 4157, with Joe Henderson, Bob Cranshaw and Billy Higgins.
- Sonny Stitt, *Constellation*, Muse 5323, with Sam Jones and Roy Brooks.

John Hicks
- Hank Mobley, *High Voltage*, Blue Note 4273, with Bob Cranshaw and Billy Higgins.

Andrew Hill
- Andrew Hill, *Black Fire*, Blue Note 84151, with Joe Henderson, Richard Davis, and Roy Haynes.

Hank Jones
- Cannonball Adderly, *Somethin' Else*, Blue Note 1595, with Miles Davis, Sam Jones, and Art Blakey. Listen to Hank's block chord solo on the title track.
- Cannonball Adderly, *Presenting Cannonball*, Savoy 401, with Nat Adderly, Paul Chambers, and Kenny Clarke.
- Kenny Dorham, *Jazz Contrasts*, Fantasy OJC-028, with Sonny Rollins, Oscar Pettiford, and Max Roach.
- Wes Montgomery, *So Much Guitar!*, Riverside 382, with Percy and Albert Heath. Also rereleased as part of the two-fer *While We're Young*, Milestone 47003.

Duke Jordan
- *The Complete Tina Brooks,* Mosaic MR4-106, with Freddie Hubbard, Sam Jones, and Arthur Taylor.

Benny Green

Photo © by James Gudeman

☰ LISTEN

Wynton Kelly
- *Wynton Kelly & George Coleman In Concert,* Affinity 54, with Ron McClure and Jimmy Cobb.
- Wynton Kelly and Wes Montgomery, *Smokin' At The Half Note*, Verve 829578, with Paul Chambers and Jimmy Cobb, one of the best albums of the 1960s.
- Wynton Kelly, *Cruisin'*, Jazzland 7.
- *Wynton Kelly*, Epitaph 4007, with Lee Morgan, Wayne Shorter, Paul Chambers, and Philly Joe Jones.
- Cannonball Adderly and John Coltrane, *Cannonball And Coltrane*, EmArcy 834588, with Paul Chambers and Jimmy Cobb.
- Cannonball Adderly, *Things Are Getting Better,* Riverside 286, with Milt Jackson, Percy Heath, and Art Blakey.
- Paul Chambers, *Go,* Vee Jay 1014, with Cannonball Adderly, Freddie Hubbard, Philly Joe Jones, and Jimmy Cobb. Listen to Wynton play the blues on "Awful Mean," and "Ease It."
- John Coltrane, *Coltrane Jazz*, Atlantic 1354, with Steve Davis and Elvin Jones.
- Miles Davis, *Friday And Saturday Nights At The Blackhawk,* Columbia 25820, with Hank Mobley, Paul Chambers, and Jimmy Cobb.
- Miles Davis, *Someday My Prince Will Come*, Columbia 8456. One of the best albums of the 1960s, with John Coltrane, Hank Mobley, Paul Chambers, and Jimmy Cobb. Listen to Wynton's solo on the title track.
- Miles Davis, *Live In Stockholm*, AVI 2004, with John Coltrane, Paul Chambers, and Jimmy Cobb. Coltrane's last album with Miles.
- *Miles Davis & Sonny Stitt*, Dragon, 129/130, with Paul Chambers and Jimmy Cobb, and one of Sonny's best albums.
- Benny Golson, *The Modern Touch*, Riverside 256, with Kenny Dorham, J. J. Johnson, Paul Chambers, and Max Roach.
- Dexter Gordon, *The Jumpin' Blues*, Prestige 10020, with Sam Jones and Roy Brooks.
- Steve Lacy, *Soprano Sax*, Fantasy OJC-130, with Buell Neidlinger and Dennis Charles. Listen to Wynton's intro and solo on the calypso standard "Little Girl, Your Daddy's Calling You."
- Blue Mitchell, *Blue's Moods*, Fantasy OJC-138, with Sam Jones and Roy Brooks.
- Blue Mitchell, *Out Of The Blue*, Riverside 293, with Paul Chambers, Sam Jones, and Art Blakey.
- Hank Mobley, *Soul Station*, Blue Note 84031, with Paul Chambers and Art Blakey. Listen to Hank's "This I Dig Of You."
- Hank Mobley, *Workout*, Blue Note 84080, with Paul Chambers and Philly Joe Jones. One of the best records of the 1960s.
- Hank Mobley, *Another Workout*, Blue Note 84431 (personnel as above).
- Sonny Red, *Out Of The Blue*, Blue Note 4032, with Paul Chambers, Roy Brooks, and Jimmy Cobb.
- Sonny Rollins, *Newk's Time*, Blue Note 84001, with Doug Watkins and Philly Joe Jones.

Kenny Kirkland
- Elvin Jones, *Earth Jones*, Palo Alto Jazz 8016, with Dave Liebman, Terumasa Hino, and George Mraz. Listen to Kenny's solo on Elvin' "Three Card Molly."
- Branford Marsalis, *Renaissance,* Columbia 40711, with Bob Hurst and Tony Williams. Herbie Hancock and Buster Williams play on one tune, Jimmy Rowles' "The Peacocks." Listen to Kenny's solo on Branford's "The Wrath (Structured Burnout)."

Ronnie Matthews
- Woody Shaw, *Little Red's Fantasy*, Muse 5103, with Frank Strozier, Stafford James, and the great Eddie Moore on drums. One of the best records of the 1970s.

Mulgrew Miller

- Mulgrew Miller, *The Countdown,* Landmark 1519, with Joe Henderson, Ron Carter, and Tony Williams.
- Mulgrew Miller, *Wingspan,* Landmark 1515, with Kenny Garrett, Steve Nelson, Charnett Moffett, and Tony Reedus. Listen to Mulgrew's great bebop solo on the title track. One of the best albums of the 1980s.
- Donald Byrd, *Harlem Blues,* Landmark 1516, with Kenny Garrett, Rufus Reid and Marvin "Smitty" Smith.
- Monte Croft, *A Higher Fire,* Columbia 45122, with Lonnie Plaxico, Gene Jackson, and Lance Bryant. Listen to Mulgrew's burning solo on the title track.
- Frank Morgan, *Yardbird Suite,* Contemporary 14045, with Ron Carter and Al Foster.
- Frank Morgan, *Reflections,* Contemporary 14052, with Joe Henderson, Bobby Hutcherson, Ron Carter, and Al Foster. Listen to Mulgrew play the blues on Sonny Rollins' "Sonnymoon For Two."
- Kenny Garrett, *Introducing Kenny Garrett,* Criss Cross 1014, with Woody Shaw, Nat Reeves, and Tony Reedus. One of the best albums of the 1980s.
- Ralph Moore, *Rejuvenate!,* Criss Cross 1035, with Steve Turre, Peter Washington, and Marvin "Smitty" Smith. Listen to Mulgrew's lovely solo on "It Might As Well Be Spring."
- Wallace Roney, *Verses,* Muse 5335, with Gary Thomas, Charnett Moffett and Tony Williams.
- Woody Shaw, *United*, Columbia 37390, with Gary Bartz, Steve Turre, Stafford James, and Tony Reedus.
- Woody Shaw, *Master Of The Art*, Elektra Musician 60131, with Bobby Hutcherson, Steve Turre, Stafford James, and Tony Reedus.
- Woody Shaw, *Lotus Flower,* Enja 4018, with Steve Turre, Stafford James, and Tony Reedus. Listen to Mulgrew's "Eastern Joy Dance."
- Marvin "Smitty" Smith, *Keeper Of The Drums,* Concord Jazz 325, with Steve Coleman, Robin Eubanks, Ralph Moore, Wallace Roney, and Lonnie Plaxico. Listen to Mulgrew's blazing solo on Smitty's "Miss Ann." One of the best albums of the 1980s.
- John Stubblefield, *Countin' On The Blues,* Enja 5015, with Hamiet Bluiett, Charnett Moffett, and Victor Lewis. Listen to Mulgrew's tune "Remembrance," and his solo on John Stubblefield's "Montauk."

Thelonious Monk

- *Thelonious Monk And John Coltrane,* Fantasy OJC-039, with Wilbur Ware, Shadow Wilson, and Art Blakey. One of the best albums of the 1950s. Compare Monk's version of his "Trinkle, Tinkle" with solo versions by Kenny Barron, Chick Corea, and Kirk Lightsey.
- Thelonious Monk, *Tokyo Concerts,* Columbia 38510, with Charlie Rouse, Butch Warren, and Frankie Dunlop. Monk and Rouse at their quirkiest—listen to Monk's solo on "I'm Gettin' Sentimental Over You."
- *The Complete Blue Note Recordings of Thelonious Monk,* Mosaic 101. A four-lp set covering Monk's recording from 1947 through 1957, with superb trio tracks. There is also an early jazz waltz—Monk's rendition of "Carolina Moon," and two tracks with Sonny Rollins, J. J. Johnson, Paul Chambers, and Art Blakey.
- Thelonious Monk, *The Complete Riverside Recordings,* Riverside 022 (a 22 lp set).
- Thelonious Monk, *Criss-Cross,* Columbia 8838, with Charlie Rouse, John Ore, and Frankie Dunlop.
- Thelonious Monk, *Thelonious In Action,* Fantasy OJC-103, with Johnny Griffin, Abdul Malik, and Roy Haynes.
- Thelonious Monk, *It's Monk's Time,* Columbia 2184, with Charlie Rouse, Butch Warren, and Ben Riley.
- Thelonious Monk, *Brilliant Corners,* Riverside 226, with Sonny Rollins, Ernie Henry, Clark Terry, Oscar Pettiford, Paul Chambers, and Max Roach.

≡ LISTEN

Horace Parlan
- Charles Mingus, *Mingus Ah Um*, Columbia 8171, with John Handy, Booker Ervin, Shafi Hadi, Jimmy Knepper, Willie Dennis, and Dannie Richmond. One of the best albums of the 1950s.

Duke Pearson
- Duke Pearson, *Sweet Honey Bee*, Blue Note 84252, with Freddie Hubbard, Joe Henderson, James Spaulding, Ron Carter, and Mickey Roker.
- Donald Byrd, *The Cat Walk*, Blue Note 4075, with Pepper Adams and Philly Joe Jones.

Richie Powell
- Clifford Brown And Max Roach, *At Basin Street*, EmArcy 814648, with Sonny Rollins.
- *Clifford Brown And Max Roach*, EmArcy 36036, with Harold Land and George Morrow.

Marcus Roberts
- Marcus Roberts, *The Truth Is Spoken Here,* Novus 3051, with Wynton Marsalis, Charlie Rouse, Todd Williams, Reginald Veal, and Elvin Jones.

Horace Silver
- Horace Silver, *The Cape Verdean Blues*, Blue Note 84220, with Woody Shaw, Joe Henderson, J. J. Johnson, Bob Cranshaw, and Roger Humphries. One of the best albums of the 1960s.
- Horace Silver, *Song For My Father*, Blue Note 84185, with Carmell Jones, Joe Henderson, Teddy Smith, and Roger Humphries.
- Horace Silver, *The Jody Grind*, Blue Note 84250, with Woody Shaw, James Spaulding, Tyrone Washington, Larry Ridley, and Roger Humphries.
- Horace Silver, *Blowin' The Blues Away*, Blue Note 84017, with Blue Mitchell, Junior Cook, Gene Taylor, and Louis Hayes.
- Art Blakey, *The Jazz Messengers At The Cafe Bohemia*, Vol. 2, Blue Note 81508, with Kenny Dorham, Hank Mobley, and Doug Watkins.

Bobby Timmons
- Cannonball Adderly, *The Cannonball Adderly Quintet In San Francisco*, Riverside 1157, with Nat Adderly, Sam Jones, and Louis Hayes. Listen to Bobby's block chord solo on Cannonball's "Spontaneous Combustion."

McCoy Tyner
- McCoy Tyner, *Expansions*, Blue Note 84338, with Woody Shaw, Gary Bartz, Wayne Shorter, Ron Carter, Herbie Lewis, and Freddie Waits. One of the best albums of the 1960s.
- McCoy Tyner, *The Real McCoy*, Blue Note 84264, with Joe Henderson, Ron Carter, and Elvin Jones. One of the best albums of the 1960s.
- McCoy Tyner, *Tender Moments*, Blue Note 84275, with Lee Morgan, Julian Priester, Bennie Maupin, James Spaulding, Howard Johnson, Herbie Lewis, and Joe Chambers. One of the best albums of the 1960s.
- McCoy Tyner, *Time For Tyner*, Blue Note 84307, with Bobby Hutcherson, Herbie Lewis, and Freddie Waits, and one of McCoy's best albums. Listen to his solo on "Little Madimba."
- Donald Byrd, *Mustang*, Blue Note 4238, with Sonny Red, Hank Mobley, Walter Booker, and Freddie Waits. Listen to McCoy's chorus in front and later solo on Donald Byrd's "Fly Little Bird, Fly."
  (The following John Coltrane albums were among the best and most influential recordings of the 1960s.)
- John Coltrane, *Coltrane's Sound*, Atlantic 1419, with Steve Davis and Elvin Jones.
- John Coltrane, *My Favorite Things*, Atlantic 1361 (personnel as above).
- John Coltrane, *Afro Blue Impressions*, Pablo 2620, with Jimmy Garrison and Elvin Jones.
- John Coltrane, *Ballads,* MCA/Impulse 5885 (personnel as above).
- John Coltrane, *Coltrane*, MCA/Impulse 5883 (personnel as above).
- John Coltrane, *Live At Birdland*, Impulse A50 (personnel as above).
- John Coltrane, *Crescent*, MCA/Impulse 5889 (personnel as above).

McCoy Tyner (Continued)

- John Coltrane, *Live At The Village Vanguard*, Impulse A 10, with Eric Dolphy, Reggie Workman, and Elvin Jones.
- John Coltrane, *The John Coltrane Quartet Plays,* Impulse A85, with Jimmy Garrison, Art Davis, and Elvin Jones.
- John Coltrane, *Impressions*, MCA/Impulse 5887, with Eric Dolphy, Reggie Workman, Jimmy Garrison, and Elvin Jones.
- John Coltrane, *The John Coltrane Group With Eric Dolphy*, Beppo 504, with Reggie Workman, Jimmy Garrison, and Elvin Jones.
- Grant Green, *Matador*, Blue Note 8159, with Bob Cranshaw and Elvin Jones.
- Joe Henderson, *In 'n Out*, Blue Note 46510, with Kenny Dorham, Richard Davis, and Elvin Jones.
- Joe Henderson, *Inner Urge*, Blue Note 4189, with Ron Carter and Elvin Jones. One of the best albums of the 1960s.
- Joe Henderson, *Page One*, Blue Note 84140, with Kenny Dorham, Butch Warren, and Pete La Roca. Original recordings of "Blue Bossa" and "Record-A-Me."
- Freddie Hubbard, *Ready For Freddie*, Blue Note 84085, with Bernard McKinney, Wayne Shorter, Art Davis, and Elvin Jones.
- Freddie Hubbard, *Goin' Up*, Blue Note 84056, with Hank Mobley, Paul Chambers, and Philly Joe Jones.
- Freddie Hubbard, *Blue Spirits,* Blue Note 46545, with James Spaulding, Joe Henderson, Kiane Zawadi, Harold Mabern Jr., Larry Ridley, Clifford Jarvis, and Big Black. Listen to McCoy's 'comping and solo on the title track.
- Bobby Hutcherson, *Stick-Up!,* Blue Note 84244, with Joe Henderson, Herbie Lewis, and Billy Higgins.
- Bobby Hutcherson, *Solo Quartet*, Contemporary 14009, with Herbie Lewis and Billy Higgins. One of the best records of the 1980s.
- Hank Mobley, *Straight, No Filter*, Blue Note 84435. Appearing on only three tracks on this album—Barry Harris and Herbie Hancock play on the others—this is one of McCoy's best. Listen to his solo on "Chain Reaction."
- Lee Morgan, *Delightfulee*, Blue Note 84243, with Joe Henderson, Bob Cranshaw, Billy Higgins, plus two tentet tracks arranged by Oliver Nelson. Listen to Joe Henderson's solo on Lee's "Ca-lee-so," and Wayne Shorter's solo on John Lennon's "Yesterday."
- Wayne Shorter, *Night Dreamer,* Blue Note 4173, with Lee Morgan, Reggie Workman, and Elvin Jones.
- Wayne Shorter, *JuJu,* Blue Note 84182, with Reggie Workman and Elvin Jones.
- Wayne Shorter, *The Soothsayer*, Blue Note 988, with James Spaulding, Freddie Hubbard, Ron Carter, and Tony Williams.

Billy Wallace

- Max Roach, *Jazz in 3/4 Time*, EmArcy 826456. Long out of print, it's hard to believe the controversy this album caused when it came out around 1958. An entire album of jazz waltzes was released at a time when musicians were debating whether or not it was possible to "swing" in 3/4 time. I went to see Max's band in Boston about a year afterward, wondering whether or not they would still be playing any waltzes. They not only played waltzes, they also played a couple of tunes in 5/4 time, and, needless to say, they swung.

≡ LISTEN

Cedar Walton
- Cedar Walton, *Eastern Rebellion*, Timeless 101, with George Coleman, Sam Jones, and Billy Higgins.
- Cedar Walton, *Eastern Rebellion 2*, Timeless 106, with Bob Berg, Sam Jones, and Billy Higgins.
- Art Blakey, *Three Blind Mice*, Solid State 18033, with Freddie Hubbard, Wayne Shorter, and Jymie Merritt. One of Art's Best—listen to Cedar's solo on the Brown-Fain standard "That Old Feeling."
- Art Blakey, *Free For All*, Blue Note 4170 (personnel as above). Listen to Cedar's 'comping and solo on Clare Fischer's "Pensativa."
- Art Blakey, *Ugetsu*, Fantasy OJC-090 (personnel as above).
- Art Blakey, *Kyoto*, Riverside Fantasy OJC-145 (personnel as above).
- Art Blakey, *Mosaic*, Blue Note 46523 (personnel as above). One of Bu's best—classic tunes such as Wayne Shorter's "Children Of The Night," Curtis Fuller's "Arabia," and Freddie Hubbard's "Crisis." Listen to Cedar's montuno on the intro to "Mosaic."
- Art Blakey, *Indestructible!*, Blue Note 4193 (personnel as above).
- Art Blakey, *Caravan*, Fantasy OJC-038 (personnel as above).
- *Art Blakey And The Jazz Messengers,* MCA/Impulse 5886 (personnel as above, except Reggie Workman on bass).
- Donald Byrd, *Blackjack*, Blue Note 84259, with Sonny Red, Hank Mobley, Walter Booker, and Billy Higgins.
- Donald Byrd**,** *Slow Drag*, Blue Note 84292, with Sonny Red, Walter Booker, and Billy Higgins. Listen to Sonny Red at his funkiest on the title track and on "Jelly Roll," Cedar's solo on "The Loner," and his 'comping on "My Ideal," and Walter Booker's "Book's Bossa."
- Steve Grossman, *Love Is The Thing*, Red Records 189, with David Williams and Billy Higgins. Listen to Cedar's solo on "I Didn't Know What Time It Was."
- Joe Henderson, *Mode For Joe*, Blue Note 84227, with Lee Morgan, Curtis Fuller, Bobby Hutcherson, Ron Carter, and Joe Chambers. Listen to the montuno Cedar plays on the intro to "Black."
- Freddie Hubbard, *Here To Stay*, Blue Note 84135, with Wayne Shorter, Jimmy Heath, Julian Priester, Reggie Workman, Larry Ridley, and Philly Joe Jones.

James Williams
- Marvin "Smitty" Smith, *The Road Less Travelled,* Concord 379, with Wallace Roney, Steve Coleman, Ralph Moore, Robin Eubanks, Kenyatte Abdur-Rahman, and Robert Hurst.

Larry Young
- Larry Young, *Unity*, Blue Note 4221, with Woody Shaw, Joe Henderson and Elvin Jones. One of the best records of the 1960s.
- Larry Young, *Into Somethin'*, Blue Note 84187, with Sam Rivers, Grant Green, and Elvin Jones.

APPPENDIX

Appendix B

Melodic Minor Scale Harmony

I — C-Δ (or) C-+7 — minor-major

II — Dsusb9, C-Δ/D, Aø/D — b9

III — EbΔ+5 — Lydian augmented — +4 +5

IV — F7+11 — Lydian dominant — +11

V — (no standard chord symbol)

VI — Aø (or) A-7b5 — half-diminished (or) Locrian #2 — b5 b6

VII — B7alt — altered (or) diminished whole-tone — b9 +9 +11 (or) b5 bl3 (or) +5

Diminished Scale Harmony

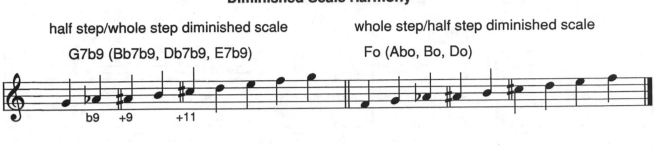

half step/whole step diminished scale

G7b9 (Bb7b9, Db7b9, E7b9)

b9   +9   +11

whole step/half step diminished scale

Fo (Abo, Bo, Do)

Whole-tone Scale Harmony

G7+5 (or) G7b13

+11   +5

☰ APPPENDIX

Appendix E

Upper Structures

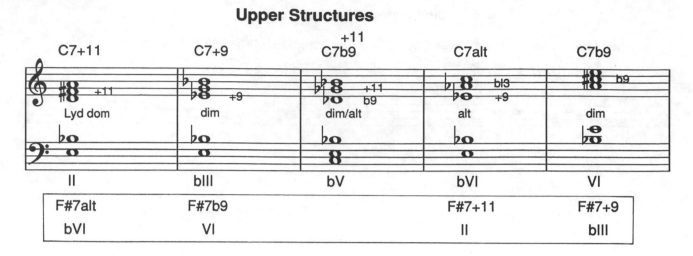

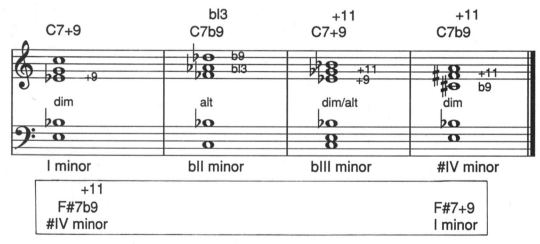

VOICING RULES: l) Inversions of triad and tritone OK
2) Doubled notes OK at or near top of voicing only
3) Add root to avoid unaltered tritone substitution

Comparison of V Scales

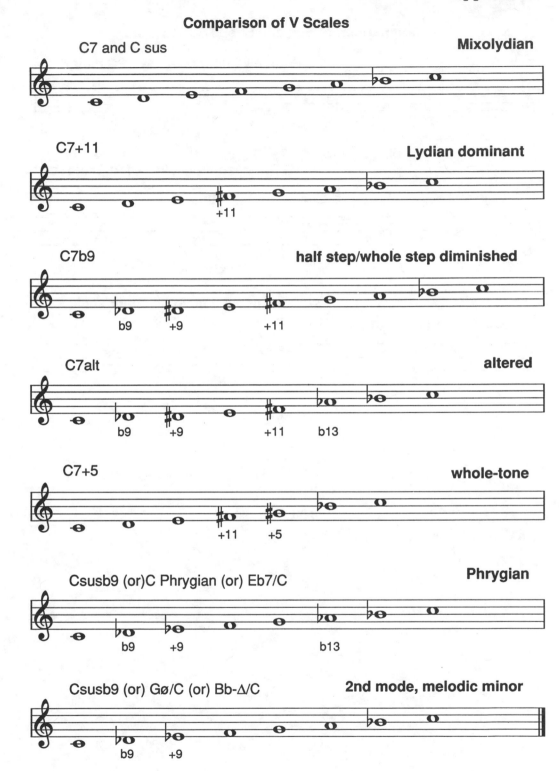

APPPENDIX

Appendix G

Comparison of Sus and Susb9 Scales

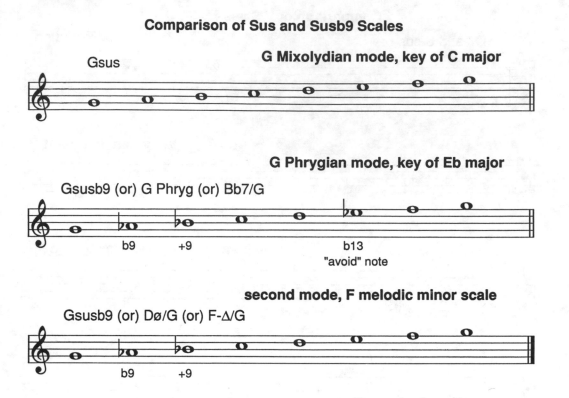

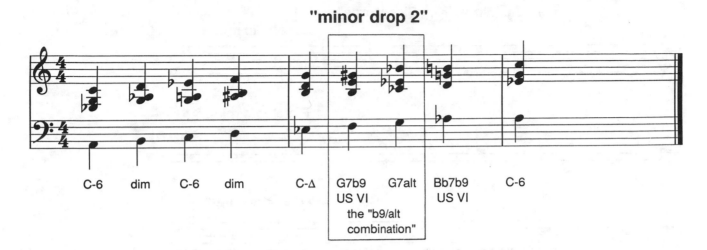

APPPENDIX

Appendix I

Melodic Minor "Key Signatures"

C melodic minor

F melodic minor

Bb melodic minor

Eb melodic minor

Ab melodic minor

Db melodic minor

F# melodic minor

B melodic minor

E melodic minor

A melodic minor

D melodic minor

G melodic minor

Latin Music Books & CDs from Sher Music Co.

The Latin Real Book (C, Bb or Eb)

The only professional-level Latin fake book ever published! Over 570 pages. Includes detailed transcriptions sof tunes, exactly as recorded by:

Ray Barretto	Irakere	Andy Narell	Ft. Apache Band	Djavan
Eddie Palmieri	Celia Cruz	Mario Bauza	Dave Valentin	Tom Jobim
Fania All-Stars	Arsenio Rodriguez	Dizzy Gilllespie	Paquito D'Rivera	Toninho Horta
Tito Puente	Tito Rodriguez	Mongo Santamaria	Clare Fischer	Joao Bosco
Ruben Blades	Orquesta Aragon	Manny Oquendo & Libre	Chick Corea	Milton Nascimento
Los Van Van	Beny Moré	Puerto Rico All-Stars	Sergio Mendes	Leila Pinheiro
NG La Banda	Cal Tjader	Issac Delgaldo	Ivan Lins	Gal Costa
				And Many More!

Muy Caliente!

Afro-Cuban Play-Along CD and Book
Rebeca Mauleón - Keyboard
Oscar Stagnaro - Bass
Orestes Vilató - Timbales
Carlos Caro - Bongos
Edgardo Cambon - Congas

(Over 70 min. of smokin' Latin grooves)

The Latin Real Book Sampler CD

12 of the greatest Latin Real Book tunes as played by the original artists: Tito Puente, Ray Barretto, Andy Narell, Puerto Rico Allstars, Bacacoto, etc. $16 list price. Available in U.S.A. only.

101 Montunos

by Rebeca Mauleón
The only comprehensive study of Latin piano playing ever published.
- Bi-lingual text (English/Spanish)
- 2 CDs of the author demonstrating each montuno
- Covers over 100 years of Afro-Cuban styles, including the danzón, guaracha, mambo, merengue and songo—from Peruchin to Eddie Palmieri.

The True Cuban Bass

By Carlos Del Puerto, (bassist with Irakere) and Silvio Vergara, $22.

For acoustic or electric bass; English and Spanish text; Includes CDs of either historic Cuban recordings or Carlos playing each exercise; Many transcriptions of complete bass parts for tunes in different Cuban styles – the roots of Salsa.

The Brazilian Guitar Book

by **Nelson Faria**, one of Brazil's best new guitarists.

- Over 140 pages of comping patterns, transcriptions and chord melodies for samba, bossa, baiaõ, etc.
- Complete chord voicings written out for each example.
- Comes with a CD of Nelson playing each example.
- The most complete Brazilian guitar method ever published! $26 including surface postage.

Joe Diorio – "Nelson Faria's book is a welcome addition to the guitar literature. I'm sure those who work with this volume wiill benefit greatly"

The Salsa Guide Book

By Rebeca Mauleón
The only complete method book on salsa ever published! 260 pages. $25

Carlos Santana – "A true treasure of knowledge and information about Afro-Cuban music."

Mark Levine, author of The *Jazz Piano Book*. – "This is the book on salsa."

Sonny Bravo, pianist with Tito Puente – "This will be the salsa 'bible' for years to come."

Oscar Hernández, pianist with Rubén Blades – "An excellent and much needed resource."

The New Real Book Series

The Standards Real Book (C only)

Alice In Wonderland
All Of You
Alone Together
At Last
Baltimore Oriole
A Beautiful Friendship
Bess, You Is My Woman
But Not For Me
Close Enough For Love
Crazy He Calls Me
Dancing In The Dark
Days Of Wine And Roses
Dreamsville
Easy To Love
Embraceable You

Falling In Love With Love
From This Moment On
Give Me The Simple Life
Have You Met Miss Jones?
Hey There
I Can't Get Started
I Concentrate On You
I Cover The Waterfront
I Love You
I Loves You Porgy
I Only Have Eyes For You
I Wish I Knew
I'm A Fool To Want You
Indian Summer
It Ain't Necessarily So

It Never Entered My Mind
It's You Or No One
Just One Of Those Things
Love For Sale
Love Walked In
Lover, Come Back To Me
The Man I Love
Mr. Lucky
My Funny Valentine
My Heart Stood Still
My Man's Gone Now
Old Folks
On A Clear Day
Our Love Is Here To Stay
Secret Love

September In The Rain
Serenade In Blue
Shiny Stockings
Since I Fell For You
So In Love
So Nice (Summer Samba)
Some Other Time
Stormy Weather
The Summer Knows
Summer Night
Summertime
Teach Me Tonight
That Sunday, That Summer
Then I'll Be Tired Of You

There's No You
A Time For Love
Time On My Hands
'Tis Autumn
Where Or When
Who Cares?
With A Song In My Heart
You Go To My Head
Ain't No Sunshine
'Round Midnight
The Girl From Ipanema
Bluesette
And Hundreds More!

The New Real Book - Volume 1 (C, Bb or Eb)

Angel Eyes
Anthropology
Autumn Leaves
Beautiful Love
Bernie's Tune
Blue Bossa
Blue Daniel
But Beautiful
Chain Of Fools
Chelsea Bridge
Compared To What
Darn That Dream
Desafinado
Early Autumn
Eighty One

E.S.P.
Everything Happens To Me
Fall
Feel Like Makin' Love
Footprints
Four
Four On Six
Gee Baby Ain't I Good To You
Gone With The Wind
Here's That Rainy Day
I Love Lucy
I Mean You
I Should Care
I Thought About You

If I Were A Bell
Imagination
The Island
Jersey Bounce
Joshua
Lady Bird
Like Someone In Love
Line For Lyons
Little Sunflower
Lush Life
Mercy, Mercy, Mercy
The Midnight Sun
Monk's Mood
Moonlight In Vermont
My Shining Hour

Nature Boy
Nefertiti
Nothing Personal
Oleo
Once I Loved
Out Of This World
Pent Up House
Polkadots And Moonbeams
Portrait Of Tracy
Put It Where You Want It
Robbin's Nest
Ruby, My Dear
Satin Doll
Search For Peace

Shaker Song
Skylark
A Sleepin' Bee
Solar
Speak No Evil
St. Thomas
Street Life
Tenderly
These Foolish Things
This Masquerade
Three Views Of A Secret
Waltz For Debby
Willow Weep For Me
And Many More!

The New Real Book - Volume 2 (C, Bb or Eb)

Afro-Centric
After You've Gone
Along Came Betty
Bessie's Blues
Black Coffee
Blues For Alice
Body And Soul
Bolivia
The Boy Next Door
Bye Bye Blackbird
Cherokee
A Child Is Born
Cold Duck Time
Day By Day

Django
Equinox
Exactly Like You
Falling Grace
Five Hundred Miles High
Freedom Jazz Dance
Giant Steps
Got A Match?
Harlem Nocturne
Hi-Fly
Honeysuckle Rose
I Hadn't Anyone 'Til You
I'll Be Around
I'll Get By

Ill Wind
I'm Glad There Is You
Impressions
In Your Own Sweet Way
It's The Talk Of The Town
Jordu
Killer Joe
Lullaby Of The Leaves
Manha De Carneval
The Masquerade Is Over
Memories Of You
Moment's Notice
Mood Indigo
My Ship

Naima
Nica's Dream
Once In A While
Perdido
Rosetta
Sea Journey
Senor Blues
September Song
Seven Steps To Heaven
Silver's Serenade
So Many Stars
Some Other Blues
Song For My Father
Sophisticated Lady

Spain
Stablemates
Stardust
Sweet And Lovely
That's All
There Is No Greater Love
'Til There Was You
Time Remembered
Turn Out The Stars
Unforgettable
While We're Young
Whisper Not
Will You Still Be Mine?
You're Everything
And Many More!

The New Real Book - Volume 3 (C, Bb, Eb or Bass clef)

Actual Proof
Ain't That Peculiar
Almost Like Being In Love
Another Star
Autumn Serenade
Bird Of Beauty
Black Nile
Blue Moon
Butterfly
Caravan
Ceora
Close Your Eyes
Creepin'
Day Dream
Dolphin Dance

Don't Be That Way
Don't Blame Me
Emily
Everything I Have Is Yours
For All We Know
Freedomland
The Gentle Rain
Get Ready
A Ghost Of A Chance
Heat Wave
How Sweet It Is
I Fall In Love Too Easily
I Got It Bad
I Hear A Rhapsody
If You Could See Me Now

In A Mellow Tone
In A Sentimental Mood
Inner Urge
Invitation
The Jitterbug Waltz
Just Friends
Just You, Just Me
Knock On Wood
The Lamp Is Low
Laura
Let's Stay Together
Litha
Lonely Woman
Maiden Voyage

Moon And Sand
Moonglow
My Girl
On Green Dolphin Street
Over The Rainbow
Prelude To A Kiss
Respect
Ruby
The Second Time Around
Serenata
The Shadow Of Your Smile
So Near, So Far
Solitude
Speak Like A Child
Spring Is Here

Stairway To The Stars
Star Eyes
Stars Fell On Alabama
Stompin' At The Savoy
Sugar
Sweet Lorraine
Taking A Chance On Love
This Is New
Too High
(Used To Be A) Cha Cha
When Lights Are Low
You Must Believe In Spring
And Many More!

Other Jazz Publications

The Jazz Theory Book

By Mark Levine, the most comprehensive Jazz Theory book ever published! $38 list price.

- Over 500 pages of text and over 750 musical examples.
- Written in the language of the working jazz musician, this book is easy to read and user-friendly. At the same time, it is the most comprehensive study of jazz harmony and theory ever published.
- Mark Levine has worked with Bobby Hutcherson, Cal Tjader, Joe Henderson, Woody Shaw, and many other jazz greats.

The Jazz Piano Book

By Mark Levine, Concord recording artist and pianist with Cal Tjader. For beginning to advanced pianists. The only truly comprehensive method ever published! Over 300 pages. $28

Richie Beirach – "The best new method book available."
Hal Galper – "This is a must!"
Jamey Aebersold – "This is an invaluable resource for any pianist."
James Williams – "One of the most complete anthologies on jazz piano."

The Improvisor's Bass Method

By Chuck Sher. A complete method for electric or acoustic bass, plus transcribed solos and bass lines by Mingus, Jaco, Ron Carter, Scott LaFaro, Paul Jackson, Ray Brown, and more! Over 200 pages. $16

International Society of Bassists – "Undoubtedly the finest book of its kind."

Eddie Gomez – "Informative, readily comprehensible and highly imaginative"

Concepts For Bass Soloing

By Chuck Sher and Marc Johnson, (bassist with Bill Evans, etc.) The only book ever published that is specifically designed to improve your soloing! $26

- Includes two CDs of Marc Johnson soloing on each exercise
- Transcriptions of bass solos by: Eddie Gomez, John Patitucci, Scott LaFaro, Jimmy Haslip, etc.

"It's a pleasure to encounter a Bass Method so well conceived and executed." – **Steve Swallow**

The Yellowjackets Songbook

Complete package contains six separate spiral-bound books, one each for:

- Piano/partial score • C melody lead sheet
- Synthesizer/miscellaneous parts
- Bb & Eb Horn melody part • Bass • Drums

Contains 20 great tunes from their entire career. Charts exactly as recorded – approved by the Yellowjackets. World famous Sher Music Co. accuracy and legibility. Over 400 pages, $38 list price.

The Jazz Solos of Chick Corea

Over 150 pages of Chick's greatest solos; "Spain", "Litha", "Windows", "Sicily", etc. for all instrumentalists, single line transcriptions, not full piano score. $18

Chick Corea – "I don't know anyone I would trust more to correctly transcribe my improvisations."

The World's Greatest Fake Book

Jazz & Fusion Tunes by: **Coltrane, Mingus, Jaco, Chick Corea, Bird, Herbie Hancock, Bill Evans, McCoy, Beirach, Ornette, Wayne Shorter, Zawinul, AND MANY MORE!** $32

Chick Corea – "Great for any students of jazz.'
Dave Liebman – "The fake book of the 80's."
George Cables – "The most carefully conceived fake book I've ever seen."

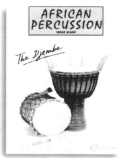

African Percussion, The Djembe

The first comprehensive djembe method book ever published.

- CD included of the author, Serge Blanc, playing each section of the book.
- Includes 22 great standards of traditional djembe music.
- Duet and trios written out so you can start playing and practising in groups.

Now Available in CD Format! - The New Real Book Play-Along CDs (For Volume 1)

CD #1 - Jazz Classics - Lady Bird, Bouncin' With Bud, Up Jumped Spring, Monk's Mood, Doors, Very Early, Eighty One, Voyage **& More!**
CD #2 - Choice Standards - Beautiful Love, Darn That Dream, Moonlight In Vermont, Trieste, My Shining Hour, I Should Care **& More!**
CD #3 - Pop-Fusion - Morning Dance, Nothing Personal, La Samba, Hideaway, This Masquerade, Three Views Of A Secret, Rio **& More!**
World-Class Rhythm Sections, featuring Mark Levine, Larry Dunlap, Sky Evergreen, Bob Magnusson, Keith Jones, Vince Lateano & Tom Hayashi